FOUNDATION FOR LIVING

FOUNDATION FOR LIVING

Charles Stewart Mott

FOUNDATION FOR LIVING

the story of Charles Stewart Mott and Flint

by Clarence H. Young
& William A. Quinn

McGRAW-HILL BOOK COMPANY, INC.

New York   Toronto   London

To
Ruth Rawlings Mott,
the Flint Board of Education,
and
The Seven Universities of Michigan—
Partners in Progress

INTRODUCTION

The memorandum I picked up from my desk concerned the fact that the year—1955—was the one-hundredth anniversary of the City of Flint. As I thought of the almost incredible sweep of forces shaping modern Flint from the little river-crossing settlement of 1855, I was somewhat amazed to remember I had shared exactly half of Flint's first 100 years.

I first saw Flint on September 2, 1905, the year the city celebrated its fiftieth anniversary golden jubilee. I found this valley of the Flint River still heavily grown with trees despite the rich harvest of pine which had brought Flint's booming lumber era. With the end of the pine had come the vehicle industry from which Flint-made wagons, road carts, and buggies rolled out to every corner of the country. Then, haltingly, after the turn of the century, automobile manufacturing began.

I held the memorandum of Flint's hundredth year in my hand, trying to visualize the factors working so mightily to shape the city.

There are no outside windows in my office in the Mott Foundation Building in downtown Flint, but I could lean back in my chair, close my eyes, and see, as if through the stone walls, the tremendous industrial establishments that mark the points of the compass from the center of the city. Flint is bounded on the north by Buick and Ternstedt, on the west by Chevrolet, on the south by Fisher Body, and on the east by the AC Sparkplug Division of General Motors Corporation. There are other industries, of course, but those are the greatest, employing some 70,000 people.

Not the wildest imagination in 1905 could have conceived of such gigantic enterprises—except, perhaps, the imagination of the man who had invited me to Flint, William Crapo Durant, key figure in so much that has happened to Flint.

The thought of Durant led me to the greatest factor of all in the destiny of Flint. Someone once said that the history of mankind is the lengthened shadow of great men. In the history of Flint, this concept has been demonstrated with particular force. It has been pointed out before that Flint, once the pine was gone, had no natural advantages of raw materials, transportation, or proximity to markets. There was no reason why Flint should have become different from other small towns in the Middle West—except for the quality of the people who settled here, and those who followed.

There were giants among the men of Flint in 1905, casting their shadows across the quiet river valley and over the future as well. The Flint we know today is a living testimonial to the stature of those men—to their vision, their courage, their ability, their hard work, and their faith in the boundless accomplishment possible for those who set their hearts and minds to a task. Then, as always, the men made the difference.

It was my privilege to know those men and work with them, and with the successors who have caried on the great traditions they established. It has become increasingly clear to me that the ideals, strength, ingenuity, daring, and hard work of individuals are responsible for Flint's remarkable record of accomplishment.

Flint's demonstration that the quality of people underlies and overshadows all other factors in existence has had a profound influence on me, and on the activities to which I have devoted my life and resources in recent years.

When a man believes that nothing else is important, really, except people, how can he implement his belief effectively? That is the question which has challenged me, and to which I have found, here in my own community, an answer that is deeply satisfying.

It seems to me that every person, always, is in a kind of informal partnership with his community. His own success is dependent to a large degree on that community, and the community, after all, is the sum total of the individuals who make it up. The institutions of a community, in turn, are the means by which those individuals express their faith, their ideals, and their concern for fellow men.

The partnership between a man and his community is often an unconscious relationship, but this fact does not make it any the less real. For me, this sense of partnership has become a growing reality over the years. In the simplest terms: Flint has given me much that is good; I try, in return, to make available to the people of Flint much that is good, placing human values first.

Flint has many splendid institutions expressing, as I have said, the faith of Flint people, their ideals, and their concern for fellow men. My own active partnership with my community is expressed mainly through another institution, called the Mott Foundation. This Foundation works principally through established community agencies, such as the board of education, to strengthen and extend their services by utilization of existing facilities to a degree far beyond the practices of the past. Further, the Mott Foundation is highly flexible, and thus is able to meet community needs not otherwise provided for, chiefly through pilot projects in new areas of community service.

This, then, is the answer I have found for my own need to perpetuate the lesson Flint has taught me—that only people are important. And since every man needs to devote as much imagination, skill, and conscience to the wise and useful spending of money as he exercised to accumulate that money, the Foundation answers this need for me also. The Foundation serves as the most effective expression of the faith, ideals, and concern for fellow men which I have acquired in my lifetime.

The objectives of the Foundation have become both deeper and wider in the course of a quarter-century of continuous growth and development. Our attempt here in Flint is to open for as many people as possible the doors of opportunity for self-advancement in health, education, recreation, active participating citizenship, technical skill, economic knowledge, and successful adaptation to every challenge of modern living. But only the opportunity can be provided, the rest is up to the individual. Our experience gives evidence that the individual responds eagerly to a down-to-earth implementation of equality of opportunity.

So broad and so deep are the objectives of the Mott Foundation that they touch almost every aspect of living, increasing the capacity for accomplishment, the appreciation of values, and the understanding of the forces that make up the world we live in. In this sense, it may truly be called a Foundation for Living—with the ultimate aim of developing greater understanding among men. We recognize that our obligation to fellow men does not stop at the boundaries of the community. In an even larger sense, every man is in partnership with the rest of the human race in the eternal conquest which we call civilization. Just as the Foundation conducts pilot projects in Flint for the sake of the whole community, so we consider the whole Foundation a total pilot project for the sake of as much of the United States and the world as may care to make a similar approach to the problems of people. We believe—and there is already a significant body of evidence to support our belief—that both the principles and techniques, such as the community-school concept, pioneered in practice by the Mott Foundation, can be utilized with excellent effect in other communities. We are happy to make available to others all the information we can provide to assist them in similar undertakings; this is a major objective of the Foundation.

For each of us, there is a time for taking stock—for comparing our intentions with our accomplishments. The thought of Flint's hundredth year, and my own sharing of half that period, brought to me the impulse for such an accounting.

Even if a man feels no necessity to justify his life to others, there is no escaping the necessity to justify it to himself. There are many ways to approach such a reckoning. Each man's life has its own private record of success and failure in his responsibilities to himself, his family, his associates, his community,

viii

and his God. It is not always easy to set forth an honest balance sheet when human and abstract values are involved, but one can try.

This book, then, is such a reckoning-up for me. Chiefly, it is the story of the reciprocal relationship ... the often unconscious partnership ... between the City of Flint and myself. And, of more importance, it is also the record of the development of a pattern of community service. As I have said, the Mott Foundation may, in a large sense, be considered a Foundation for Living; for me, in another sense, it is a foundation for living—the realization of the purpose of my life. Above all, I hope that this record may prove illuminating and useful to others who share the same belief in the importance of people and the same need to do something effective about that belief.

Charles Stewart Mott

ONE

On Charles Stewart Mott's thirtieth birthday, June 2, 1905, it would have seemed easy to predict the pattern of his future life. Within another two weeks, he would be celebrating the fifth anniversary of his marriage. He was the father of two children, and was already firmly settled in Utica, New York, as president and general manager of the Weston-Mott Company. The company had made the transition from bicycle wheels to automobile wheels and axles, and was showing a steady advance in production and sales. It would have been a fair assumption that C. S. Mott's future would be devoted to continuing the development of this family company in Utica. The event that changed this prospect was a very short letter to Mott from W. C. Durant, written just two days after Mott's thirtieth birthday.

BUICK MOTOR COMPANY
OFFICE OF SALES DEPARTMENT

Jackson, Michigan
June 4, 1905

Mr. C. S. Mott, Pres.,
    Weston-Mott Co.,
        Utica, N.Y.

Dear Sir:—
    Would you entertain a proposition of removing or establishing a branch factory at Flint, Michigan, provided the business of three or four large concerns was assured for a term of years? Flint is in the center of the automobile industry, a progressive city, good people, with conditions for manufacturing ideal.
Yours very truly,
W. C. Durant

c/o Durant-Dort Cge. Co.
    Flint, Mich.

This letter, written only six months after Durant had entered the automobile industry with Buick, already shows him thinking in wide concepts. It suggests his ability to influence, if not control, "three or four large concerns for a term of years." Durant's characterization of his home town, Flint, as being "in the center of the automobile industry, a progressive city, good people, with conditions for manufacturing ideal" was to become increasingly accurate.

The almost casual letter from the unpredictable genius of the automobile industry stirred Mott's imagination. He had then, as always, an instinct for change, variety, growth, and development in his activities, for new opportunities to challenge his energy and ingenuity. Mott replied immediately.

WESTON-MOTT COMPANY

UTICA, N.Y., U.S.A.

ESTABLISHED 1884

June 6, 1905

Mr. W. C. Durant,
    Durant-Dort Carriage Co.,
      Flint, Mich.

Dear Sir:—

Your letter of the 4th inst. is received.

The writer expects to visit Jackson either Monday or Tuesday of next week, and as I presume you are called there frequently on business, could you not arrange to meet me there at that time, when it would be possible to go into the matter suggested in your letter more fully than can be done by correspondence?

It has been proposed to us once or twice to consider locating in the West, especially since the automobile industry has become so important in your state, but the proposition we looked into did not prove sufficiently attractive to offset the disadvantage of moving an established business to new territory.

The idea of a branch factory does not appeal to me as there is so much detail to our business that it is important that constant oversight be given, and should this factory remain here and a branch factory be established there, the time consumed in traveling would be considerable and would cause a large amount of physical and mental strain that would undoubtedly cause the business to suffer. We might entertain a proposition provided it were sufficiently attractive to remove our plant to a new place. We own our plant, free and unencumbered here and it would be a difficult proposition to dispose of it to advantage if it were vacated. Our plant here meets our requirements, although it is not a building of heavy construction. It stands on our books at about $25,000. (building).

We are doing a very satisfactory business and it has steadily increased, and it has grown only because we have given it constant attention and have endeavored to increase the quality of our goods to meet the requirements of the trade.

If you could, before the writer leaves for the West, outline more fully what you are in a position to propose, it might facilitate matters and then enable me to go into the project more fully with Mr. Doolittle, who is equally interested with me in our company. You may be sure that we shall give careful consideration to any proposition you may care to make. We cannot go into the matter hurriedly, and since looking into the question two years ago, we put the question of removal out of our minds.

Very truly yours,
Weston-Mott Co.
C. S. Mott
President

This letter is perhaps equally revealing of the man who wrote it. Mott speaks as a practical businessman first of all, yet between the lines there is evident the drive toward larger fields of activity. The rejection of the "branch factory" idea because of the difficulty of exercising "constant oversight" is a principle which has guided Mott consistently. He has acted on the belief that a man should attend to his business personally if he expects it to develop and prosper, and he has generally concentrated his major interests where he could give exactly that kind of personal attention to them. Equally typical are both Mott's request to "outline more fully what you are in a position to propose" and his remark, "we cannot go into the matter hurriedly. . . ." Mott's loyalty to his associates is also demonstrated in his careful specification that Mr. Doolittle "is equally interested with me in our company."

Weston-Mott had furnished chain-drive rear axles and front axles to the Buick Motor Company in Flint even before Durant had taken command of Buick. There were Weston-Mott axles on the sixteen Buicks made in 1903, and on the thirty-seven that followed in 1904.

Mott visited Jackson the next week and Durant gave him a glowing amplification of the advantages in moving the Weston-Mott factory to Flint. Though impressed with the drive and certainty of Durant, Mott made it nevertheless clear that no decision could be reached until his partner, William Doolittle, also had an opportunity to hear the whole proposal directly from Durant. Mott invited Durant to visit Utica, look over the Weston-Mott operations and talk with Doolittle. Durant accepted but remained vague about a definite date for his visit. His immediate concern was with securing bevel-drive rear axles and he asked Mott to prepare samples and cost estimates on two models.

Back in Utica, Mott wrote Durant to reaffirm that nothing further could be said on moving to Flint until Durant had reached an understanding with William Doolittle. Remarking also that there had been no further word from Durant on the bevel-drive rear axles, Mott implied his feeling that Durant could be quite casual in matters of detail. Durant was given to large visions, with his swirls of projects giving rise to many vistas of a golden future. Mott, on the other hand, was and is a practical man, looking directly at what is ahead, planning for it with skill and certainty, but taking one step at a time.

Having once considered the possibility of moving to Flint, Mott persisted in following up. But Durant's attention was apparently elsewhere. Thus the correspondence between the

4

two men, which had begun with such promise of rapid action, seemed to have reached a dead end. But the need for axles was a reality Durant could not escape. After a long silence he sent Mott a wire that he and J. Dallas Dort would visit Utica to look over Weston-Mott and talk with Mott and Doolittle. They came on September 1, 1905.

In spite of the unpromising situation created by Durant's lagging correspondence, the famous magnetism of his presence offset any doubts Mott and Doolittle might have entertained. Durant was at his persuasive best in outlining the advantages of moving the Weston-Mott Company to Flint. The future was all one expanding golden horizon in his eyes, and no one was more adept in communicating this vision to those who listened. He was impressed with the combination of the practical and the imaginative in the Weston-Mott operations. He saw how methodically, yet how rapidly, the Weston-Mott people had made change after change, developing new products to fit altering markets. He found Mott to be both a sound businessman and a mechanical engineer of remarkable ingenuity. Mott found Durant to be the intense, fast-moving, big-planning genius who held open the door to a vast and challenging future. Durant pressed for a decision and Mott and Doolittle agreed to make an immediate trip to Flint.

The Motts and Doolittle arrived there on September 2, 1905 and spent a few days. Before they returned to Utica, the decision to move had been made, signed, and sealed.

The Motts and William Doolittle were not too happily impressed with the superficial appearance of Flint in 1905; they saw it as a "hick town" in comparison with Utica. But the people they met in Flint gave them quite another impression. Among them were John J. Carton, for many years attorney for the Buick Motor Company; Arthur G. Bishop, of the Genesee County Savings Bank; and William S. Ballenger, one of the original organizers of the Buick Motor Company. Arthur Bishop gave the visitors from Utica a dinner party at his home, where they met many interesting and influential men including

William F. Stewart of the Stewart Body Company; Francis Rankin, publisher of Flint's *Wolverine Citizen;* Robert Armstrong, of the Armstrong Spring Company; F. A. Aldrich, secretary-treasurer of the Durant-Dort Carriage Company; Fenton McCreery, distinguished American diplomat, and a number of others.

It was clear to Mott that Buick gave great promise, and that, with the larger-than-life figure of Durant dominating the situation, and a body of able men concerned in the enterprise, all the constituents of success were at hand. Yet, if there was a good deal to gain, there was also a good deal to lose. The woods were full of new automobile companies in those days; they were already falling by the wayside, as hundreds more were to do until only today's handful would remain. Mott had brought his company well into the black in five years; he possessed security and all the assurance of a pleasant future in Utica. But security was not enough; he saw the enlarged potential of a Flint location, with much of the automobile industry shaping up in Michigan. He had already done substantial business with Oldsmobile in Lansing and Cadillac in Detroit, and now with the promise of all Buick axle business, plus the other advantages offered, the risk was worth the try.

Mott once summed up this turning point in his life with this statement:

> Our trip to Flint... was an immediate decision, as was our decision to move our plant from Utica to Flint, instead of simply establishing a branch in Flint. We felt that Michigan contained the majority of automobile production, and was the important place to locate our factory, and that we would do better to operate one factory than two. . . .
>
> Mrs. Mott and my partner were perfectly agreeable to our moving to where there were business advantages. . . . The upshot of our visit was that before we left Flint the day following Labor Day, we had signed a contract whereby we were given a good-sized site at the corner of Hamilton and Industrial Avenues, on which to erect a new plant, alongside of a pro-

posed Buick plant, and arrangements were made to form the Weston-Mott Company of Michigan to take over the business of Weston-Mott Company of Utica, capitalization $500,000, of which Flint citizens were to subscribe $100,000. Also, Weston-Mott Company was to receive contract from Buick Motor Company for all of its axle requirements on a percentage basis. In this new Weston-Mott Company, C. S. Mott was president, John J. Carton was vice-president, and W. G. Doolittle was secretary-treasurer.

This, then, was the decision made on that long weekend of September 1905 which brought C. S. Mott to Flint. It was arrived at quickly, but not without a thorough review of the circumstances that had brought Mott to the point where he had the power to make such a move of cardinal significance. What had been decided was to have a profound influence on Mott's own future and on the future of Flint. Here Mott was to build the career that led him to a vast fortune and an amazing roster of accomplishments. And in Mott, Flint not only encountered the man it would elect as mayor seven years later, but the man who would become the greatest benefactor of the community within a half century.

TWO

Charles Stewart Mott was born on June 2, 1875, in Newark, N.J. His twenty-six-year-old father, John Coon Mott, was devoting himself to the family cider and vinegar business in New York City. At the age of twenty-two, he had married Isabella Turnbull Stewart, daughter of the proprietor of Stewart's Hotel, Old City Hall, Newark.

Mott has traced the ancestry of his father back nine generations to one Adam Mott who came to America from England before 1645. Mott's mother was descended from Col. Charles Stewart, who came to America from Ireland in 1750, settled in New Jersey, and fought in the Continental Army during the Revolutionary War from 1777 to 1782. Family pride in this ancestor—who commanded a battalion of the First New Jersey Regiment of Minute Men and later a regiment of the line, and still later served on Washington's staff—accounts for the first two of Charles Stewart Mott's names.

In 1880, the family moved from Newark to New York City, where Mott had his early education. His notes indicate that he attended five different public schools before he entered Stevens High School at Hoboken, N.J., in 1888.

Mott likes to refer to his ancestors as "sod-busters." They had been farmers for generations, and his father had grown up on the family farm. "Summertimes," he recalls, "I was sent up to Boucksville, in central New York, to spend vacations in the country with my grandparents, and those were happy days." In the best American rural tradition, the Mott family life was close-knit; affections within the family were deep, solid, and understood beyond the need for much obvious display. There were only the two children, Charles and his sister, Edith, two years older.

In one of Mott's notes, he writes: "When my parents wanted to punish me I was kept in my room, where there was running water to drink, and I was given bread only to eat—a bread-and-water diet. But that was not very severe punishment to me, for bread satisfied my hunger and I occupied my time reading books. I think I read everything that was written by Jules Verne, Dumas, and many other similar authors. I probably read more books then than I ever have since."

Although the family was prospering, they kept to conservative customs. Mott notes: "Mother used to make my clothes from material from Father's suits. Short pants and so tight that the boys used to ask if I was poured into them. Mother sewed them on a 'chain-stitch' sewing machine. I used to skate a lot —went to school in New York on roller skates. One day a little over-exertion broke a stitch, and presto—my pants were in two pieces, one on each leg—and I walked home hanging one skate in front of me and one in the rear."

The interest in mechanics, which was to lead Mott into mechanical engineering, emerged in his early years. He remembers making his own toys as a child, and the most vivid of his boyhood memories has to do with experimenting with photography when he was thirteen years old. He writes in his notebook:

My first camera was a plain black box with a piece of glass in front; it was almost a lens, and in front of the lens a pinhole. There was no plate-holder. Instead, the camera was taken into a dark room and a $3\frac{1}{4}$- by $4\frac{1}{4}$-inch plate inserted, and closed up. All pictures were 'time exposures'; on a bright day it took five seconds, on dark days a minute. We had a Camera Club—developed our own plates and made our own prints. We even made our own lantern slides, and believe it or not, I still have a few which I made at that time, and they are as good as I could get made now.

Mott's interest in mechanics, coupled with a happy aptitude for manual training and shopwork, took the form of a specific ambition to which Mott held firmly. He planned to study mechanical engineering and hoped to become first a draftsman and then an engineer in a bridge-building company. Mott's devotion to this definite ambition ran counter to his father's equally definite hope to bring his son into the family business. This difference was bridged by compromise: The son *did* work in the family business, and the father *did* agree that the son should study mechanical engineering.

In 1888 the family moved to East Orange, N.J. and Mott entered Stevens High School in Hoboken. He was graduated in 1892 and continued his education at Stevens Institute of Technology in mechanical engineering.

Restless energy, the need for action, was his characteristic trait even then, and this restlessness of spirit found a satisfying outlet after his second year at Stevens. That summer, Mott joined the New York State Naval Militia, with headquarters on the USS *New Hampshire,* berthed at the foot of East 28th Street. He had a tour of duty as seaman in the old cruiser, USS *San Francisco.* Thus, at nineteen, Mott encountered two of the major interests of his life: military service and the sea.

The same year brought another adventure. When he returned from the naval militia cruise, his father—then head of an amalgamation of cider and vinegar making companies, the Genesee Fruit Company—suggested that his son go to Denmark and study the science of pure yeast culture at a school conducted by a Dr. Jorgensen in Copenhagen. Young Mott immediately obtained a certificate from Stevens Institute permitting him to re-enter the college a year later without re-examination and prepared for the trip to Europe. It is apparent that the elder Mott was deeply anxious for his son to enter the family business, and that the trip abroad was probably as much designed to accomplish this end as to make available new techniques in cider and vinegar making.

On August 8, 1894, Mott boarded the 10,000-ton White Star liner *Majestic,* bound for Queenstown, Ireland. He took along only a small amount of baggage and a Palmer light-weight bicycle. The fare was $50. On the voyage, Mott arranged for membership in a large English bicycle group,

10

Cyclist Touring Club, which provided its members with credentials, road maps, and complete information on hotels, restaurants, and lodging houses. Thus equipped, Mott set out on a bicycle trip that included Cork, the west coast of Ireland, and the lakes of Killarney. From Killarney, he went by train to Dublin and took a night boat to Liverpool, then rode the bicycle to Chester.

The trip was an important experience for Mott. He was on his own, plunged into the Old World at an age when his whole life could be influenced deeply. He enjoyed every aspect of the adventure, and still remembers the warm hospitality extended to him in both Ireland and England.

From Chester, Mott pedaled on to Birmingham, which fascinated him as an industrial city, then to Coventry, Stratford-on-Avon, and Bristol. Bristol's famous suspension bridge, and the gates to lock high-tide water in the harbor, held the interest of the mechanical engineering student who hoped himself to become a builder of bridges. He rode on to Totnes, and there visited the Symons family, with whom his father had done business. He was graciously received by the family, and was impressed by their courtesies and by their fine old house. Continuing his journey, Mott visited the Isle of Wight, and then went on to London.

Next came a boat trip to Rotterdam, then more bicycling to Delft, where he visited a plant that made alcohol from root vegetables and used what was left of the vegetables as feed for cattle. He visited Amsterdam, Haarlem, Scheveningen, Berlin, and Kiel—then reached his destination, Copenhagen, and Dr. Jorgensen's laboratory.

Mott found lodgings at a Fru Maar's *Pensionat*, on the fourth floor of a large apartment building, and began his studies of yeast culture at the laboratory. His notes describe the nature of those studies:

I spent almost five months there, learning the techniques of making yeast cultures, and separating and growing pure varieties from single cells. I learned how famous breweries used yeast which was originally grown from a single cell. After de-

11

termining that such a yeast produced exactly the quality of beer desired, the yeast was propagated and kept pure to that variety thereafter. I worked on the separation and pure culture of yeast from wines and ciders. I learned that a yeast culture propagated from grapes grown in one particular section of France, for example, could be taken to a distant location, and that when this culture was used in fermenting grapes in the new area, the wine produced would have many of the characteristics of the wine made in the section from which the original yeast culture had been derived.

Mott found the arrangement of daily meals in Denmark strange. "After rising, we had coffee and zwieback, and then went to work, returning somewhat before noon for breakfast, and then having another meal around four or five o'clock, and a final meal about nine o'clock."

Perhaps the most illuminating aspect of his experience in Denmark was the new kind of social life in which he found himself. He remembers the Copenhagen Opera with warmth and pleasure, and notes that he "even went to a dancing school run by one of the dance teachers of the Opera House . . . meeting and dancing with people from various places, very few of whom spoke my language. . . ."

From Copenhagen, Mott went to Munich for further study of the chemistry of fermentation. In the laboratory of Dr. Lintner, in Munich, Mott learned to make the analyses fundamental to fermentation processes, including study of the kinds of sugar and determination of sugar content. He encountered a new breakfast pattern: *Bratwurst und Semmel*—which the porter brought to the laboratory. Mott continued his newfound interest in the opera at Munich; he remembers that he almost always occupied standing room instead of a seat. Three months completed Mott's special studies in Munich. He visited Paris on the way back to London to take ship for home.

In April, 1895, Mott rejoined the family in New York. That summer, he carried on some experiments utilizing the new scientific techniques he had learned in Europe. With only one

12

apple crop a year, and little research work already done in this field compared with the long tradition of similar study with regard to grapes in Europe, he realized it would take far too many crops—and years—for him to arrive at any practical results. Also, he had never lost any of his love for mechanical engineering. With his father's agreement, he re-entered Stevens Institute in September, 1895, for the junior year of his mechanical-engineering course.

The father's persistent wish to interest the son in some aspect of the family business became evident in another form. The elder Mott had acquired a carbonating company which was engaged both in building beverage-carbonating machinery and in importing carbonic gas from Germany. In 1896, this company was reorganized and named the C. S. Mott Company. The young man whose name the firm bore was very active in the affairs of the company during his last two years in college—active in every aspect, from management and manufacture to the hard work of installing equipment.

Many years later, Mott's good friend, Alfred P. Sloan, Jr., in his autobiography, *Adventures of a White Collar Man,* was to write of Mott:

> But about the time I was starting in at Hyatt as a draftsman, this tall, blue-eyed young fellow, a mechanical engineer, had been working in overalls. He and his father had a small business, manufacturing soda-water machines. Charley Mott, between classes at Stevens Institute, installed the machines in drug-stores and confectionery shops. These appliances were hard to sell, but the Motts were pretty ingenious about it. They would permit a store owner to pay installments amounting each month to no more than he had previously been paying for tanks of carbonated water.

What Sloan calls a "pretty ingenious" way of selling the carbonators was a financing plan which Mott recalls in these words: "Payments were in the form of notes—one of the first, if not actually the first, form of installment selling. As there was some delay in our bank's notifying us of the payment of

13

notes sent for collection, we attached a printed postal card to each note, and when customer paid said note the collecting bank would sign and mail the postal to us and we would deposit the postal with our bank and get credit for same."

Mott received his degree as a mechanical engineer from Stevens in June, 1897, and occupied himself during the next year with developing the carbonating company. He was a personable young man, not only tall and blue-eyed, but distinctly handsome and of commanding appearance. Also, he had no objection to wearing overalls and working with his hands. The ingenuity Sloan noted has characterized Mott always. Being a mechanical engineer has meant more to Mott than merely having a degree. Not only was much of his early success based on his dogged ability to apply engineering principles to any new product problem, but the habit of mind he developed as an engineer—the same practical, methodical, logical progression from facts to decisions—has served him consistently in widely varied fields of application.

The Buffalo World's Fair in 1901 was to bring a striking instance of Mott's versatility as an engineer-manufacturer. The fair brought a request for forty carbonating machines which were to be "electrically operated and completely automatic." There had been no such machines—but Mott built them and delivered them on schedule.

Three years before that, Mott joined the U.S. Navy. This was on April 26, 1898, the day after the United States declared war on Spain. Mott is proud to remember that his organization was reported to be the first National Guard unit to join. They were assigned to the USS *Yankee,* a cruiser hastily converted from the Morgan Line's *El Norte.* Mott, a gunner's mate first class, was responsible for the four forward guns on the main deck; the ship was armed with a total of ten 5-inch guns, using fixed ammunition. The *Yankee* put out to sea from Brooklyn Navy Yard, and on May 12, took up the somewhat dreary duty of patrolling between Block Island and Cape Henlopen for a period of two weeks. Detached from patrol duty, the

Yankee was sent to join the Cuban blockade on May 29, 1898.

Young Mott was a good correspondent, and he wrote frequent letters to his parents, grandmother, and sister. One of these letters covers the famous incident in which Hobson scuttled the collier, *Merrimac,* in the channel at Santiago, and the next describes the *Yankee's* part in its first real action, the bombardment of Santiago on June 6, 1898, and subsequent activities.

Bahia de Guantanamo
Tuesday, June 7, about noon

Dear Father:

I presume the letter I wrote on Sunday will have reached you safely. On Sunday there was "nothing doing" and we got as much rest as possible. At night the lookouts were doubled. When day began to break about 4 A.M., Monday, we were called to quarters and we came most of us with but a pair of trousers on. We cleared for action and had a hurried bite and cup of coffee. Then the fleet, with the *New York* (flagship) at the head and the *Yankee* second, went into line of battle, and after an hour or so the ball began.

I think that anyone near the fort must have thought that hell was let loose. During the bombardment we threw about 200 five-inch shells and 300 six-pounders into the fortifications, and things were pretty well torn up. Of course, the other ships all did their share.

Our mark was the battery of six guns on the eastern side of the channel entering into the harbor. It was located on a very high rocky cliff, but I guess we played havoc pretty well with it. Below this battery there were other guns masked, but they did not shoot long. On the western side there was a good deal of firing, but I think that the battleships which shot at long range took good care of them and probably blew up their magazine, for there was a big fire and explosion. We opened fire at about 4000 yards and went in to 2000; were probably nearer all the time than any other vessel. Our skipper believes in being right in it. I was quite busy and the smoke was very dense, but I could see that no one did better shooting than the *Yankee.*

15

A little later in the day the *Dolphin,* which was near shore well east of the fort, discovered a trainload of Spanish soldiers creeping along the shore; they immediately let fly with six-pounders, and the train backed into a cut, from which they could neither advance nor retreat without being seen. Then a lot of shells were dropped near them. It is said that Garcia was aboard the *New York* yesterday, and he reported that great damage was done to the forts, in which 120 Spanish were killed; said that the *Dolphin* killed 112 on the train. Also that one of the large shells passed over the fort and landed on the forecastle of the *Vizcaya,* destroying one of her largest guns and killing 13 men.

At 12 o'clock that night we (*Yankee*) left for Guantanamo, about 40 miles east of Santiago; there we destroyed a block-house on a bluff, and threw a lot of shells into their fort, about 7000 yards up the bay. In front of the fort was a gunboat and a torpedo boat; it is believed that we hit the former. They threw some shells at us, but with no result.

The *St. Louis,* which was with us, remained outside and cut some cables.

On Tuesday night we went back to Santiago, where we remained for 24 hours. Last night we left for St. Nicholas Mole, Hayti. This morning we were ousted at 4 o'clock, when we sighted what proved to be a British tramp steamer.

St. Nicholas Mole, June 9—3 P.M.

No sooner was breakfast over than we had quarters, and then the "gunners' gang" had the lovely job of putting all the empty cartridge cases and boxes below. There were all of those from the two bombardments. I think it was the warmest work I ever did. The temperature on the deck is very high, but below it was terrific, and the air was not sweet. The nine of us had nothing on but shoes and stockings, and they were soaked through; it took us two hours to do the work. When I came on deck I nearly had a chill—it was so much cooler; had a brine-bucket salt-water bath afterwards.

Bumboatmen have been alongside selling oranges, limes, and bananas at N.Y. fancy prices; sour was no name for them.

We got here about noon and our boats are still ashore; don't know how long we shall stay here. It seems to me quite likely that we shall go to some place like Dry Tortugas, or Key West, to get troops; I don't see how we can ever accomplish much at Santiago or any other place in Cuba without them. My idea is bombardment, to be followed up by the landing of troops.

We have been fortunate in moving around; have had various experiences and seen quite a number of places for the length of time we have been in the service: Block Island, Delaware, and patrol service, then these three forts south here and taking a very prominent part in the Santiago bombardment and doing the Guantanamo alone. Have been with what is probably the largest American fleet, and had the excitement of blockading and being shot at and "torpedoed at."

Santiago, June 10

We left Hayti last night at about 8; at nearly midnight we were hustled out to quarters and found several lights in view; two of the ships had search lights; for the first time we did not chase them, but put on extra steam and came here flying. This morning, some hours after our arrival, a number of ships came in; they look to be transports and probably have many men aboard. I imagine that an attack will be made on the fort tomorrow.

The weather continues fine and hot. Suppose you are having it a little warm in the city.

Hope that this will reach you before the war is over. Love to mother, grandma, Edith and yourself and all.

Stewart

A hint of the heroic atmosphere which prevailed in this war is evident in Mott's letters. The former militiamen were careful to say from time to time that they knew they were not on a picnic—yet something of delighted excitement and boyish adventure is still apparent in both their actions and their reports. Bits from some of Mott's letters to members of his family show the enthusiasm, the pride of accomplishment, and the zest for living which he brought to this adventure in warfare:

Things seem to run much smoother now; mess, work, and everything. I think that just a little more discipline will make everything perfect. Give us about another month. Even now we get to our guns and man them in a way that pleases the Captain. In the daytime now we always wear clean whites, and no dirt goes. We have to scrub and wash clothes every other morning. In the evening we wear blues, which is regulation. Such beautiful skies and blue water I never saw before, it is simply great. Expect to see a great deal that is interesting and beautiful.

The *Yankee* had a part in nine engagements, and was at Guantanamo August 14, 1898, when signals were flashed from the flagship, "Peace protocol signed." The *Yankee* crew received a rousing reception when mustered out in New York; they were reviewed by President McKinley and Mayor Van Wyck. Thirty years later, when the members of the *Yankee's* crew published a book, *The USS Yankee on the Cuban Blockade,* the former Lieut. John Hubbard, executive officer of the *Yankee,* was a rear admiral, and was included with the commanding officer, Rear Admiral Willard H. Brownson, and Capt. William Butler Duncan, Naval Militia of New York, in the affectionate and respectful dedication of the volume. Hubbard's brilliant contribution to the volume makes clear the factors which had created some bitterness and friction aboard the *Yankee* on its wartime cruise—the gay, casual, informal, amateur approach of the well-educated young militiamen conflicting with the "Old Navy" regimen of discipline, smartness, and speed in carrying out orders.

It is significant that none of Mott's letters reflects any bitterness toward the officers; he apparently had much more realization than many of his fellow crew members of the necessity of discipline, smartness, and efficiency. This wartime experience taught him a great deal about men under stress; it gave him pride in his own accomplishment, as he demonstrated repeatedly his ability to hold his own as a man among men under difficult and strenuous conditions. He had been very much of an individualist; he remained an individualist. However, he also learned to work, as an individual, in effective cooperation with many other men for a common end. He learned to respect discipline as a major means to cooperative accomplishment in an organization.

After his discharge, Mott continued to serve as chief gunner's mate in the New York Naval Militia. He also resumed his activities with the carbonating company which bore his name, and worked with his father in the management of the Genesee Fruit Company and in the other interests the family had acquired, which included acting with his father as sales representatives for the Weston-Mott Company, manufacturers of wire wheels.

On Mott's twenty-fourth birthday, June 2, 1899, his father, forty-nine years old and at the height of a successful career, died suddenly. Thus Charles Stewart Mott began his twenty-fifth year with a burden of sorrow and responsibility. By January, 1900, one of his uncles had taken over much of the management of the Genesee Fruit Company, and it was suggested that Mott go to Utica, New York, as secretary and superintendent of the Weston-Mott Company.

In 1896, while Mott had still been at Stevens Institute, his father and uncle had bought I. A. Weston and Company, Jamesville, N.Y., manufacturers of bicycle hubs and wheels since 1884. The company had been reorganized as the Weston-Mott Company, with the uncle, Frederick G. Mott, as president and manager, and with C. S. Mott as a director. In 1898, the Weston-Mott Company had been moved into a new factory in Utica. At about the same time, the demand for bicycle wheels had dwindled. The Weston-Mott Company had struck out in several directions at once: drop-forged axles and wire wheels with cushion rubber tires for a new type of light carriage; wire wheels for push carts, implements, and wheel chairs—even wheels for jinrikshas—and, last, wire wheels for automobiles. Acting as New York sales representatives for the Weston-Mott Company, C. S. Mott and his father had, in

1898, sold wire wheels to such early automobile makers as Canda Quadricycle Company, Grout Automobile Company, and the Autocar Company.

To the young man who had been bent since boyhood on mechanical engineering, the affairs of the Weston-Mott Company held deeper interest than the business of the Genesee Fruit Company. It is likely that young Mott's concern with mechanical engineering had been a factor in his father's decision to buy into the Weston-Mott Company in the first place.

For the first six months of 1900, Mott divided his time between Utica and New York City, acting as superintendent of Weston-Mott, and carrying on the activities of the C. S. Mott Company in manufacturing carbonators.

Mott had another reason for spending most of his weekends in New York City; he was engaged to Miss Ethel Culbert Harding, whose mother had been a girlhood friend of his mother. Miss Harding's father, Herbert Brunswick Harding, was manager of a medicine company, "Humphrey's Homeopathic Medicines," which was reputed to have an advertisement once a week in every newspaper in the United States.

Charles Stewart Mott and Ethel Culbert Harding were married at All Angels Church in New York City on June 14, 1900. After a wedding trip to New Brunswick, Canada, where the Harding family had a long and distinguished history, the Motts settled in Utica. They visited New York City from time to time, and often attended the opera. Mott continued to manage his carbonating company, and later moved it to Utica, where he kept it operating for some years until he became too busy to attend to it. Eventually the Duffy Company bought the original Mott cider and vinegar company, although to this day the name Mott is retained on cider and other products sold by that firm.

Gradually Mott took over purchasing and engineering in the Weston-Mott Company, as well as acting as its secretary and superintendent. Frederick G. Mott, president of the company, was in the process of withdrawing from active management. In addition to bringing his nephew from New York, he interested a Utica man, William G. Doolittle, in joining the company as part owner and treasurer. The Weston-Mott Company struggled to adapt to the changing developments in vehicle manufacturing. In the year from January 1, 1900, to January 1, 1901, the company had sales of $149,891, but showed a loss of $1,480 and a depletion of operating surplus to $10,303.

The fight for business involved rapid change of products to meet shifting demands. It was apparent that the future of the Weston-Mott Company lay with the rising automobile industry. Mott's notes of those years include the following:

In 1900, R. E. Olds decided to put on the market the new curved dash runabout he had designed. We got his order for 500 sets of wire wheels, and that order was duplicated a number of times during the following few years until we had furnished about 3,000 sets, which was enormous business for that time. We also made wire wheels for many automobile manufacturers, including my much respected friend J. W. Packard of Warren, Ohio—founder of the Packard Motor Company. It was J. W., who, when demand changed from wire to wood wheels, told me that he regretted it, and that he only hoped that the wood wheels would stand up as well as our wire wheels. And when that change occurred, cars were quoted with wire wheels as standard and wood wheels $100 extra. Years later, after wood wheels had become standard, demountable wire wheels were offered at $100 per set extra.

But back to 1902: We were receiving large quantity orders for wire wheels from R. E. Olds. He hung on to the use of wire wheels longer than anyone else. We were running night and day. Then, during 1902, he cancelled all orders and shut us down. The bottom dropped out of the wire wheel business, and the management of Weston-Mott Company went to other activities, and I was left with responsibility of a factory and payroll, and very little business or income.

It was up to me to do something, and I went out on the road to meet for the first time the automobile manufacturers, and to try to sell them artillery wood wheels with which we had neither experience nor production.

Sales were impossible; they wanted to buy front and rear chain drive axles with their wheels. Previously they had built their own tubular frames of different construction from what they now wanted. In fact, there was only one other source producing something of the type of what was desired.

So, we had to design axles of our own—make drawings and blueprints of what we had never produced, and solicit business for a line of goods with which we had no experience. But before I went home, I had secured orders for a volume of business greater than we had ever done in one year, and still we had never built an axle.

Those were not the days of the 40-hour week. Our factory started at 7 A.M., and ran until 6 P.M.—with one hour out for lunch—10 hours a day, 60 hours a week. I used to get to the factory at 6 A.M., taking my lunch with me, and work until 7 P.M., trying to construct axles which would do the job. It was several months before that was accomplished.

What now seems very simple was very difficult because no one had ever done it before. Suitable material, knowledge of design, and experience—were mighty scarce. At last we produced something. Today, I should not be very proud of the result, but at least it was as good as anything anybody else had. It showed wear with use, of course, but it stood up well, and did not break down, as was the case with the product of others. We used ball bearings in the front, and Hyatt Roller Bearings in the rear. Differentials were purchased from the Brown-Lipe Company.

The Cadillac Company started in 1902, and contracted with the American Ball Bearing Company, of Cleveland, for 3,000 sets—but these axles did not stand up, and the Cadillac Company turned to us for supply. During 1903, we furnished them with 1,500 sets of axles. The Hyatt Roller Bearings were run directly on shafts and the interior of tubes. They did not break—and that fact enabled the Cadillac Company to produce and sell cars. Later, shafting material was changed. Still later, Hyatt Roller Bearings were ground, and run on hardened sleeves on the shafts, and hardened sleeves within the tubes.

In those early years, Mott and Doolittle each received $100 a month as salary. They contracted with two men to true-up wire wheels, and those men, on piecework, often earned more than the superintendent and treasurer. A foreman once left without notice; so Mott put on overalls and acted as foreman of the rim department for some time, along with his other responsibilities. He was not satisfied with the rim machinery and arranged to have it changed so that the rollers could be opened up and rims could be replaced in the machine for further operations after welding.

Life was not all work and business; Mott and his wife enjoyed the social life of Utica and their regular visits to New York City. Their first daughter, Aimee, was born April 15, 1902.

In September, 1901, Mott bought his first automobile, a Remington. He still has the original invoice on the letterhead of the Remington Automobile and Motor Company of Utica:

REMINGTON AUTOMOBILE AND MOTOR CO.

Utica, N.Y.
Sept. 10 '01

Remington Automobile & Motor Company,

Sold to   Mr. C. S. Mott
          Weston Mott Co.
          Utica, N.Y.

Terms—NET

One Remington motor complete with dynamo, batteries, carburretter, muffler, etc.	$175.00
One Style "C" body complete	75.00
One water and gasoline tank	9.50
Tools, pump, oil-can, bell	3.25
One pair "Baby Square" lamps, No charge.	
One transmission gear, special price	50.00
One set foot levers, rods, etc. complete	6.50
One radiator complete with attachments	10.00
Ironing body for motor and to gear	10.00

Labor on complete job, at cost 25.00
(Other parts furnished by C. S. Mott) ....
                                            $364.25

PAID

Sept. 26, 1901
Remington Automobile & Motor Co.
L. Malcolm Graham Treas.

Mott drove his Remington in a "Horseless Carriage Run" in 1902. He was a charter member and first president of the Automobile Club of Utica, and he was one of the founders of the American Automobile Association in Chicago. On September 4, 1902, Mott traded in his first Remington, being credited not only with the full amount of the original purchase price, but also receiving an additional allowance of $135 for "running gear, steering levers, wheels, tires, and compensating gear" which he had furnished for that first car. The net difference he paid for his new "special 1903 Remington" on September 4, 1902, was $140.75.

Mott worked furiously. Now, at last, he had full scope for his engineering ability. His uncle, Frederick G. Mott, became interested in oil lands in the West, and offered his Weston-Mott stock for sale. Mott and William G. Doolittle purchased this stock and other outstanding stock in the Weston-Mott Company in 1903. They were equal partners in the enterprise, with Mott being president.

In 1901, the company's sales had risen to $195,076, with a profit of $11,303, all of which was added to the operating surplus. From January to September, 1902, Weston-Mott sales were $159,547, with a total profit of $19,004. A 3 per cent dividend amounting to $1,500 was declared, and the operating surplus was increased to $40,610. In 1903, sales were well over $200,000.

The partnership between Mott and Doolittle was a pleasant and effective relationship, with Doolittle attending to the financial problems of the company and Mott handling the other major aspects of the business. Mott and Doolittle drew up a contract by which the life of each was insured in favor of the other, and by which, in the event of the death of either partner, the other might purchase the deceased partner's stock at a set figure if he wished—or, even if he did not wish to do so, the surviving partner might be required by the deceased partner's heirs to purchase the stock, but at a lower figure.

The business flourished, adapting rapidly to the many changes required by the developing automobile industry. The size of the factory at Utica was doubled, and doubled again, and the number of employees increased accordingly. From August 15, 1903, to August 1, 1905, just before that first visit Mott and Doolittle paid to Flint, the company's earnings were $601,572, and the operating surplus was increased to $191,073.

THREE

The September, 1905, visit of Mott and Doolittle to Flint came just after the city, in its golden jubilee, had taken a long look at its own story. The celebration was in honor of Flint's fiftieth anniversary as an incorporated city.

In 1855, there had been about 2,000 people in Flint when the community became a city. Lumbering was already the chief industry, and it was to dominate the scene for a quarter-century and to develop its great men. Perhaps the most impressive of those great men was Henry H. Crapo. He contributed mightily to Flint's lumber boom and at one time had as many as five lumber mills in operation simultaneously. He was also an ardent agriculturist and, inaugurated as governor of Michigan in 1865, a distinguished public servant. The Flint and Holly Railroad, built by Governor Crapo and his friends, was an essential step in Flint's progress. Lumber from Flint went to every corner of the world, and the city enjoyed rising prosperity until the pine had been harvested.

With the end of the pine, the people of Flint had to look for other types of employment. Their energy, ingenuity, and enterprise were equal to the problem. A variety of industries developed, mostly concerned with aspects of woodworking. Among these, the most important was wagon-and-carriage making. W. A. Paterson had opened a carriage and repair shop in Flint in 1869.

In 1886, an apparently minor event took place which was to have an immeasurable effect on the future of Flint. William Crapo Durant, grandson of Gov. H. H. Crapo, learned that for $2,000 he could buy the Coldwater Road Cart Company. He entered into a business partnership with a friend, J. Dallas Dort, and they bought the road cart business. This inconspicuous fact provided the foundation which was to make Flint first "The Vehicle City," celebrated for its wagons and carriages, and later, "Auto-maker to the World."

The Durant-Dort Carriage Company, the W. A. Paterson Company, and the Flint Wagon Works, were notably successful enterprises and attracted many skilled craftsmen to Flint. By 1905, Flint's population was estimated at 16,000.

In 1903, the pioneer qualities of enterprise and ingenuity which have always characterized Flint had led J. H. Whiting, of the Flint Wagon Works, to venture into the automobile business by buying the Buick Motor Company from the Briscoe brothers, and bringing inventor David D. Buick and his one Buick car to Flint. It seemed perhaps logical that a wagon-and-carriage maker should simply place engines in his carriages and thus make the transition to the automobile age. It proved, of course, much less simple than that, and in the course of time J. H. Whiting called on another carriage maker to carry on the faltering development of the Buick Company.

That man was W. C. Durant, who had already made a fortune and a national reputation for success with his Durant-Dort Blue Ribbon carriages and road carts. Durant hesitated, investigated, then made up his mind. He poured all of his vision, energy, organization, and financial genius into the Buick Motor Company. It was typical of his foresight that one of the first major acts in his development of Buick, shortly after he had assumed responsibility for the management of the company, was to invite the Weston-Mott Company to move to Flint so that there would be an unfailing supply of axles for Buicks.

In response, Mott faced away from the East he knew so well and ventured his whole future in Flint with complete confidence. His foresight was never more accurate than at that moment. When Mott and Doolittle returned to Utica they lost no time in developing their plans for the move to Flint. On September 16, 1905, a notice was sent to all Weston-Mott employees explaining the several reasons for moving the plant to Flint, and expressing the "earnest desire that the men who are now in our employ shall accompany us." Four days later, an announcement of the move was sent to Weston-Mott customers, assuring them that the "removal can be made without interfering with this season's business," and that "when we are in our new home we can promise, not only continued satisfaction from a mechanical point of view, but also first class deliveries."

The business continued in Utica while construction was started in Flint. As building advanced, machinery was shipped from Utica, although manufacturing operations were maintained there until the Flint plant opened. Meanwhile, the Motts continued their pleasant life in Utica. Their oldest daughter, Aimee, had been born in 1902; their second child, Elsa Beatrice, had come along in 1904, and their third child, Charles Stewart Harding, was born in 1906.

The Weston-Mott Company had to decline some business during 1906 because of the difficulties of keeping up production while transferring operations. Many other problems were involved in the transition from Utica to Flint. One of them was finding housing for the 100-odd Utica employees who planned to move to Flint with the company. Weston-Mott was at that time employing about 240 men in Utica and was expecting to be able to give employment to 350 men in Flint. A local committee was formed to compile lists of available houses.

In June, 1906, the Weston-Mott Company of Utica, New York, became the Weston-Mott Company of Flint, Michigan. A board of directors was elected: William G. Doolittle, Charles S. Mott, and Frederick H. Hazard of Utica, New York; Arthur G. Bishop and John J. Carton of Flint. The directors elected as officers: C. S. Mott, president; J. J. Carton, vice-president; A. G. Bishop, secretary; W. G. Doolittle, treasurer. Capitalization was $500,000.

On August 8, 1906, the power was turned on for the first time in the Weston-Mott factory of Flint, with twenty men already employed and a small proportion of the machinery ready to run. The formal opening of the new plant was postponed until September. In addition to the machinery shipped from Utica, new machines had been ordered and it was expected to run the new plant with a total of 400 machines. The factory was praised as one of the finest and most modern, providing ample light and ventilation for workmen.

By early August that year, a number of the company's Utica employees had moved to Flint. Though many stayed behind, most key men chose to move with the company; of these, several were to play important parts in the future of both Flint and the automobile industry. One of them was Harry H. Bassett, who had been with the Remington Arms Company for fourteen years when Mott hired him. He was effective and adaptive and soon became assistant manager. He was appointed factory manager on March 25, 1907, when Hubert Dalton, his predecessor, resigned.

During this period, Buick, spurred by the driving genius of Durant, was taking tremendous strides. In 1905 Buick made more than 600 cars, and in 1906 about twice that many and had orders for almost 900 more. Buick output was increased by 50 per cent in 1907, not withstanding the panic in the country. Durant looked forward to the time when he would be making 50,000 cars a year. The carriage industry was still very much alive. In fact, it was on September 29, 1905, the same month that Mott and Doolittle had made their decision to move to Flint, that the Durant-Dort Carriage Company received the largest single order in its history. Through Durant's connection with the Durant-Dort Carriage Company, he was able to draw upon both the financial resources and the other facilities of the carriage company to assist the expanding Buick organization. In the panic of 1907, when many automobile companies were falling by the wayside, Durant conceived the idea of showing Buick automobiles in Durant-Dort Carriage display rooms throughout the country, which is said to have been the beginning of the auto showroom in America.

The new Weston-Mott plant, located at the corner of

Hamilton and Industrial Avenues beside the new Buick plant, covered 60,000 square feet but soon became inadequate. Buick and Flint were leaping ahead, and since Weston-Mott production was primarily tied to Buick production, the company had to match the expansion of Buick at every step. In February, 1907, Buick made news by consigning 90 Buicks—the regular 2-cylinder, model F—to the Pense Auto Company of Minneapolis, all shipped on one special 30-car train.

Almost every week saw some new report of Buick plans for enlargement of production facilities, with orders exceeding capacity. More than 4,000 men and women were employed in the more than 80 "manufactories" in Flint. In December, 1907, the W. F. Stewart Body Company found it necessary to schedule evening overtime to meet the demand for buggy and automobile bodies. But these were not the only vehicles being built in Flint. The W. A. Paterson Company reported having built and sold nearly 3,000 sleighs in the current season ending the day before Christmas.

With all these signs of progress and expansion in Flint, the year 1907 was difficult in many ways. Among the voluminous notes Mott has kept, there is one which states:

> Back about March, 1907, there was a "Bank Freeze-up" of funds, and there was cash available only for minimum payroll. All automobile manufacturers except W. C. Durant quit production, but not the visionary W. C., who kept on full-steam-ahead, and as cars could not be sold because no one had money to pay for them, Durant filled all available warehouses with Buick cars, and when in the course of months the money market "unfroze" Durant had the finished cars to sell—and how he sold them and made a lot of money with which he enlarged Buick to make more cars, was really something—and gives you an idea of the kind of man this Billy Durant was. . . . All of our customers except Buick held up their orders and we could make no collections. I can't remember how we scraped together enough money to meet payrolls. I visited all of our customers and prevailed upon them to settle their accounts with us, with bunches of notes

of $1,000 or so each, and then I undertook to settle my accounts payable with these notes endorsed. Many came back to me with the statement that they had to have the money. I had to again send them the notes with invitation to come to Flint and help us get cash on percentage basis. The notes were accepted and, I presume, passed on to our creditors' creditors, and we discovered a new elastic currency. When, later in the year, the panic passed, and cash was available, these notes were paid off while other creditors were getting notes. And Durant and Buick made a killing with the large stock of cars they had accumulated while other manufacturers were shut down.

Within a year after Mott moved to Flint, his partner, W. G. Doolittle, died. This threw the entire responsibility for the financial aspects of the business on Mott, in addition to production and sales. According to the contract between the two men, Mott exercised the right to purchase the deceased partner's stock at the stipulated figure. This made him sole owner of the Weston-Mott Company.

Buick expansion continued, both in production and in the building of additional plant space. In June, 1908, the Buick plant was reported to be turning out a complete car every 12 minutes, and output was increasing. The plant operated 18 to 20 hours a day, and total output that June was 1,654 cars. Buick won more racing trophies in 1908 than all other cars combined, and that was the year when the famous Buick model 10 captured the imagination of men and women throughout the country. The boom was on for Buick, for Weston-Mott, and for Flint. It carried into 1909, when Buick production passed the 10,000-car mark.

As for Weston-Mott, in the year beginning August 1, 1908, the company's sales topped $2 million for the first time. Of that sum, more than $500,000 was accounted total profit. The next year, the original $500,000 capitalization of Weston-Mott was increased to $1.5 million and sales were more than $5.5 million. Such increase of production could be accomplished only by tremendous expansion of plant, facilities, and working force. In October, 1908, the Weston-Mott Company contracted for a plant expansion to provide 105,000 additional square feet of floor space. The company had about 500 employees and the new addition was to make room for 250 more.

This was a period of highly diversified and intensive activity for Mott himself. He hired most of his executives during this period, and functioned as sales manager and chief salesman for the company. He also found time to follow his interest in engineering and design. Mott notes: "For the first years there was a question whether the engineer or I designed the axles. In other words, I would explain the thing, talk it over, and decide what we wanted to do, how we wanted to do it, and the engineer would put it on paper. But I'm not trying to take anything away from the engineers. In the course of time, it became the responsibility of the engineering department, but for a long time it was my responsibility." Among those Weston-Mott engineers was F. A. Bower, later to become a distinguished chief engineer of Buick and one of the most active citizens of Flint in civic affairs.

No matter how busy he was, Mott held fast to his belief in personal management. While able and willing to delegate both responsibility and authority, he has never relinquished his own sense of personal responsibility for accomplishment of established purposes in the most effective possible ways. He also found time for interests and activities outside the immediate scope of the Weston-Mott Company. Asked if he would like to become a director of Genesee County Savings Bank, Mott accepted on the basis that he had had no experience in banking but thought it was a good time to learn.

1908 was a great year for Flint in many ways. It saw the final transfer of all Buick operations from Jackson to Flint and the increase of employment at the Buick plant to about 2,500 men. Albert Champion came to Flint and, with others, founded the Champion Ignition Company. The Flint *Journal* reported: "Mr. Champion is said to be the world's champion motor-cyclist. He has taken prizes in almost every land, it is stated, and has paced the greatest bicycle riders of the world. The devices which will be manufactured by the new concern are stated to be entirely his own invention." Champion was to remain an important and colorful figure in the automotive world, and his initials are still embodied in the name of the AC Spark Plug Division of General Motors.

The most significant event of all in 1908 was the birth of General Motors, with the official certificate of incorporation filed in New Jersey, September 16, 1908. Durant's urge for expansion, founded on the success of Buick and the necessity for increased facilities to meet the rising demand, was driving for new channels. One of the first acts of General Motors was the acquisition of 49 per cent of the stock of Weston-Mott Company, leaving Mott still in control but tied closely to the future of General Motors. Within another year, General Motors acquired some twenty companies in the automobile industry including Olds, Cadillac, and Oakland, so that several Weston-Mott customers became part of General Motors, thus increasing the already close relationship between the two companies. Weston-Mott, however, still had outside customers.

A letter Mott addressed on July 31, 1909, to Durant illuminates the problems accompanying ever-increasing production and the need for perpetual expansion.

July 31st, 1909

Mr. W. C. Durant,
   c/o General Motors Co.,
   New York, N.Y.

Dear Sir:-
   Enclosed please find copy of letter which I sent over to Mr. Little yesterday and which we have gone over in detail with him today. In further explanation will state that the outside contracts that we have taken on amount to about 30,000 sets and we presume that we have turned down other business of equal amount. The 30,000 plus the 44,000 that we had figured for General Motors Co., would have taken our capacity and we should have had to work night and day to take

care of it. The additional 30,000 that you require is in excess of what we feel we can take care of with present plans for factory and equipment. The new factory Mr. Wood is going to put up for us back of Imperial will be 400 ft. long, 74 ft. wide, two stories and basement and he said he could have this ready within three months from the time we placed order three weeks ago, but we presume we will be lucky if we get into it early in November.

Mr. Bassett feels that if we give him another factory same size as above mentioned to be placed along side of it back of the Imperial that he can equip that factory for front axles using our present factory for rears and thereby be able to get out the 25,000 Model 10's and 5,000 deliveries that we would otherwise be unable to produce. He feels that that will be all of the output we could expect to obtain from the new factory this year but that in 1911 these additions would enable us to considerable increase in our output.

Mr. Wood is out of town today but we presume if we placed order with him at once that it would be December first before he could get the building finished.

Regarding amount of funds necessary to handle this extension, will say that we should want to cover the building, additional machinery and equipment, the stock and increased account at least $400,000.00 more than our present plans, and in order to take care of these we should require $100,000.00 of it available in September, $100,000.00 October, $100,-000.00 November, and $100,000.00 December, to be borrowed on notes maturing not earlier than August or September 1910. This money we would want to borrow aside from our present sources of supply for in order to carry out our present plans to get out the original 75,000 sets we figure that we would want to increase the capital stock by $300,000.00 cash—one-half by General Motors Co., and one-half by myself. What additional money we needed we would be able to borrow from banks with which we are at present doing business, this with the understanding that we can depend upon your advice that you have an outlet where we can use all of the General Motors constituent companies' notes which we may receive in payment of account. Furthermore, it is with the understanding that the Weston-Mott Co., will not be called upon to furnish any additional cash capital or cash loan to the Oak Park Power Co., for if it is up to us to do this we shall have to have borrowing capacity for just that much more.

Mr. Little requested me to write you in full as above stating that you would be in New York on Tuesday and would wire me as to whether or not to proceed on above basis with your assurance that the financial proposition would be taken care of as above outlined.

The material situation is very serious with us and we have requested Mr. Chapin of Brown-Lipe Gear Co., to be here on Tuesday and the Union Drop Forge Co., on Thursday.

Trusting that this covers the ground and awaiting your wire, I am,

Very truly yours,
C. S. Mott

These immediate problems were solved temporarily, as were the hundreds of others that came up every week. Designs also changed, and there was a perpetual need for new engineering and production developments. Weston-Mott had been buying differential gears from the Brown-Lipe Company and was that firm's largest customer. A decision was made to use a new bevel-gear differential for Buick, Cadillac, Olds, and Oakland. Mott called H. W. Chapin, secretary of the Brown-Lipe Company, to Flint and asked him whether his company was prepared to make the new bevel gear. Chapin realized that tooling costs would be tremendous, but made an immediate decision to undertake the manufacture of the new design. Additional financing was needed, and as a result the Brown-Lipe-Chapin Company, with Mott furnishing half the capital, was organized to handle the production. The company entered into a contract with General Motors in February, 1910, and later became part of General Motors.

The Weston-Mott Company, for all its close relationship with General Motors, still maintained its separate entity, and Mott had no hesitation in exercising the control represented by his 51 per cent of the stock.

On May 6, 1910, Durant sent Mott the following telegram:

WOULD IT INTERFERE WITH BUSINESS AND WOULD YOU CARE TO ACCEPT MEMBERSHIP GENERAL MOTORS DIRECTORATE? EXPECT TO ORGANIZE PERMANENT BOARD NEXT WEEK. PLEASE WIRE.

Mott telegraphed the following reply:

VERY MUCH COMPLIMENTED BY YOUR OFFER BUT FEEL THAT UNTIL WE CAN MAKE AXLE SUPPLY SUFFICIENT AND SATISFACTORY TO OUR CUSTOMERS AS WE EXPECT TO DO DURING COMING SEASON THEY WOULD FEEL THAT WE WOULD BE PREJUDICED IN OUR SHIPMENTS AND FEARING HOLDUP AND POOR SERVICE AS AT PRESENT TIME THEY WOULD REFUSE TO CONTRACT WITH US FOR NINETEEN ELEVEN REQUIREMENTS. I WOULD NOT HESITATE IF I COULD FOR ONE SEASON GET ENOUGH MATERIAL AND DEMONSTRATE OUR ABILITY TO MEET SHIPPING SPECIFICATIONS. I, THEREFORE, BELIEVE THAT IT WOULD NOT AT PRESENT BE TO BEST INTEREST OF WESTON-MOTT COMPANY FOR ME TO ACCEPT.

The difficulty to which Mott referred in this telegram— getting materials and supplies to keep up with increased orders —applied with even more force to General Motors as a whole. This problem of getting materials, coupled with an almost incredible program of expansion, brought General Motors into troubled times in 1910. In spite of enormous sales, expansion had been so rapid, and so many companies had been purchased, that a great deal of money was needed. When Durant found that the only way to secure the money was to relinquish his own management of General Motors, he did so. In September, 1910, General Motors gave a five-year 6 per cent note for $15 million and common stock worth $2 million to get $12,750,000 in cash to meet obligations. The Eastern bankers who made the loan were also given control of the company through a voting trust. It is a tribute to the vitality of the young General Motors Company that it was able to survive such a crisis. Durant remained a director, but busied himself with other interests.

1910 had begun as a boom year in Flint, with a happy

accounting of the fantastic gains of 1909. Buick introduced two new models, the No. 19 touring car and the No. 14 runabout—along with continued production of the pioneer model F, and the No. 10, No. 16, and No. 17. A state labor-bureau report showed that average daily wages had increased from $2.20 to $2.62 in 1909. Almost 500 women were employed in Flint factories, and their average daily wage had also increased —from $1.13 in 1908 to $1.18 in 1909. Flint entered 1910 as fourth city in Michigan in the number of wage-earners employed, having more than doubled its number of workers during 1909. There were more than 10,000 employed in Flint factories at the beginning of 1910, compared with 4,449 in 1908.

The automobile was beginning to become a major item in world commerce, with the United States second to France in the value of cars exported. Buick was sweeping along triumphantly, having made 4,437 cars in the last quarter of 1909— more than twice as many as Cadillac. Buick's output in that quarter almost equalled the combined production of Reo, Hudson, Regal, Franklin, Peerless, Pierce-Arrow, Mitchell, and Stoddard-Dayton cars in the same period. It was claimed that half the cars sold in Detroit in 1909 were Buicks. In the first quarter of 1910, Buick made 6,478 cars, an increase of nearly 50 per cent over the last quarter of 1909.

Flint was at the peak of activity, and in August, 1910, the following official census figures summarized the story of the growth of Flint:

Year	Population
1855	2,000
1860	2,950
1870	5,386
1880	8,409
1890	9,803
1900	13,103
1910	38,550

It was in the midst of this roaring boom that the General Motors expansion stumbled over its own magnitude and almost crashed of its own weight. More literally, the demands of expansion went millions of dollars beyond available funds —and the day came when Durant negotiated the incredibly expensive loan from Eastern bankers at the cost of his personal control of the company he had created. Through the whole difficult period, Durant issued optimistic statements. Although the group providing the new financing insisted upon Durant's relinquishing control of General Motors, they accepted his recommendation that Charles W. Nash—then superintendent of the Durant-Dort Carriage Company—be made general manager of Buick. The announcement of this fact was made September 17, 1910, in a Flint newspaper, in the customary euphemistic terms—requiring more than a little reading between the lines.

C. W. NASH TO BE GENERAL MANAGER OF BUICK PLANT

Charles W. Nash, of this city, will assume charge of the plant of the Buick Motor company on Monday as general manager of that big industrial institution. This change comes as a sequel to a readjustment of the business of the company which has been in progress for the last several weeks. The appointment of Mr. Nash was made at the insistence of W. C. Durant under whose direction the plant has been operated and who has found it necessary to relinquish official duties which have called for more time and attention than he could well spare from the General Motors company and other interests with which he is actively identified.

The business of general manager was tendered to Mr. Nash by Mr. Durant six months ago, but its acceptance was delayed until the present time, owing to the fact that Mr. Nash had made all arrangements for an extended trip abroad from which he recently returned. It is understood that Mr. Nash will have full charge and control of the business of the Buick Motor company in all its departments and that he will devote his entire time to its interests.

Mr. Nash has heretofore been prominent in the industrial affairs of Flint having been for a number of years general superintendent of the associated factories of the Durant-Dort Carriage Co. as vice-president of that organization and a director of the Flint Varnish Works. Mr. Nash has been in Boston for the last few days on business connected with the Buick Motor company and is expected to return to this city tomorrow.

There are seven models in the Buick line for 1911, and all of them give promise of meeting with a favorable reception at the hands of the trade. The company is behind in its orders and is turning out cars at the rate of about 65 per day. The shipments for the 6 working days of last month amounted to an even 400 cars, and the plant is working today to produce 102 cars to bring the total for this week up to the same number as last week. The number of cars turned out for this week up to last night was 298. The number of men employed in the several mechanical departments of the Buick plant is upwards of 2300; the exact number on the payroll yesterday, being 2393.

At the same time, there were cautious reassurances to a worried Flint that "arrangements" had been made to secure the financial stability of General Motors. In the meantime, the working force at Buick had dropped under 2,500, and there was considerable delay in getting the 1911 models ready. In late September and early October, the details of the new financing reached the public. By October 10, the plant-expansion activities were resumed at the Buick drop-forge plant. By February, 1911, Buick employment was back up to 4,800, and Weston-Mott had 1,000 workers.

FOUR

The fears and uncertainties of 1910, as they affected Flint people, contributed to one rather remarkable event in the town's political history: Flint elected a Socialist Mayor in 1911. This distinct shock to the "old Flint" people and the business and industrial men suggested the unpredictability of the thousands of "new" people who had been drawn to Flint from every point of the compass. Indirectly, it had a strong influence on Mott's future.

A Detroit newspaper story of May 30, 1911, gave the public a hint of what Durant had been doing with his time since relinquishing active management of General Motors. It also introduced a new automobile name, but no one could have guessed then just how large that name would be written on the futures of Flint, General Motors, Durant, Mott, and the automotive world.

W. C. DURANT TO START AUTO PLANT

W. C. Durant of the General Motors company and racer Louis Chevrolet, one of the speed wonders of the day and a co-worker with Mr. Durant in the manufacture and exploitation of fast cars, will establish a factory in Detroit for the manufacture of a new high-priced car whose chief distinctive feature will be an engine perfected during the last winter by Chevrolet assisted financially by Durant.

After Chevrolet goes through the 500 mile race on the Indianapolis speedway today he will enter a commercial race for those rich rewards that go not to the drivers but to the manufacturers of automobiles.

For the first time since his retirement last October, Chevrolet is expected to be in the big auto racing event of the year today. He was at first listed as a relief driver but on

40

petitions of the pilots entered he was announced to drive a Buick in the contest.

Last winter at a garage on Grand River Avenue in this city, Chevrolet experimented secretly with a new type engine that is to be the chief selling advantage in the new car. Chevrolet is of French-Swiss birth. He came to America in 1900 after securing in France a complete education in automobile construction and driving where he made a record as a racing driver and expert. He has been a winner in many races of national fame. After severing other connections he engaged with Buick in 1908. As a skilled mechanic he was retained in a business way by Mr. Durant.

The new Durant-Chevrolet car, it is stated, will be of high grade. Mr. Durant will make his headquarters in Detroit though he will retain his interest in the carriage works in Flint with which he has been identified for many years.

On July 31, 1911, a second Durant activity emerged—the Mason Motor Company. On October 30, 1911, a third Durant project was announced: the Little Motor Company of Flint. The company was named for W. H. Little, former Buick factory manager. Little, and two other notable Flint men, C. M. Begole and W. S. Ballenger, appeared as incorporators of the new company, but it was known, of course, that Durant was the "moving spirit of the enterprise."

The old Flint Wagon Works plant had been acquired with 871,000 square feet of floor space, and Durant said its capacity would be 15,000 cars a year. He planned to make a 4-cylinder runabout with self-starter—to sell for $600. He also planned a 24-horsepower 6-cylinder car to be sold at $1,400. Thus in a year the irrepressible Durant bounced back with three companies sustained at first chiefly by the magical luster of his name and the confidence of his old friends—among whom Mott was one.

In November, 1911, Mott was making his second trip to Europe—this time as a member of the Society of Automobile Engineers. He made H. H. Bassett general manager of the

Weston-Mott Company and felt freer than ever before to permit himself outside interests. Bassett announced that Weston-Mott business was unusually good, and that the company's employment had reached 1,400, with still more being added as fast as materials could be secured for them to work on. He also mentioned the fine business during 1911 with the new demountable wheel rims invented by E. K. Baker.

Mott, of course, had not been unaware of Durant's new gestures in automobile manufacturing. In August, 1911, Durant had invited Mott to join the Chevrolet venture.

> Cadillac Hotel,
> Detroit, Michigan,
> August 22, 1911.

Mr. C. S. Mott,
Flint, Michigan.

My dear Mr. Mott:

I have reserved $250,000 worth of stock for you in our new company and you can send me check for the whole or any part of it at your convenience.

We have decided to establish permanently in Detroit and have secured an ideal location. Construction work will commence this fall. The arrangement of the plant will be similar to the Buick but somewhat larger.

Everybody goes in on the same basis excepting Mr. Little, who subscribes for $250,000 of the stock, paying in $125,-000 and giving his notes (twenty-five for $5,000 each, drawing interest at the rate of 5%) for the balance, secured by the $125,000 stock issued against the notes. As the notes are retired, an equal amount of stock is to be released. In case he becomes incapacitated and is unable to give his undivided attention to the business, any remaining unpaid notes are to be cancelled and the stock returned to the treasury of the company. All of the subscribers will agree to the above, everyone of whom are on the same basis excepting Mr. Little.

I think you will be quite pleased with the plan, policy of the company and product. I will explain more fully when I see you.

If you prefer, the subscription can be made and the stock issued in the name of some other party and endorsed over to you.

Address next ten days care Cadillac Hotel this city.

Yours sincerely,
W. C. Durant

P.S. I would very much like to have you actively interested.

Mott did not write in reply at the time, but discussed the offer with Durant somewhat later. At the beginning of October, Durant wrote again, this time with an invitation to subscribe for stock in the Little Motor Car Company.

October 2nd, 1911.

Mr. C. S. Mott,
  Flint, Michigan.

Dear Mr. Mott:

A new organization for the manufacture of motor cars in Flint is contemplated and the property of the Flint Wagon Works has been secured for the purpose.

The plant will be entirely remodeled and when completed will have approximately 350,000 sq. feet of floor space with a capacity of 20,000 cars per year.

The new company, which will be called the Little Motor Car Company, will have a capitalization of $500,000 preferred and $700,000 common, of which $207,000 of preferred and $469,100 common has been subscribed.

The company has obtained a contract and license from the Chevrolet Motor Company for a term of years which enables it to manufacture an attractive line of motor cars without experimental or engineering expense (the heaviest expense items connected with the motor car business) and by reason of this arrangement will be able to turn out a finished product in ample time for the 1912 trade.

I propose to give my personal attention to the building up of the organization and am in hopes of restoring to Flint one of its oldest and until recent years one of its largest manufacturing institutions.

$293,000 of preferred stock (the balance of the capital

43

stock) is being offered at par with a bonus of 50% of common stock and $10,000 of this subscription is allotted to you. Will you advise promptly if you are in position to handle it or to what extent I can count upon you for financial support in this undertaking?

It is necessary for me to add that I recommend this investment.

Yours very truly,
W. C. Durant

P.S. The principal subscribers to date are as follows: C. M. Begole, $138,000 preferred, $69,000 common; W. S. Ballenger, $69,000 preferred, $34,500 common.

Mott replied immediately, accepting the offer. In March, 1912, Durant wrote to Mott again on the question of the Chevrolet stock reserved for him. Mott's reply is of special interest because it reflects his belief that a man should be able to observe and follow up an investment; he was not inclined to make an investment in Detroit business because he did not expect to be in Detroit. Further, the letter expresses his increasingly warm feeling for Flint, its people, and the men of his own organization.

March 29, 1912

Mr. W. C. Durant,
   c/o Chevrolet Motor Co.,
    Detroit, Michigan.

Dear Mr. Durant:—

I have just received yours of 21st inst. on my return from New York City where I spent a few days with Mrs. Mott, who has been indisposed for past six months.

There was a time when, especially through my friendship with Bill Little, I felt I would like to have an interest in the Chevrolet Company, but much time has since elapsed during which I have turned the matter over in my mind considerably and discussed it with my people in the East, and I have come to the conclusion that ultimately I will find my way back to New York State, where I was born and brought up, and have many friends and relatives of my wife's as well as my own, and I, therefore, feel it inadvisable to make a large investment in Detroit.

I have, as you are aware, subscribed for Little Motor Car Company and Copeman Electric Stove Company, stock which was allotted me, and thus am with you to a certain extent at least. I like Flint people and have many friends here from whom it would be hard to break away, and I do not think I will ever do so absolutely. I have developed the Weston-Mott Co. to such an extent for the past twelve years at the expense of my energy, and there are so many of my boys in my organization that I naturally want to see them and the business thrive and prosper, no matter who owns the stock or whether I am financially remunerated or not. My feeling toward you, Bill Little and the old crowd has not changed, but my Western interests will be confined to Flint.

Trusting that you will understand me better than I can write and with kind regards, I am,

Very truly yours,
C. S. Mott

When he replied to Durant's letter Mott had already demonstrated a new interest in Flint. On March 7, 1912, he had been nominated as the Independent Citizens' Party candidate for mayor of Flint—with a majority of 635 votes over the other three primary candidates in the heaviest primary vote recorded in Flint to that time.

Flint's election of a Socialist mayor, John A. C. Menton, in 1911, had jolted Flint business and industrial people. With the 1912 campaign coming up, Republicans and Democrats joined forces in a new Independent Citizens' Party, and a group of Mott's friends persuaded him to become the new party's candidate for mayor. With Bassett carrying more of the load at the Weston-Mott Company, Mott felt relieved of many obligations. Asked many years later why so many people wanted him to run for mayor, Mott remembered casually: "I was a businessman who had conducted a good-sized business on a safe and sound basis. I was friendly with everybody, and I didn't have any enemies. They probably thought that a successful businessman could do more for the city than a Socialist mayor."

Mott's first public statement after announcing his candidacy on the Independent Citizens' ticket has that straightforward, down-to-earth quality which has always been characteristic of him.

This is my platform. I have no radical ideas on city government.

I am in favor of public improvements—good schools, good and properly cared for streets, public parks, and free public baths.

The city of Flint should have a sufficient supply of good water and it should have as much in the way of public convenience as any other city of its size in the country has.

I believe that a mayor should endeavor to enforce the laws and ordinances on the statutes, to assist in the passage and enforcement of additional regulations for the proper protection of life, health, and property and for the general welfare of the community without regard to personal or party prejudices.

If I am elected mayor of Flint, I shall endeavor to cooperate with the common council along these lines for the benefit of our city at large.

I am not an orator. I am not given to flowery speechmaking. I do not believe in bull-dozing. The people who vote for me with the idea that I am going to carry things with a high hand in the council will be disappointed if I am elected. I will use my own methods to bring about the passage of any measures that I advocate, but my methods will always be fair and above-board. The political preferment of the men with whom I might be working would not influence me in any action that might be taken or anticipated by the council. The making and enforcing of laws for the betterment of the city as a whole and for the people of the city as a whole would be my sole aim.

This is the platform upon which I stand today and upon which I will continue to stand throughout the tenure of my office if I am elected. My interests are coincident with the city at large and with the business, professional, and working men and their general welfare. I have the time to give much of my attention to the affairs of the city and will not do it sparingly if elected.

I feel under a compliment to Flint. Its people have been very kind to me since I came here a stranger five years ago and if a majority of them express their preference for me to handle their affairs as the city's executive officer I will reciprocate to the very best of my ability.

The campaign received great publicity, in which the most impressive theme was that Mott was the "candidate of the factory men"—meaning the hourly rated workers—as much as he was the candidate of business and industrial leaders. His easy victory in the primary was greeted by enthusiastic statements from many of Flint's outstanding citizens.

As the campaign continued, there seemed almost to be a competitive spirit to find new ways of endorsing Mott's candidacy—both by the city's leadership and the men in the shops. There were also long debates about socialism in the papers. Of the seventeen points in the Socialist platform, the seventh may well have made a lasting impression on Mott's memory: "We insist that school buildings shall be open for the use of the public, when not in use for school purposes." It is a delightful irony that this Socialist demand of 1912 should have been brought into rich realization twenty-three years later in Flint by Mott as a demonstration of capitalist democracy at work.

In the campaign, the Socialists attacked Mott as "Flint Representative of Wall Street Interests," and claimed that he wanted to be mayor in order to have his taxes reduced. They asked him to permit the use of his factories during the noon hour to hold Socialist meetings—presumably to advance the candidacy of his opponent, Mayor John A. C. Menton. Mott declined.

Amid Socialist talk of exploited workers, the papers friendly to Mott announced that the Weston-Mott average wage for factory men—excluding foremen, superintendents, and office men, but including skilled and unskilled labor, boys, laborers, and sweepers—was 27.25¢ per hour, the highest rate known anywhere in the country. Amazing as that figure is to us now, it may also be noted that in Flint, at the same time, No. 1 round steak was 12¢ a pound, No. 1 regular sugar cured hams, 13¢ a pound; sausage 10¢ a pound; corned beef, 10¢ a pound; eggs, 22¢ a dozen; ginger snaps, 4 pounds for a quarter; "women's 16 button, high cut, velvet shoes," $1.98; men's spring suits and overcoats, "made to your order," $15 to $27.50.

A Chicago Socialist, Edward J. McGurty, was brought in to conduct the campaign against Mott and teach the Socialist economic concept to Flint so that the people who were coming from all over the country for Flint's relatively high wages could make the astounding discovery that they were being exploited. It is another of those cyclic humors of the years that, in 1957, Mott was to give the University of Chicago $1 million for a building to house a staff concentrating on teaching everybody the economic ABC's.

In 1912, the attacks were hot and heavy, personal and vitriolic. Socialist atheism and free love were much discussed on the one hand, and taxdodging, labor blacklists, and Wall Street bosses on the other. Everyone, it seemed, felt deeply and spoke loudly.

As the campaign drew to a climax before the April 1 election, each faction had a mildly embarrassing bit of adverse publicity. Mott's good friend Charles W. Nash, the man Durant had recommended as general manager of Buick, was arrested. The Flint *Journal* story made a virtue of necessity, but the Socialist press was quick to say, "The man arrested for working boys overtime will vote for Mott." The *Journal* story is worth quoting; if public relations people are seeking examples of sincere and graceful handling of an embarrassing situation, here is a classic:

> Charles W. Nash, general manager of the Buick Motor
> company, was arrested Tuesday afternoon on a charge of vio-

lating the state labor laws. The specific charge was that boys under the age of 18 years had been kept at work by the Buick Motor company for more than 54 hours a week. The warrant was served on Mr. Nash by Chief of Police McCall and followed a complaint made by William E. Washburn, state labor inspector, of Owosso. Mr. Nash was arraigned in Justice Halsey's court and pleaded guilty. He was fined $5, which he paid.

"I am glad that this case was brought against us," said Mr. Nash to the Journal this morning. "It will serve as a warning to our foremen and superintendents to not violate the law. The trouble in this particular case is that a number of foremen and superintendents were not familiar with the law. This is the reason it was violated. I wrote a letter to the state commissioner of labor this morning congratulating him on having an inspector who was attending to his duties at all times.

"There are a large number of people who believe that state officers are inclined to wink at violations of the state laws by large corporations. I want it thoroughly understood that the Buick Motor company does not wish to be winked at. We propose to run our business in accordance with every letter of the law. I hope that should there be any more violations of the state labor law in our factory that the inspectors will proceed just as they did in this case."

Inspector Washburn gave the following statement in regard to the case:

"The complaint in this case came in the form of a letter to the state labor commissioner's office. The violations were alleged in several parts of the Buick factories.

"In fairness to both Mr. Nash and his assistant, Mr. Allen, I wish to state that I am convinced they were perfectly innocent of the fact that the law was being violated. They are very fair-minded men and were perfectly willing to correct the conditions. Mr. Nash has seen to it that notices of the 54-hour law have been posted in every department of the factory and is supporting me every way he can in the enforcement of the law."

The Flint *Arrow* published a story about the arrest of the Socialist candidate for supervisor of Flint's third ward, who had "careened around Police Headquarters" daring the police to arrest him. The story continues, "After listening to his drunken abuse for half-an-hour and making repeated efforts to have the inebriated candidate for civic honors go home peaceably, Night Sergeant McLean took his dare and had him locked up in the county jail." The next morning the candidate pleaded guilty, and was given a suspended sentence.

April 1 came, and Mott and the other Independent Citizens' Party candidates were swept into office. Mott received 3,920 votes to Menton's 2,358. Mott issued the following statement:

> I will stick to my platform.
>
> I will be mayor for ALL of the people of Flint.
>
> I want to compliment and congratulate the men and women of Flint on the splendid showing they made Monday in the complete victory with tremendous majorities for the Independent Citizens' Party.
>
> All of the wards did splendidly, and the 1st, 5th, and 6th wards particularly so.
>
> I am sure that every man elected has the interest of the public at heart and we will all cooperate and work hard to give the city the best there is in us.
>
> I am grateful to the electors for their confidence and their support.

Mott took office on April 8, 1912, and began devoting himself to learning the complexities of Flint's municipal problems. Sewers were of insufficient capacity, where they existed at all. Streets were inadequate and in poor condition. The water supply was in question. Fire protection was in serious need of improvement. There were some 40,000 people living in a city with municipal facilities for 10,000 people.

A sane and perceptive editorial in the Flint *Journal* of April 2, 1912, recognized the functional, if strange, contribution of the Socialists to Flint's awakening in the matter of effective government.

> When the electors of Flint voted to place Charles S. Mott in the mayor's chair and elected all of the candidates of the

Independent Citizens' party they declared for a business administration of the city government with a capable business man at the head. An analysis of the returns will show that it was not a vote of class against class, but a vote of the majority of the citizens of Flint for a party ticket which stood upon a platform of progress, efficiency and desired reforms. Leaving all isms, economic, and other side issues out of the question, the real determination of the electors was to place in office the men who they deemed big enough to handle the problems before the people at this time. . . .

Credit must not be taken away from the party which was defeated in yesterday's election. The Socialists came into the city government of Flint at a time when there was a widespread protest against existing conditions. They awakened the people of Flint to the need of a business administration, and although the Socialists were selected as the ones to suffer as the result of the awakening which they themselves had brought about, it must be acknowledged that their advent into city affairs has galvanized into renewed life the public conscience, which henceforth will see that city affairs are rightly conducted. The people of Flint were suffering from the hookworm in their city affairs until the Socialists pricked them and awakened the electors to the fact that Flint ought to have a business administration and an efficient city government.

The prospects for the coming year are bright. Men devoted to the city and its advancement have been chosen, and their ability is unquestioned. This year should be one of the best in the city's history, from the standpoint of capable government.

FIVE

Mayor Mott began his administration with a frank announcement that he had a lot to learn about city affairs, but that he was in the process of getting the facts. He proposed to keep the public informed as to actions contemplated and taken, and the reasons for those actions so that the public would really know what was going on in Flint's city government. He also stated another principle for the city which he has followed consistently in his own business affairs: getting the greatest value for every dollar spent.

Of all Flint's problems, the need for storm sewers was the greatest. Many years later Mott made these notes about the sewer situation in Flint in 1912:

> It was only a few days after I took office as Mayor of Flint, in April, 1912, when we had a heavy rain storm. The next morning a woman living on Avenue A or B, and just off Detroit Street phoned me and told me that the sewer had backed up into, and filled her cellar with water and sewage, and she invited me to come up and look at it, which I immediately did, and found that it was five or six feet deep in her cellar.
>
> Up to that time storm water catch basins, etc., were led into the only sewer pipes which we had; namely, sanitary, and when these were overloaded from higher ground, and capacity at lower end was over-taxed, it caused backflow, with results as indicated. Then, too, in North end of city (that would be northwest of the corner of Leith Street and Industrial Avenue), there was no provision for getting rid of storm water, and one bad storm that we had flooded that entire section, several feet deep, and even up to the kitchen stoves on the first floor. . . .
>
> I called into consultation Professor Riggs of Department of Sanitation at the University of Michigan, and he sent over Professor Hoad and Assistants, and they undertook and pro-

duced a complete set of sewer plans for the city of Flint. Up to that time the plans, or records of sewers put in were drawn on sheets of paper of various sizes, and no record of relation to each other, or to a standard "bench mark." And, in many cases it took actual digging to determine this relation.

Complete plans for the city were made, and practically all sewers at present existent were planned for exclusive sanitary use, and together with extensions, etc., and then a complete layout of storm water sewers adequate for the purpose. As had been the custom here-to-fore, assessments were made against the property benefited, but in the case of storm water sewers the property owners objected, and won a suit against the City, and the City had to put in the storm sewers at its own expense.

About this time *Labor News* ran headlines, "Why Does Mayor Mott Want Storm Sewers?" The next day in Flint *Journal* were large reprints of pictures I had taken of the Leith Street Industrial Avenue section under flood, and under pictures was printed "Mayor Mott's Answer As To Why Storm Water Sewers Are Needed."

Mott also found that he was an ex-officio member of the water board, and that there was no official record of the underground system—since the only man who knew the location of the water mains apparently considered that his special knowledge made him indispensable as long as it was not committed to paper. Mott prevailed upon the water board to secure a complete set of records of all water mains.

Mott also notes a special problem of insurance classification:

> During my first term as Mayor, local insurance agents got after me, and said that Flint was in the third rate classification, and that if we could get into the second class, then insurance rates on property in Flint would be reduced.
>
> I took the matter up with the National Board of Fire Underwriters, and was told that I had a lot of nerve in asking for improvement in classification when, as a matter of fact, they said they had already made a report showing what we had to do in the way of improvement in order to keep from being

put into fourth class, where they said we belonged. I told them that I had seen the report, but it was too technical, and asked them to send one of their engineers to Flint, which they did, and I made a list of his requirements as to additional mains and connections, valves, hydrants, and enlarged pumping equipment to be put in. Also, list of additional fire-fighting equipment, fire hose, etc., etc. And he said that when we could accomplish all of those things we could get into second class.

I got the approval of the Board of Aldermen, and the Chamber of Commerce and others, towards working on such a program, and in the course of years we got what was required, and got into second class.

In a rather unusual way, Mott made use of the newspapers to reach the public directly, with open letters telling everyone about the specifications of paving, about the operation of Flint's Hurley Hospital, and asking for public reactions and suggestions on various questions such as additional street lighting. He also made his own position on each issue very clear by this means.

Mott called upon the public to take a real and active interest in city activities; he presented information about city affairs and problems through the press in a continuing attempt to have the public well-informed so that it could share the responsibility for all city actions. A water filtration plant was built, and sewer construction was under way—interrupted by complaints from property owners about their assessments. Mott spent virtually full time on his $100-a-year job as mayor, and insisted that the voters, as "stockholders" in the City of Flint, had the duty of keeping informed on all problems involving the city.

Mott's innovations in city government included a suggestion that a "municipal housekeeping commission" made up of women be appointed. This immediately aroused the suspicion of the Flint Equal Suffrage Association. Mott then proposed that the association nominate the members of such a commission. Mott also committed himself as a believer in equal suffrage with this statement:

> I believe in equal suffrage particularly for the benefit of the thousands of working women who are supporting themselves and sometimes their families and who have no one to represent their interest. It is absurd to argue that if women gave proper attention to their homes and families they would take no time for voting. Men are able to carry on large business enterprises and still devote a part of their time to political affairs. The average woman has as much leisure as the average man in which to inform herself on public questions and if she wishes to, can give her thought to them while performing household tasks that are purely mechanical. I have never heard any logical argument against woman suffrage.

During the same period, two of Durant's Flint enterprises were flourishing: the Little Motor Car Company and the Mason Motor Company. A. B. C. Hardy was manager of the Little Motor Car Company, and, by the arrangement with the Whiting interests under which the old Flint Wagon Works had been secured, he had to manufacture buggies as well as cars. A newspaper item of June, 1912, mentions that 3,600 buggies had been turned out, as well as an increasing number of the popular Little cars. Mr. Hardy later stated that only $36,500 in new cash was put into the Little Company—and $10,000 of that was a claim which the Weston-Mott Company had against the Wagon Works for axles.

In August, 1912, it was announced that Flint was to get the Chevrolet Motor Company plant. Several factors made it advantageous for Durant to consolidate manufacturing operations in Flint, rather than continue to make Chevrolet in Detroit. Out of the Little Motor Car Company, the Mason Motor Company, and Chevrolet, was to develop the powerful Chevrolet Motor Company which was to take such a dominant position in the automobile industry in years to come.

By September, 1912, Weston-Mott was employing 1,675 men, and hiring more every day, in addition to working overtime. The company was making more than twice as many axles, hubs, and rims as any of its competitors. Its customers outside General Motors included many truck, electric car, and other automobile companies.

Flint's growth was indicated by the 1912 school census, showing 1,190 more children of school age than in 1911—an increase from 6,687 to 7,877. Bank deposits showed increases in all five Flint banks, and Flint tax valuations jumped several million dollars.

By October, Flint's total employment in the plants was reported as 8,000, an increase of 2,500 from the previous year. Buick's September production, 1,657 cars, exceeded any previous record. Former President Theodore Roosevelt visited the Buick plant, asking many questions of Nash, and talking with Mott in the Buick offices. Roosevelt expressed himself as amazed at the immensity of the operations.

In November, 1912, Charles W. Nash was elected president of General Motors. Mott's affection and admiration for Nash are based on the long close friendship the two men enjoyed. Mott found in Nash that rarest and most misnamed of qualities, "common sense." Nash had the true genius of perception, the ability to weigh and relate causes and effects and to project them to their inevitable results. The Flint *Journal* published a thumb nail sketch of Nash's career at the time of his election as president of General Motors. The amount of formal education Nash received can be guessed from the fact that he was "bound out" at the age of seven.

1864—Born in DeKalb Co., Illinois on a farm.

1866—Came to Forest township, Genesee Co., with his parents.

1871—Bound out to Robert Lathrop of Flushing to work 14 years for $100 and three suits of clothes.

1876—Ran away because of the irksome apprenticeship and hired out to work on the farms of L. J. Hitchcock of Grand Blanc and Alexander McFarlan in Mt. Morris.

1881—Made his first business venture of any account when he entered haypressing partnership with W. J. Adams.

1884—Married Miss Jessie Hallack of Burton.

1889—Took job as clerk in grocery store of W. C. Pierce.

1890—Went to Flint Road Cart Company, now Durant-Dort Carriage Company to work as a carriage trimmer for $1.00 per day.

1910—Appointed general manager of the Buick Motor Company.

1912—Elected president of the General Motors Corporation.

Among the notes Mott has made from time to time about men he knew well, there is none so appealing as this incident he reports of C. W. Nash—a man who never lost his simple, down-to-earth humanity for all the magnitude of his accomplishments.

Charles Nash

All through his life, Charlie Nash was a kindly and considerate friend to mankind. I have hunted deer with him in the Upper Peninsula of Michigan and in the southern part of Texas. We have slept close together on cold nights. He was very handy at butcher work on the farm, and in hunting, and also an excellent cook in camp.

One day I went bird hunting with him and several others quite some distance north of Bay City. He had arranged with a chap as guide, and this guide had an excellent bird dog that he valued highly.

During a successful day's hunting, Charlie noticed that the guide seemed to have something very much on his mind. When we got back to camp and were eating supper, he managed to get out of the guide what the trouble was. The guide had a fourteen year old daughter who was troubled with a pain in her side, which seemed very serious. But the old local doctor said it was nothing but a "belly ache." Charlie got the idea that it might be something different, so quickly after supper he and the guide got in an automobile and drove some miles to the guide's home.

Charlie examined the girl and came to the conclusion that she had an attack of appendicitis. He had the guide drive over to a place where they could telephone, and Charlie telephoned the Pere Marquette people in Bay City and, through his influence as President of Buick, got the Pere Marquette Railroad to stop their midnight train at the small local flag stop, at which time Charlie loaded the guide and his daughter on the train for Bay City. When they reached Bay City, Charlie had telephoned and arranged for an ambulance and doctor. The child was taken to hospital and successfully operated on for appendicitis and her life was saved.

A few weeks later, Nash received a crate—and in that crate was the wonderful bird dog—the guide's most prized possession, the only gift he could find adequate for the man who had surely saved his daughter's life.

It is said in Flint that W. C. Durant, one day observing Charles W. Nash cut a lawn, admired the way he worked, and offered him a job with the Durant-Dort company in the lowest common-labor classification. From this, Nash worked his way up to become superintendent of Durant-Dort—and when the Eastern bankers wanted a man to head Buick at the time they displaced Durant's control in 1910, they accepted Durant's advice to put Nash in charge, although Nash had had no auto-making experience. Nash did a truly magnificent job with Buick, and in rebuilding the fortunes of General Motors. It is one of the most singular ironies that Nash resigned as president of General Motors later because Durant—the man to whom he owed the two greatest opportunities of his life—had come back into power. The fault was neither Nash's nor Durant's; there was no fault, really; there was only an irreconcilable difference between the ways in which the two men operated—a difference deeply rooted in the essential natures of the two men. Mott has always had the most profound admiration for both men, but for Nash he has also a warm personal affection.

58

Weston-Mott wound up the year with awards and paid-up insurance policies for sixty-two employees who had been with the company five years or longer. Mott, in turn, was presented with a loving cup by his department heads as a Christmas gift. Mott received another present, a Christmas stocking five feet long, presented to him at his office in the Flint City Hall. It contained samples of many Flint-made products, and toys symbolizing the many civic improvements he was trying to secure for Flint. It was a friendly gesture expressing the gratitude of the city to a man who was devoting full time to the presumably honorary job as mayor. Major problems as 1912 ended were still a sewer plan, a park plan, a street-improvement plan, and a proposed charter revision which would provide an appointive executive staff for the city.

At the beginning of 1913, Flint took stock of itself—and found a great deal to be proud of. Its factory production for the year just completed was valued at $30 million. There were 8 theaters, 10 hotels, 25 churches, and 30 church societies. There were 150 miles of streets and 10 miles of pavement. There was a new water-filtration plant. There were 21 public schools and one parochial school. There was the largest auto plant in the world, covering 56 acres. There was a city trolley system, covering 12 miles. The tax rate, at $19.90 per $1,000 of assessed valuation, was said to be the lowest in any Michigan city. The population was estimated above 42,000. The average daily wage for 1912 had been $2.79—one of the highest in Michigan.

As 1913 proceeded, there was much discussion of whether Mott would run for mayor again. A newspaper reported his statement that he would run as an independent and not on any partisan ticket, if at all: "There are many things yet unfinished, which I would like to follow out to ultimate termination. As far as the position of mayor is concerned, I will be only too glad when I am freed of the duties of that office. It is not the office that I want, but the work than can be accomplished by the holder of that office."

A People's Party was formed—a somewhat different group

59

from the former Independent Citizens' Party—with Mott as candidate for mayor. Mott recommended a bond issue involving some $300,000 for the needed work on sewers, roads, parks, and paving, to be voted on in a special election, March 20, 1913. Four of the six items were approved by the voters, and Flint was in a position to expand its municipal facilities to match its tremendous growth of population.

The first part of 1913 brought an anti-vice crusade, a series of prosecutions of coal dealers for short-weight loads, and a campaign to establish a YMCA in Flint. The Socialists found ways to criticize Mott's "business administration," but the campaign had none of the fireworks of 1912. Mott received 4,290 votes to 2,341 for Menton, again his Socialist opponent.

Although there were no Socialists among the aldermen elected this time, the administration ran into difficulties in getting the sewer program accepted when individual assessments were protested by real estate men. The common council yielded to pressure and cut down the proposed sewer construction plan—only to face other pressure from those who wanted the whole program carried out. Mott kept issuing statements to the public to clarify the situation, but it seemed impossible to secure any meeting ground between the two opposing schools of thought. The controversy continued and held up other city improvement work also—since paving was not to be done until after the sewers were in. Objections and injunctions continued to hamper the planned sewer construction.

Other matters showed definite progress. The YMCA campaign was highly successful, and plans were made to construct a building. A sum of $112,000 had been raised, $12,000 more than the original goal. The city enacted a pure-food ordinance, regulating standards of meat and milk. Action was taken, at the instance of the feminine Municipal Housekeeping Commission, to abate the smoke nuisance. The council also passed a child-welfare ordinance, providing for one or more nurses in the city health department to have charge of child welfare work in the city.

Throughout 1913 Flint was surging onward with production and employment. The number of men in the larger plants increased from 6,000 in August to 8,000 in October.

For Mott, it was a year of decision. In 1908, General Motors had acquired 49 per cent of the stock of the Weston-Mott Company; in 1913, Mott transferred the remaining 51 per cent to General Motors on a straight exchange-of-stock basis. "General Motors didn't have to put up a cent," Mott recalls. "It was paid from cash, property, and stock that the Weston-Mott Company owned. The balance was made up in General Motors stock—so that all that General Motors did was to give me stock for the Weston-Mott Company. The exchange of stock was on the basis of book value."

Considering that Weston-Mott sales exceeded $6 million in the 1912–1913 fiscal year, the value of the company—and the consequent stock holdings resulting from selling the remaining 51 per cent of it—explain Mott's basic acquisition of General Motors stock. This was to become worth many millions of dollars over the years and to make possible the establishment and development of the Mott Foundation.

It was understood that Mott was to remain in charge of the Weston-Mott Company. In 1910, when Durant had invited Mott to become a director of General Motors, Mott had declined on the basis that it would prejudice the position of Weston-Mott in relation to its non-General Motors customers. This factor no longer applied, and in November, 1913, Mott was elected a director of General Motors—a position he has retained continuously ever since, the only 1913 director still on the board.

From 1907, when the Motts moved to Flint, to 1913 when Mott disposed of his final Weston-Mott holdings to General Motors, both Buick and Weston-Mott had grown by leaps and bounds. In the course of this tremendous expansion, Weston-Mott, like Buick, was hiring and training the perpetually increasing supply of workers coming to Flint. The wages paid were considered excellent for the time, and the surviving wagon and carriage companies lost many skilled workmen to the automotive plants.

As for Flint, the quiet "hick-town" the Motts had first observed in 1905 was changing rapidly; the old patterns were breaking up; the new social order had little homogeneity, because the changing population had little in common except source of income. The people came in waves and surges, from all over Michigan, from the South, from Europe, from almost everywhere. They could not be assimilated by Flint's small-town social patterns, so Flint simply added masses of people who brought with them problems and differences which were to result in social chaos for years to come. Drawing in these masses of people, in the process of building automobiles, Buick and Weston-Mott were unconsciously creating vast human problems in the community, problems which were to become increasingly apparent, and which were to require—and receive—an answer unique in American civic history. By a kind of magnificent justice which seldom strikes so grand a balance, Charles Stewart Mott, one of the dominant figures in the industrial enterprise which brought this multiplied population to Flint, was to do more than anyone else to provide that unique answer to the problems Flint's heterogeneous population created---through the Mott Foundation.

SIX

In January, 1914, Mott stated that he would be a candidate for re-election—on "an independent ticket and no other." Mott's announcement included the statement ". . . I believe that national politics has no place in municipal government. . . ." Asked to amplify his formal announcement, Mott said:

> I started in nearly two years ago to give the people of Flint what they needed in the way of improvements and what I believed and still believe that they want. It has been an almost overwhelming task and by no means a pleasant one. If I had completed the work that I set out to do I would retire now. But I have not completed it. Of course, if the people of Flint do not want it finished, well and good. That is for them to say. But I will not be the one to back down. I would consider that I had neglected a duty to Flint if I retired at this time.

Nash wrote a letter to the Flint *Journal* the day after Mott's announcement and, with characteristic common sense, pinpointed the problems of the city as providing water supply, sidewalks, sanitary sewers, and other facilities for the dwellings that had sprung up in outlying districts of Flint to house factory workers:

> Now, this work cannot be done without considerable cost and the cost raised by taxation. All this work, I am satisfied, has been undertaken by Mayor Mott because he wants to see our factory people, who are really the people who are keeping Flint alive, to have favorable conditions under which to live, as other cities have. I have heard it said that Mayor Mott was too much interested in the people who work in the north end factories. I think this is unfair criticism. Although they may live in the outlying districts, I believe the men who work in

these factories are entitled to the same consideration that is accorded the people in the downtown district, who are otherwise employed. That Mayor Mott has not completed the work he set out to do for the people of Flint is due to an unfortunate set of circumstances for which he can be in no way held responsible. . . .

Charges of waste and extravagance were leveled against Mott's administration. Mott and his backers publicized actual savings achieved by his administration. Mott also recommended resubmitting the problem of continued storm sewer construction to the voters. He stated repeatedly that he did not propose to have the city provide services the people did not want—but that since the city was larger, bills were greater for the services people wanted.

At a Progressive Party meeting, a speaker said of Mott: "Mayor Mott is an honest man and a gentleman and he has done a lot for the city, but he bores with too big an auger." There was also some skepticism about the proposed charter, and more than a little discussion of the purchase of voting machines which Mott had ordered as an economy measure. At a council meeting, Alderman William H. McKeighan presented a resolution which would prevent use of the voting machines in the coming elections. Mott stated that he had been expecting such a gesture—but from the Progressive Party, not from a member of his own administration. He had prepared a statement on the speed, efficiency, and economy of the voting machines. McKeighan's resolution failed to pass.

A Mott-for-Mayor Club publicized the accomplishments of Mott's administration in public health, increased fire protection, lower insurance rates, and in other fields. Eventually there were three tickets: Citizens Independent, Progressive, and Socialist—with Mott, John R. MacDonald, and Menton, nominated in the primaries.

With all Flint's needs for municipal improvements, and the projects undertaken in the preceding two years, Mott was still able to point to the fact that Flint's tax rate was lower than the rates in Bay City, Port Huron, Detroit, Saginaw, and Grand Rapids. For 1914, the city's proposed budget was $12,975 lower than for the previous year. Mott was also able to note substantial balances in the lighting, fire, police, building, salary, street, and bridge funds, totaling $88,900.

Looking over the Flint political situation with sharp but somewhat cynical eyes, a Detroit *News* correspondent wrote that Flint politicians were accounting for Mott's running for a third term as mayor on the basis that he wanted to run for Congress. The reporter pointed out that the Progressive candidate, MacDonald, was "credited with having a speaking acquaintance with as many Flint voters as any man in the city, and far more than the usual run of candidates have. Flint has been his home for 35 years." This reporter's analysis of public attitudes toward Mott's administration is illuminating:

Mayor Mott has conducted the mayor's office like he conducts his factory, which means on strictly business lines. But there has been a lot of grumbling, the main cause appearing to be that he inaugurated so many public improvements, largely in the way of sewer and paving extensions, that during his administration taxes have reached a new high-water mark, notably for special assessments. Last summer when taxes were payable, there were angry protests at the city hall by hundreds of people whose only taxable property are the homes where they live. They tell now that being a very rich man, Mayor Mott doesn't seem to be able to see the tax situation from the angle of the poor man. That is, his political opponents say this.

Mott immediately denied that he was running for re-election as mayor as a prelude to a try for Congress in the fall; he stated that he would not be a candidate for Congress on any ticket if re-elected mayor—but that he might consider running for Congress if not re-elected mayor.

Nash, busy as he was as president of General Motors, wrote a long and thoughtful letter to the Flint *Journal* in which he said that the factory interests and the interests of the people of Flint were identical. He also said good things about Progressive candidate MacDonald, but devoted strength and persuasiveness to reminding people of Mott's accomplishments for the city, and the need to continue Mott in office to permit him to complete the work he had undertaken for the good of the community. Nash evidently could feel that the confusion of issues, parties, personalities, rumors, prejudices, and mistaken impressions had reached such a point as to leave the election of Mott in doubt. The Flint *Journal* underscored Nash's letter with a strong editorial derived from it, and continued to back Mott's candidacy with full force.

To add to all the cross-currents of confusion, on April 3, before the April 6 election, there was some highly mysterious activity reported at the Genesee County court house in Flint —centering in Judge C. H. Wisner's private chamber. The judge, the prosecuting attorney, the sheriff, various police officers, and a stranger were involved. Mayor Mott was reported to have entered the circuit judge's room for a few minutes. Arrests made public were for violation of the local-option law by selling liquor, and it was reported that a corps of detectives had been making an investigation for several weeks. Two former mayors had been called in for testimony. Mayor Mott was reported to have been present throughout the proceedings, but would say nothing except, "You will learn all this when the election is over." It was surmised that political issues were involved, but the judge kept a tight hold on release of information. What effect the mysterious activities in the court house may have had on the April 6, 1914, election can scarcely be determined, since there were already so many curious influences and factors at play.

MacDonald, the Progressive Party candidate, carried 11 of the 14 precincts—with 3,193 votes to 2,445 for Mott and only 492 for Flint's 1911 Socialist mayor, Menton. The new charter was defeated—but the bonding issue to continue storm-sewer construction was carried. The results of the election were known a few minutes after the polls closed—thanks to the voting machines which had been a major point of attack on Mott during the campaign.

As Flint shook itself after the bitter election, Mott issued this statement:

> As I am just completing two years' experience on city work, I do not feel that I can conscientiously congratulate Mr. MacDonald, and he will understand me when he gets through. But I do assure him of my continued friendliness and best wishes for a successful administration and I stand ready to co-operate with him and lend him all assistance possible, whenever or if ever he may see fit to call on me.
>
> I congratulate Flint that Mr. MacDonald has a reputation for straightforwardness and independence, and I believe that he will do things for Flint's best interests, irrespective of those who would have him do otherwise.

Mayor-elect MacDonald also issued a graceful statement, concluding with these words, "Am gratified to feel that at all times I will have the benefit of the knowledge and valuable experience in city matters of my worthy predecessor, Mayor Mott, for whom I have the very highest regard."

Actually this defeat had been somewhat of a blow, and was not without its aftertaste of bitterness. Mott was grateful to Flint for the opportunities he had found in the city. He felt that he was making a real and effective contribution to his community by serving as mayor, spending full time at a job which was considered primarily an honorary function. He believed in business methods and principles—and in getting the greatest possible value from every tax dollar spent. He had disciplined himself strictly to carry out only and exactly what Flint people indicated they wanted the city government to do. He had kept an open door to the public—had invited everyone to keep informed and, in effect, to police all city activities. He had been meticulously conscientious about his duties and responsibilities as mayor. Mott had used all available media of public information to keep Flint people aware of city activities and plans. He had, indeed, in all matters, acted in what he believed to be the best interests of the whole city and all its people—and he had accomplished an amazing number of improvements. And now when he was willing to continue another year to complete the program Flint people said they wanted, the voters repudiated him. Yet in the same election they approved continuation of the storm-sewer construction he had undertaken as perhaps the greatest necessity of all for the city.

Smarting inwardly under the defeat, although bearing it outwardly with good grace, Mott felt the need to get away from Flint for a time. He and Mrs. Mott set out on a tour of Europe. After visiting England and Holland, the Motts were joined in Paris by Mr. and Mrs. Alfred P. Sloan, Jr. and by Mrs. Mott's parents. Early in July, the Motts returned to Flint. Mott's friends, including Flint's most distinguished citizens, held a banquet in his honor. W. W. Mountain was toastmaster, and he began the tributes to Mott, lauding him for "Betterment of Flint Both from the Civic and Industrial Standpoint." W. H. Little talked about "Old Associations," remembering the days when Mott had first come to Flint. Little's sense of humor was foremost, as always. He described Mott's invention of a demountable rim which was very easily removed from the rim. In fact, according to Little, the real problem was to keep it *on* the wheel.

C. W. Nash spoke on "Manufacturing Interests as Related to City Government," tracing the growth of Flint's industry and consequent growth of the city's civic needs, and pointing out that Mott had understood those needs and had done a great deal to help meet them. Nash also paid a personal tribute to Mott, saying that Mott's advice and counsel had been very helpful to him—and expressing satisfaction that Mott had been made a director of General Motors so that Nash would have that advice and counsel available.

J. D. Dort spoke on "The Ideal City," relating how much Mott had done in helping Flint toward becoming a finer community for all its people. Last, in a generous tribute to Mott, Dr. C. B. Burr pointed out that Flint had already benefited and would continue to benefit from the constructive ideals and thorough performance of Mott. Dr. Burr then made the presentation of the evening to Mott—a handsome silver loving cup inscribed:

*Presented by His Friends and Fellow
Townsmen to*

HON. CHARLES S. MOTT

Twice elected on a non-partisan ballot

MAYOR OF FLINT

1912–1913

*In grateful recognition of his unselfish
devotion to the public welfare
and his insistence upon the
application of business
principles in municipal
government.*

The tremendous attendance at the banquet, and the good words from leading men in Flint, made Mott feel that Flint had not really rejected him after all—and that there was understanding appreciation of his intentions, efforts, and accomplishments among those about whose good opinion he cared most. The loving cup, and the ceremonies attending its presentation, served to wash away the tinge of bitterness Mott had felt on losing the election.

Michigan's Gov. Woodbridge N. Ferris laid the cornerstone of the new YMCA building, and Mott, who had taken a leading part in the fund-raising campaign for the building, was named chairman of the board of directors. Mott still operated the Weston-Mott Company for a General Motors flourishing under the direction of Nash. Nash and Mott liked and understood each other. They were alike in integrity, common sense, and the belief in hard work and thoroughness. Each depended upon the advice of the other.

SEVEN

In its New Year's Day editorial, January 1, 1915, the Flint *Journal* noted: "To Flint, the Old Year has brought prosperity almost unlimited. It has seen the transition from the country village of yore to the modern city practically completed." Flint's population had pushed beyond 50,000, and it was no longer easy to predict what would happen in the growing community. People were boasting that their city was spending more than half a million dollars on improvements and, in general, was riding the crest of a wave of prosperity. To Flint, the war in Europe was exciting but still remote.

The war was rolling back and forth across Europe; England and Germany were both grumbling at the United States. A threatening financial crisis in the United States was scarcely felt in Flint. America was becoming more and more enthusiastic about automobiles—and both Buick and Chevrolet were doing well. Flint was still making buggies, too—and the Executive Committee of the Carriage Builders National Association recommended that a standardized buggy be adopted by the trade.

General Motors common stock was quoted at $99. Louis Chevrolet was coming out of retirement to resume auto racing. An Auto Page became a feature of the Flint *Journal* —advertising the Saxon Roadster at $395, the new 1915 Maxwell at $695, the Chevrolet Baby Grand Touring at $985, the Chevrolet Royal Mail Roadster at $860, and Fords at $450 up. The Buick plant was called the largest manufacturing plant in the world except the Krupp Gun Works and Baldwin Locomotive Plant.

Not without misgivings, Mott was persuaded to run for mayor again in 1915; he was not enthusiastic about the idea but accepted it as a duty. Again he insisted on running on a Citizens Independent Party ticket. Alderman John G. Windiate and Alderman William H. McKeighan filed petitions for the primary on the Republican ticket.

Statements of the candidates were reasonably typical of the men. Windiate said in part: "The main issue in this campaign is the enforcement of law and order. . . . In a general way, I stand for a reasonable amount of necessary improvements but not to such an extent that they will become a burden to the small taxpayer."

His opponent in the Republican primary, McKeighan, said only, "Tell them that I will be mayor for all the people."

Mott said:

I am not seeking the office of mayor, and had no thought or desire to run until the eleventh hour, when I was approached by men who think that city affairs should be taken out of national party politics, and who desire that the business of the city should be conducted on business principles—and I consented to the use of my name. Acceptance of office would mean much personal sacrifice for me, but if elected I should devote most of my time to the upbuilding of the city, as I have done in the past.

In the Republican primary, Windiate represented the conservative "old Flint" part of the population, which was being inundated by the waves of "new people" from everywhere, who were still coming to Flint in vast numbers for jobs. McKeighan was the young, handsome hero of the "North-end new people" —a political charmer with a sound feeling for political expediency and the kind of oratory which fills the ears and churns the emotions without involving the intelligence.

On March 3, the largest vote in Flint's primary history was cast—and McKeighan beat out Windiate for the Republican nomination by some 250 votes. Mott, unopposed for the Citizens Independent ticket nomination, received an unimpressive token vote. In editorial comment, the Flint *Journal* meditated gloomily, "There is a question, and it is a very serious one, whether there can be such a thing as a representative vote in Flint." This question was raised by the fact that some 2,000 had voted for the first time in the primary—and, while they had been in Flint long enough to satisfy legal voting requirements, they were in large part "transients" in a real sense. Nobody could predict what Flint voters would decide about anything.

The really exciting issue of the coming election was not electing a mayor, but deciding the "wet or dry" issue. Flint's local-option laws were not highly respected by much of the population, and the "wets" organized as the "Genesee County Liberal Association," worked aggressively to restore the free flow of liquor.

McKeighan was elected with almost 1,200 more votes than Mott, and Genesee County remained "dry" by a majority of 612 votes. In a somewhat shoulder-shrugging editorial, the Flint *Journal* pointed out that surprise and disappointment at the results of the election would have been on one side, if not on the other—and that what was in the best interests of the people was the only important thing. Clearly, Flint was changing so rapidly that a "realistic" policy on the part of the newspaper required consideration of a completely new set of values.

Mott issued a characteristic statement:

> I would like to express my sincere thanks to the many friends who sought so diligently to bring about my election. It is a satisfaction, indeed, to know that so many of them demonstrated their desire to see me elected, entering into a campaign with an enthusiasm unbounded and carrying on the work with a spirit of personal interest that one neither asks nor expects from even a friend. What regrets I may have are in their disappointment rather than my own, for it was my own desire merely to be of service to Flint if the people of Flint desired my services.
>
> In view of the odds with which we had to contend I feel that I have reason to be extremely gratified over the showing, not that I personally but that my friends have made for me.

We were all working against overwhelming odds, a fact that is apparent on the face of the returns which show a Republican majority in the city of better than 5,500. When one stops to think that practically every vote cast for me was a split vote, by men who sought to give preference to me over the candidate on their own ticket, and sought out my name from its obscure place on the ballot, there is, in my opinion, every reason to be gratified.

As in 1914, many factors combined to defeat Mott in 1915, but this time the loss was rather a relief than a source of bitterness. Mott had been willing to serve out of a sense of civic duty; his defeat relieved him of that particular obligation.

Flint kept on growing, and again the need of additional housing became acute. A company to promote the building of houses in Flint was formed, with Mott and Dort each subscribing $10,000 toward setting up a $250,000 fund; Mott was made head of this company. Pledges to construct 280 houses were made at the first meeting of the group.

September, 1915, brought news that Chevrolet Motor Company of Delaware had been incorporated by W. C. Durant with $20 million capital. Although there were plants in various parts of the country, the main manufacturing units were to be in Flint. Chevrolet stock had reached $250 a share.

Thus Mott's willingness back in 1912 to accept stock instead of the cash he could have demanded from the Little Motor Car Company—one of the basic companies combined into Chevrolet—began to appear as a sound investment instead of merely a helpful gesture.

Through Chevrolet Motor Company of Delaware, Durant —by trading Chevrolet stock for General Motors stock— was able to regain control of General Motors on September 16, 1915—exactly seven years after he had organized it. A dividend of $50 a share on General Motors common stock was declared, a fact which is the more impressive when it is remembered that at one point in 1913 the stock had sold for as little as $25 a share. Under the Nash management, and with the added impetus of the "munitions boom" through these years, General Motors had prospered remarkably. Weston-Mott, as a unit of General Motors, had shared this vigorous growth—and Mott, as a General Motors stockholder and director, grew both in fortune and in prestige. He maintained the most friendly of relations with all the major figures in General Motors, from Pierre S. du Pont, the new chairman of the board of directors, to Durant, Nash, Chrysler, and the rest. Never carried into extreme or emotional partisanship in the areas of conflict which arose within the organization, he was trusted by all. He took strong positions on issues of policy, but only on the basis of what he considered best for the company as a whole—without regard for the special interests of individuals. Mott's impartiality, clear vision, wide experience, and common sense have always been a stabilizing factor in the direction of General Motors.

Flint's automotive and subsidiary plants were kept busy through 1915—with Buick, Chevrolet, Paterson, Dort, and Monroe cars in production. There were four Flint men on the General Motors board of directors: Mott, Nash, Durant, and A. G. Bishop, of Genesee County Savings Bank. Nash announced in November that, after distribution of the $50 dividend on each share of common stock—some $11 million—General Motors was still in an excellent cash position, and that all subsidiaries were operating on a paying basis. Nash also announced that Buick expected to double its output in the following eight months—and would add employees in Flint accordingly. He expected that 3,000 more houses would have to be built in Flint for additional employees.

Surging production and employment went on into 1916, with 15,000 men working in Flint plants at the start of the year as compared with 8,000 at the beginning of 1915. Flint banks boasted over $9 million in savings deposits, and 1,400 new construction building permits had been issued in 1915. The new Flint YMCA had a thousand members.

Early in January, it was announced that General Motors

common stock had been put on a permanent dividend basis of 5 per cent quarterly—with the first 10 per cent payment, representing the past and current quarter, payable February 15. It was feared that this low rate of return—a mere 20 per cent per year—would be disappointing and discouraging to investors, and would cause a drop in the price of the stock. It was explained that higher dividends *could* be paid—since the net earnings of the company in the six months ending February first were estimated at $12 million—but the directors preferred to be conservative, with the expectation of declaring an *extra* dividend over and above the 20 per cent at the end of the year.

On June 1, 1916, Nash resigned from General Motors, and Durant assumed the presidency. Nash must have been deeply conscious of the debt he owed to Durant for the two great opportunities of his life: his first job with Durant-Dort Carriage Company, and his first job with General Motors. Yet so greatly had Nash grown with the stature of his accomplishments that he felt he must resign from General Motors when Durant regained control, although apparently Durant wanted Nash to stay. Durant's confidence in Nash's extraordinary abilities had been more than justified, since Nash had, in the years between 1910 and 1916, brought General Motors into a position of triumphant security, solvency, and competitive strength. Nash went on to develop his own company with continuing success.

Later in 1916, Harry H. Bassett, general manager of Weston-Mott, became assistant general manager of Buick—under Walter P. Chrysler, president and general manager. Chrysler had been brought to Buick by Nash in 1912, and had proved a remarkably effective works manager. Both of these men were close to Mott. Bassett was the young man Mott had hired from the Remington Arms Company back in 1905; Chrysler was one of Mott's closest friends. With that insight into character which has served him so well over the years, Mott had recognized the capacities of both men. It was in 1916 that Mott became a vice-president of General Motors.

With the entry of the United States into World War I in April, 1917, all General Motors plants were put at the disposal of the Government, and there were many changes. Also in 1917, the separate companies held by General Motors were absorbed as divisions. General Motors had become an operating company rather than a holding company with the change in organization, although the divisions retained a degree of autonomy.

In February, 1918, it was announced that Chevrolet would at last become part of General Motors. Capitalization of General Motors was increased to $200 million. Although there was some disruption of production in the transition to war work in the plants, most General Motors units were rapidly utilized for war production.

Because of the complexity of new problems brought to city administration by the war situation, Mott was persuaded to become a candidate for mayor of Flint again in 1918. Flint's 1917 mayor, George C. Kellar, stated, "... I can best serve this community by withdrawing in favor of Mr. Mott. The emergency demands the ability and courage of a citizen such as Mr. Mott has always shown himself to be." Kellar, a good friend, had urged Mott to enter the campaign. This time, Mott ran on the Republican ticket and was opposed in the primary by George H. Gordon. The only other candidate was John S. Tennant, running on an Independent ticket, so it was generally assumed that nomination would be tantamount to election.

Five days before the March 6 primaries, the Flint *Labor News* devoted its full front page to support of Mott's candidacy. The headline was: "WHY MOTT FOR MAYOR?" The subhead continued " 'Mott for Mayor' Should Be the Slogan of Every Citizen Voter Who Desires a Just and Efficient Administration of Local Government for Progressive Flint." There followed a solid page of editorial comment noting Mott's many services and contributions to the community, praising his character, and recommending his election in the strongest possible terms.

76

On March 6, 1918, Mott was nominated for mayor with a majority of 1,577 over his opponent.

On the day after the primaries, the Flint *Journal* reprinted part of an editorial it had presented after Mott's defeat by MacDonald in 1914, noting that the future would rightly place the credit Mott's constructive services as mayor had deserved.

Mott's after-nomination statement was: "I wish to thank sincerely all of the men who have by their efforts and votes made yesterday's results possible, to affirm again my belief in and friendship for the people of Flint, and to state that if elected it will be a pleasure to me to serve this city to the best of my ability." His final election was almost a taken-for-granted formality. Among his first problems as mayor was urging people to buy the kinds of coal then available in anticipation of the next winter's needs. Soft coal was on hand but hard coal was scarce.

EIGHT

An atmosphere of excitement prevailed throughout Flint—
with Liberty Loans, Red Cross, and the war news. In May,
Mayor Mott found it necessary to issue the following statement
for publication:

> *To whom it may concern:*
> Flint has always had a reputation of being a law-abiding,
> as well as one of the most patriotic places in the United States,
> and I feel sure that you wish your reputation sustained.
>
> Unpatriotic citizens and pro-Germans deserve more severe
> punishment than they can possibly get, but the officials of this
> city and county cannot take that as an excuse for mob-rule
> and law breaking.
>
> Take notice that the police department has been instructed
> accordingly.

Flint's first full-time health officer, Dr. William DeKleine,
found real backing for his various health programs with Mott
as mayor. By this time, the salary of the mayor of Flint was
$2,500 a year, and Mott asked DeKleine what the doctor
could do with a gift of the mayor's salary to the health department. DeKleine answered that he wouldn't know what to do
with $2,500, but would know what to do with $5,000. He
wanted to employ a dentist and organize a dental department
to go into the schools to correct the dental defects of children.
Mott took the suggestion to the school board, and the board
matched his $2,500 with an appropriation of the same amount,
and Dr. DeKleine put his school dental department into operation.

The year 1918 brought into General Motors one of Mott's
old and close friends, Alfred P. Sloan, Jr. Sloan was president
of the group of parts manufacturers Durant had originally

78

organized as United Motors. When the group was acquired by General Motors, Sloan also moved to the corporation he was later to head. Thus an association between Mott and Sloan, going back many years, continued even more actively in the years to follow.

Another long-time friend of Mott was highly active in Flint city affairs in 1918—Roy Brownell, then Flint's prosecuting attorney, later to be associated closely with Mott over many years.

In July, 1918, Maj. George D. Wilcox, Detroit District Manager of the Motors Branch of the U.S. Army Quartermaster Corps, urged Mott to take charge of production for Michigan and Indiana. Mott went to work the next day, and was told to pick his own men. He chose men from the automobile industry to carry out the work in production of vehicles for the army; these included a number of Flint men. Many years afterwards, Mott noted: "We had first-class men in my outfit. I picked the kind of men who had been doing the same type of work they would be needed for. And they were the men who did the work while I was thrashing the thing out with Washington. We were stock-chasers. That was my job: Top stock-chaser."

Mott worked both as Flint's mayor and as Chief of Production of the Motors Branch of the Army Quartermaster Corps. In November, his commission as major was formally issued, which required him to resign as mayor of Flint. His resignation was announced November 8, 1918—the same day that newspaper headlines were black with the fact that the previous day's "armistice report" had been false. In his letter of resignation to the Flint Common Council, Mott expressed regret in resigning, but stated that he felt the War Department had first call on his time.

In acknowledging Mott's letter of resignation, Flint's aldermen congratulated him upon his appointment, expressed appreciation of his financial assistance for health services, and noted: "This council desires to express its own sentiment and that of the people of this city upon your resignation from the office of mayor. We feel that the services you have rendered to our city were greatly in excess of mere duty, were in fact the product of devotion to the highest ideals of public service."

On the day Mott was honorably discharged from his job in Detroit by the War Department, January 31, 1919, the Flint Board of Commerce held a banquet honoring W. C. Durant. In the course of his talk that evening, Durant spoke with warm affection of Flint, and the men who had worked with him in the development of General Motors. He paid special tributes to Walter P. Chrysler and to Pierre du Pont. Durant also read to the 550 men present at the banquet a letter he had received from Winston Churchill, then minister of munitions for Great Britain. The letter, addressed to Durant as president of General Motors, stated:

My Dear Sir,

Sir Percival Perry has reported to me concerning his recent mission in the United States of America, and I am advised of the valuable and enthusiastic assistance rendered by your executive officers and organizations.

I desire personally to thank you and your staff for the help which you rendered, and to express my appreciation of the fact that the enthusiasm and interest which was exercised was something more than ordinary commercial considerations would demand.

A cessation of hostilities has been secured without application of the special means which you so wholeheartedly undertook to contribute; yet I am sure you will agree with me that the advent of peace is a reward sufficient to compensate for all endeavour.

Believe me
Yours sincerely,
Winston S. Churchill

With the permission of the group assembled, Durant cabled the following reply to Churchill:

Hon. Winston S. Churchill,
Minister of Munitions,
White Hall, London, England.

At the third annual meeting of the Board of Commerce of Flint, Michigan, held last evening, attended by 550 members, at which I was the honored guest, I took the liberty of reading your personal letter of December 3 appropriate to the occasion in the review of recent events and because Flint, Michigan, is the birth-place of the General Motors Corporation, the pride of every Flint citizen, everyone without exception interested in the development, progress, ideals, and standards of that organization.

I join with the members of the Board of Commerce in hearty greetings of good will and sincere thanks for your courtesies and much appreciated compliment.

W. C. Durant

At the banquet, Durant spoke in glowing terms of the future growth of both Flint and General Motors. He also spoke of the responsibility the company felt in providing housing for its employees—which resulted in the Modern Housing Corporation development by which many homes were built in Flint. General Motors had expanded tremendously in 1919, buying a number of companies, and constructing the $20-million General Motors Building in Detroit, as well as purchasing a controlling interest in Fisher Body Corporation.

In the fall of 1919, Mr. and Mrs. Mott, with a group of other General Motors executives and their wives, visited and inspected industrial establishments in France, Italy, and England. The group included: Mr. and Mrs. Alfred P. Sloan, Jr., Mr. and Mrs. Walter P. Chrysler, Mr. and Mrs. Albert Champion, and Mr. and Mrs. C. F. Kettering.

On November 1, 1919, Walter P. Chrysler resigned as president and general manager of Buick and first vice-president in charge of operations for General Motors. A few months later, he joined the Willys organization. Mott remembers that Chrysler was often frustrated by Durant's casual way of overriding plans others had made. Although Chrysler had been made executive vice-president, he could never know when Durant would change policies. Mott recalls a particular instance in which he and Chrysler had left Flint at six in the morning for a meeting in Detroit with Durant. The meeting went on and on without even a break for lunch. Chrysler's temper mounted with his hunger, and the discussion degenerated into quarreling. Later, Mott mentioned to Durant that it might have been helpful to send out for sandwiches and coffee. Mott regretted seeing Chrysler leave General Motors, but he knew that Chrysler could no longer tolerate the situation under which he was working.

1920 opened with every expectation of another big year for Flint, with 29,000 men working in Flint factories, and plans for further industrial expansion. Mott once more entered politics—at the strong urging of his friends Charles Greenway, Leonard Freeman, and others—as candidate for the Republican nomination for governor of Michigan, issuing the following statement:

> If nominated and elected, I promise the state will be honestly and effectively administered. I am an engineer by education, an executive by training, and three terms as mayor of Flint have given me an insight into what ails government and what may reasonably be done to improve government through careful planning and prompt execution. It is not for me to say what my chances are; but if the people of Michigan want me as badly as my friends say they do, I am their man from now on. Needless to say, the letter and spirit of the corrupt practices act will be scrupulously observed during my campaign. I would count it an honor to have my name appear on the same ballot with electors pledged to the Republican ticket, Harding and Coolidge.

Mott's close friend, John J. Carton, campaigned vigorously, and Flint organized effectively to back Mott's candidacy, but Mott was not well enough known in the rest of the state. There were, of course, attacks based on the idea that General Motors was seeking control of state affairs; Mott's headquarters countered the accusation strongly, pointing out that the same claim had proved to be unfounded during Mott's terms as mayor of Flint. Mott's showing—third in a field of nine candidates—was considered to be very good considering that he was neither a politician nor an orator. He received an overwhelming vote in Genesee County.

In mid-1920, the postwar depression began to affect General Motors—then in the midst of expansion in many directions. Inventories piled up—falling grain and livestock prices hurt automobile sales and proved disastrous to the tractor subsidiaries. A falling stock market drove General Motors stock down, and Durant bought enormously in an attempt to keep the stock above $20 a share. Eventually, his commitments went millions of dollars beyond his personal resources—and it was necessary that someone with considerable financial capacity take over those stocks to prevent their being unloaded on an already depressed market. The du Ponts, with the help of J. P. Morgan & Company, took over the stocks—averting their complete loss by Durant, and preserving the credit and standing of the company.

For the second time, Durant left General Motors—on November 30, 1920.

In the changes affecting General Motors in 1920 and 1921, Mott, as always, was a stabilizing influence. Neither a "Durant man," nor an "anti-Durant man," he was, in his own phrase, "in the good graces of the whole outfit." Years later, Pierre du Pont referred to Mott as having been "a tower of strength during the Durant debacle." The reorganization of General Motors in 1921 brought Mott into his most active and effective service to the corporation through a new job. The following announcement from the Flint *Journal* of April 11, 1921, appears to have been devised carefully for its effect on the strong-division or strong-central-office schools of thought.

MOTT MADE CHIEF OF ADVISORY STAFF OF GM

C. S. Mott, who has been a vice-president and director of General Motors Corporation for more than six years has been made chief of the advisory staff of the corporation with headquarters in Detroit. Mr. Mott succeeds Alfred P. Sloan, Jr., in this capacity following a decision to place an officer in the Detroit offices while Mr. Sloan is needed in the production branch which is operating from New York.

Mr. Mott, who returned Saturday from New York, said he was assuming the new responsibility at a cost of considerable personal inconvenience to himself and his family, since it will require that he spend a large part of his time in Detroit and he has neither the desire nor the intention to give up Flint as his residence, but as it seemed advisable to take care of the condition at this time he decided to take up the work.

Mr. Mott will represent the corporation in its Detroit office and will head the advisory staff which consists of such men as A. B. C. Hardy, director of advisory purchase section; C. F. Kettering, director of advisory engineering section; Norval A. Hawkins, director of advisory sales section; Henry L. Barton, and a number of others. Mr. Mott is well-known and well-liked by the members of the organization with whom he will come in contact and his appointment will do much to set at rest the minds of those who may have thought the corporation was working towards centralized operation; Mr. Mott's ideas as to maintaining the integrity of divisions and their operation are well-known to his associates.

In spite of the inconvenience of being away from his home in Flint so much of each week, Mott enjoyed the activities of his Detroit job. There was concentration on improving the quality of Chevrolet, Oldsmobile, and Oakland. Mott was working with the people he knew, on exactly the kinds of problems to which his engineering background, wide production experience, and notable common sense could contribute most. Where others became emotionally involved with one group or cause, he remained calm, concentrating on the end products.

Flint, sharing the uncertainties of 1921, suffered unemployment, but by the end of the year production was going up again in the factories. One of Flint's earliest giants of the vehicle and automotive industry died in 1921: W. A. Paterson, who had opened a carriage shop in Flint in 1869. Later, he had manufactured carriages, and road carts made for Durant and Dort, and, still later, Paterson automobiles. He had also been one of the original stockholders and directors of the Buick Motor Company. He, like Mott, had served as mayor of Flint.

Harry H. Bassett, who had replaced Chrysler as general manager and president of Buick, was succeeding brilliantly with the original keystone of General Motors; the abilities Mott had recognized in him so many years before now found full scope. Albert Champion, one of Mott's favorite people, after a notable record in spark-plug production during the war, was developing the AC Spark Plug Division into the largest business of its kind in the world.

Mott has many pleasant memories of the colorful Champion, including the time that Champion came to Mott's office in Detroit with the request for an appropriation to buy a small piece of land on Dort Highway—part of the Dort property. Mott asked if Champion wouldn't soon need the old Dort building and the large section of land that went with it. Champion said that he would need it, but doubted that he could get it. Mott said, "You couldn't unless you asked for it." Champion revised his request, and Mott secured approval from Sloan on the whole purchase—the land where the enormous AC plant now lies along Dort Highway on the east side of Flint.

Mott has many interesting memories of the years in Detroit, and a number of accomplishments to his credit. He is most proud of having hired William S. Knudsen. Mott says, "In some book it said that Knudsen went to Sloan and Sloan hired him; well, that is not true. I take the credit for hiring Knudsen. I had him about a month and then there was a break-up in the Chevrolet organization and we needed a man to take care of things so we put Knudsen in charge of that because he was able. . . ."

Knudsen's effectiveness with Chevrolet, from March, 1922, until he moved up to become executive vice-president of General Motors in 1933, made automotive history. Mott preserves with pride a 1932 telegram from Knudsen on the tenth anniversary of the day on which Mott had hired him, February 23, 1922.

Among Mott's other accomplishments as chief of staff for General Motors in Detroit were promotion of the use of ethyl gasoline by General Motors men—and the use of Duco as finish for General Motors cars. There was hesitation on the part of General Motors men to use ethyl gasoline, although it had been developed by General Motors research under the direction of C. F. Kettering. This reluctance was based on a theory that ethyl gasoline burned up the valves of cars. There was a garage for the use of General Motors executives in Detroit, and Mott had all other motor fuels taken out except ethyl gasoline—so the General Motors men used ethyl gasoline and found that the rumor about its burning up valves was untrue.

Mott also remembers a number of instances when he did not get his ideas accepted:

> I wanted to use common bodies, but I couldn't get that across—also to use common doors. I promoted that and failed but somebody else got it across later. I was responsible for the Pontiac car. I said, "Here is a Chevrolet 4-cylinder. Why can't we build a 6-cylinder at Pontiac, using the Chevrolet body, axles, and everything else, and have another outfit make it at a higher price?" Fisher Body was making the bodies, so Red Fisher said, "Well, if you are going to get more money for it, then it should have a bigger body." That was against what I wanted to do. They built it and made all special tools, since they didn't want the car to look like a Chevrolet. Well, when at last they built the car, which I named, and had it at the show in Lexington Avenue—on one side was the Chevrolet, and on the other was the Pontiac, but they had painted the two cars exactly the same and you would have sworn it was the same body. I would have used the same body, but painted the cars a different color.

Flint kept on growing through the twenties. Durant brought his new company, Durant Motors, to Flint and manufactured Flint and Star automobiles in the big plant he built in the south

86

end of the city. He also made a number of other cars but none was able to hold a dominant position in public confidence.

At Buick, Bassett was highly successful, reaching production above 200,000 cars in 1923. Bassett was also successful in another way—in his dealings with the people who worked for him at every level. His genuine concern for all employees was not an expedient affectation, but a real and personal facet of his nature—and the employees knew it.

Other General Motors developments of the period included absorption of the Brown-Lipe-Chapin Company, of Syracuse, N.Y.—and of Flint's Armstrong Spring Company. General Motors also purchased and established the famous proving ground near Milford—with a wide choice of terrain ideal for giving cars grueling tests. There are two small lakes on the proving ground,—a nice one, named for Sloan, and a small, muddy one named for Mott—the latter being chiefly inhabited by turtles. Flint's population kept on increasing, and the social chaos increased proportionately—but few thought much about it with the prosperity of the times.

The Secretary of War, John W. Weeks, appointed Mott as civilian aide for Michigan; the special responsibilities of this job included promotion of recruiting for the Citizens Military Training Camp at Camp Custer. Mott was continued in this appointment as civilian aide for Michigan to the Secretary of War from 1924 until 1934.

It was rumored in 1924 that Mott was a candidate for the Republican nomination for Governor of Michigan. This, Mott denied flatly, stating, "I am neither a candidate nor have I any intention of becoming a candidate this year."

The Motts had many good friends and a highly active social life. Walter P. Chrysler was an especially close friend; Mott was godfather to the four Chrysler children. He also kept up his contacts with his Weston-Mott men and maintained a wide circle of friendships.

The Mott children had enjoyed it when their father was mayor because he brought home free passes to the movies for them, which supplemented the strict allowance established to teach them the value of money. Always very much aware of the fact that a bit of success or prosperity, however achieved, does not lift the possessor out of the human race, Mott took all possible care to preserve his children from the infections of snobbery as they grew up. He has always regarded himself as just an "ordinary guy" who might be operating a New York State farm except for the fact that his father moved to New York City to sell the family farm products, and later invested in the Weston-Mott Company. Mott's friendships include people of every background. He has resisted by all means the tendency of money to set a wall between himself and others. His evaluation of people has been on the basis of personal qualities rather than bank balances, and he has always wished to be similarly considered by others. This concept—a fundamental belief in and practice of democracy in its most real sense—he has consistently attempted to inculcate in his children. In simplest terms, he has taught them that the fact they happen to have more money than most people does not make them better or different from anyone else; on the contrary, it imposes special obligations.

Harding Mott has many vivid memories of his childhood: his father's reading Kipling's *Captains Courageous* and other stories aloud to the children . . . frequent horseback rides out in the country with his father . . . many family trips including visits to the Hardings and Mother Mott at Christmas and summer visits at Seabright, New Jersey . . . a family visit to California in 1917 when both Aimee and Harding contracted typhoid fever and had to stay for weeks in the Good Samaritan Hospital in Los Angeles . . . a family trip to Europe. . . . The rewarding tradition of the close-knit family which Mott had known as a boy carried over to his own family, and they did things together as far as possible. In the summer, the children usually went to some camp; Harding attended Boy Scout camp and the state YMCA camp. Aimee and Elsa went to Camp Aloha, Fairlee, Vermont.

After grade school, the girls attended the Emma Willard

School at Troy, New York, for four years; Aimee went on to Vassar, Elsa to Smith. Harding went to Hotchkiss, then to Antioch College (in which C. F. Kettering, Mott's close friend, was deeply interested), then to Yale, where he majored in industrial engineering at Sheffield Scientific School. Harding also attended Citizens Military Training Camp at Camp Custer at the age of seventeen. Harding Mott remembers that when he was fourteen Kettering—whom his father always liked and admired greatly—gave him his first airplane ride . . . in a biplane with an air-cooled motor, using ethyl gasoline.

One year, Mott rented a houseboat on the west coast of Florida, and he and Mrs. Mott voyaged in the Ten Thousand Islands area.

Mott liked hunting and fishing, and grew to enjoy golf and tennis. He has always had a particular fondness for the West —with Arizona as his favorite State. For years, he managed a few weeks each winter at Jack Van Ryder's, at Camp Verde, Arizona. Rough-country hunting and camping trips get away from artificial standards rapidly—and back to the realities of individual character, which is something Mott has always cherished. Also, rugged cowboy life contributes greatly to that physical fitness which Mott has always regarded as one of the primary obligations of an intelligent and self-respecting man. He has set his children an example in this regard—with horseback riding, hunting, fishing, sailing, and other strenuous activities. Mott set examples, too, on the cultural side—with a deep and intelligent interest in music, art, and literature. His special affection for the West is reflected in his Frederic Remington paintings and sculpture, and his impressive art collection also includes a wide range of excellent pictures.

In 1918, Mott secured two adjoining pieces of land between Kearsley and Court Streets, and there established an estate called Applewood, which has embodied and expressed many of his interests and ideas. Buying 26 acres from Dort and 38 acres from Nash, Mott was able to create a somewhat remarkable farm in the middle of Flint. His brother-in-law, Herbert E. Davis, designed a splendid Tudor mansion, which was built in 1918. A big barn was also built, and an impressive chicken house—and for twenty-five years, Mott raised livestock as well as maintaining large vegetable and flower gardens. The family moved into this big new home in 1919. Mott had a pipe organ built into the great living room, and many of the fine paintings of his collection are also displayed there. Trees, shrubs, and flowers have always been among Mott's interests, as Applewood demonstrates. Growing up in New York City, he had always yearned for the farm life his father had left— and he attained his own version of it in Flint.

In June, 1924, the happy life of the Motts was broken by tragedy. Mrs. Ethel Harding Mott, who had been in poor health for some time, suffered a fatal accident. While the rest of the family was at breakfast, Mrs. Mott fell from the window of her bedroom in the second story of their home, sustaining injuries from which she died a short time later. There are probably few to whom family and home have meant quite so much as to the Motts—and Mrs. Mott had been the central and presiding grace of the lives of her husband and children. She was known to her Flint friends for her gentleness, goodness, affection for her family, and activities in many charitable organizations.

The unexpected and untimely death of his wife broke the patterns of living Mott had worked for. He maintained Applewood and continued to work in Detroit from Monday mornings until Friday afternoons—but nothing was quite the same for this man whose life was centered in his home. In 1925, Mott took his three children, accompanied by their aunt, Mrs. E. A. Tauchert, and her son, on a European tour. After that, the children were in college. For Mott, there was work, plus hunting, fishing, and sailing trips. Within the next six years, he made two attempts to re-establish the kind of home-centered life which meant so much to him—the first being ended by another untimely death, the second by divorce. Not until 1934 was he to find the person with whom he was once more able to develop the splendid family life which has always been among his ideals.

NINE

After May 10, 1923—the date Sloan became president of General Motors—Mott and Sloan worked together more closely than ever before. Sloan in New York and Mott in Detroit made their special contributions to General Motors through a period of solid development in which the trend of the buying public demonstrated increasing confidence in General Motors products. Sloan and Mott liked and understood one another; each was an engineer, with the habitual need to get down to the facts of any situation; each had a very real social conscience, too—a sense of clear-cut obligation to his fellow men; each was capable of large vision, while not losing sight of the very down-to-earth practical detail work necessary to hammer vision into reality. They were explorers rather than adventurers, working by carefully devised plans rather than by inspiration.

In *Adventures of a White Collar Man,* Sloan expressed the satisfaction of this relationship: "I liked to work with Mott. His training had made him methodical. When he was confronted with a problem, he tackled it as I did my own, with engineering care to get the facts. Neither of us ever took any pride in hunches. We left all the glory of that kind of thinking to such men as like to be labeled 'genius.' We much preferred the slow process of getting all the available facts, analyzing them as completely as our experience and ability made possible, and then deciding our course."

In Flint, employment dipped in 1920, with the postwar depression, but came back by 1923—the year Flint's population hit 135,000. There was another drop in employment from March to November, 1924—but after that, rising employment prevailed. At times the need for employees was so great that advertising and recruiting programs were used to bring more and more workers to Flint. Highly skilled men were sometimes difficult to find—and at one period there was an influx of excellent mechanics from the New England States, many of them accustomed to small dies utilized in making watches and similar small items, to whom the gigantic dies of the automobile industry were somewhat amazing.

A School of Trades had been started at the Flint YMCA in 1918—sponsored by the Industrial Fellowship League and the Flint Vehicle Workers Mutual Benefit Association. Under the guidance of Albert Sobey, this school became the Flint Institute of Technology in 1919, and ultimately developed into General Motors Institute. Harry Bassett is credited with having interested General Motors in backing the school. The Flint Vehicle Workers Mutual Benefit Association and the Industrial Fellowship League evolved into the Industrial Mutual Association (IMA), which developed both indoor and outdoor recreational programs for shop workers and their families.

At the time Sloan became president of General Motors, B. C. Forbes had wanted more information about him, and had turned to Mott as the logical source. In *Automotive Giants of America,* which Forbes co-authored with O. D. Foster, the sketch of Sloan includes these paragraphs:

> When I wired one of Mr. Sloan's oldest and closest friends and associates, C. S. Mott of Flint and Detroit, to specify some of the qualities which had won Mr. Sloan such signal promotion, he immediately telegraphed this illuminating reply:
>
> "Alfred Sloan is an indomitable worker; a systematic and persistent organizer; a stickler for procedure; a crystallizer of corporation policies for the benefit and protection of the customer, the stockholder, and the members of the General Motors organization. His many years of training and experience in shop work, followed by taking over sales and executive duties, combined with natural ability and an open mind, make him an ideal man to direct the affairs of General Motors Corporation. Sloan and I have been warm personal friends

ever since we started doing business together over twenty years ago. The satisfaction derived from my personal relations with him could not have been greater if he had been my own brother. I think he inspires the same confidence in all with whom he comes in close contact."

Mott's is one of the twenty pen portraits included in *Automotive Giants of America*. The 18-page sketch of Mott is highly perceptive. It begins:

Charles Stewart Mott is an example of a new type of citizen America is producing. This new type is the brainy, busy, successful businessman, willing, while still in the very prime of life, to enter the stormy political arena and fill public office, thereby necessitating the giving up, either partly or entirely, of money-making pursuits.

Forbes secured from Mott a statement of the basis upon which he had taken an active part in government.

We business men have been content for the most part merely to rail at the doings and the misdeeds of those filling public offices. We often talk sneeringly of this, that and the next foolishness indulged in by the "politicians." But what have most of us done to try to better matters? Not a thing.

Years ago I gave the subject of a citizen's responsibility toward his community, towards his fellow men, very serious thought, and I decided that I could not very well retain my self-respect unless I were prepared to undertake such public responsibility as others might wish to call upon me to undertake. Here I was, comfortably situated financially, so that my family would not suffer were I to withdraw from daily business. I possessed robust health. I had enjoyed technical training as an engineer, fairly wide experience in the handling of men, experience also in conducting rather large business affairs, thus, presumably, fitting me to some extent at least for dealing with many of the duties connected with administration of civic and state affairs.

It was because I had reasoned things out in this way and had reached a definite decision that it was incumbent upon me, if I desired to retain in the fullest degree my self-respect, to respond, when possible, to any call that might be made upon me to discharge public duties, that I consented to become mayor of my town years ago, when the people were clamoring to be delivered from the unpleasant conditions brought about by a Socialistic mayor.

It was in exactly the same spirit that I later consented to allow my name to be put up at the primary as a candidate for governor of the State. The fact that I did not head the poll did not—could not—alter my carefully-reasoned-out attitude towards the shouldering of public responsibilities whenever called upon to do so.

America has afforded me opportunity to make reasonable headway in the world and to provide for my family. Why should I not stand ready, like a loyal soldier—I served six years in the Naval Militia and through the Spanish War in the Navy—to take orders from my fellow-citizens and obey any summons to serve my country in any capacity they might consider me fit to undertake?

In comment, Forbes noted:

Outside of his own State and his own industry, Charles S. Mott is not very widely known, largely because he is no seeker after publicity, no courter of the limelight. He is, and always has been, a doer rather than a talker. His brain works better than his tongue. He is not a glib orator. He is content to be simply himself—an undemonstrative, serious-minded, hard-working citizen, intent upon getting worthwhile things done efficiently, smoothly, expeditiously, leaving the results to speak for themselves.

Forbes also pointed out the importance of Mott's job in General Motors:

General Motors has its financial headquarters in New York, but its operating activities center around Detroit, and other parts of Michigan. C. S. Mott has always been high in the operating councils of General Motors. It is to him that his fellow-members of the executive committee look for unfailing co-operation in guiding and directing the operations of the various huge automobile and other plants that form General Motors.

After a biographical sketch of Mott, and a resume of the development of the Weston-Mott Company, Forbes stated: "From a concern worth perhaps $100,000 when Mott joined it in 1900, Weston-Mott had grown so rapidly and so soundly that by 1913, it was worth fully $3,000,000—a very substantial return for thirteen years of intense application."

Explaining that he had "tried to get Mr. Mott to tell how a man can best cultivate executive qualities," Forbes continued:

But Mr. Mott is a poor talker about himself or his achievements. With much prodding, I did succeed in getting this much out of him:

"The first consideration in business is to see to it that you produce something for which there is a demand.

"The next thing is make the thing right, and the next—as important as any—is to make the price right.

"You must exercise eternal vigilance in watching overhead. Many little expenses run into a large sum in the end. Some concerns concentrate almost wholly upon reducing production costs and neglect selling costs. Economic distribution is just as essential as economic production.

"Get facts. Never guess. Keep statistical records. Know every month exactly what your business has done in all its departments. Don't merely have these statistics compiled: study them, analyze them, use them as a basis for your reasoning, as a foundation for your vision of the future and your planning. Get down to the bedrock of things. Investigate things to the bottom. Think things through.

"Devote careful attention to training other men to shoulder and properly discharge responsibilities. When you get towards the top, or to the top, organize yourself out of a job. Encourage your best co-workers to reach out for greater responsibilities.

"Don't look over others' shoulders every moment of the

day to see what they are doing. Give them scope. Give them latitude. Encourage them to think for themselves. Encourage them to develop initiative. Don't pounce on them when they make mistakes; sit down and reason things out with them so that, while they won't make the same mistake again, they won't be afraid to exercise originality again lest they might make another mistake."

The Forbes interview also quoted Mott on another special characteristic—one that has been influential in many ways throughout his life—his sense of the importance of health, and every man's responsibility to maintain his own good health at best:

I am a great believer in keeping physically fit. I think this is of tremendous importance for any man who is in earnest about accomplishing the very most of which he is capable.

I go in for horseback riding, for farming, for hunting, for fishing whenever I can contrive to find the time. But I don't take vacations to do these things. I believe a man can keep himself in better condition while working and sticking to his job than when he goes away on a vacation and does nothing else but pursue recreation and amusement and exercise. After such a vacation, there comes a relapse. Instead of taking an overdose of exercise for a week or two at a time and then taking little or no real exercise for weeks or months at a stretch, it is better, I believe, to stick right to one's job and squeeze in a rational amount of exercise and recreation right along. This keeps the muscles as well as the mind in condition regularly. It flattens out the health curve, so to speak, instead of sending it away up one week then letting it slump.

In this interview, Forbes also commented on one of the paradoxical features of Mott:

I have already recorded that Mr. Mott isn't of the "regular fellow," "good mixer" type. Indeed, he gives strangers the impression of being rather austere, unbending, even cold. Yet I discovered, in the course of my investigation, that Mr. Mott, as one of his intimates put it, "has a heart as big as an ox."

He gives a great deal of money to the Flint YMCA (of which he has been president), to community chests, to the church, to philanthropic societies, and to other worthy or public purposes. But he does it so quietly that few people catch a glimpse of this side of his character.

We are indebted to B. C. Forbes for this portrait of Mott at the age of fifty-one, during his most active years as a business executive guiding the destinies of General Motors operations as chief of staff in the Detroit office. There have been many interviews with Mott, many stories written about him and his activities, but none other has caught so much of the quality of the man himself, or embodied such clear statements of the basic principles by which he has worked and lived.

In 1926, Mott took a step from which great strides in community development would come. That step was the formal establishment of the Charles Stewart Mott Foundation.

The factors leading to this action were several. Mott remembered the complexities of settlement of his father's estate, and had a strong belief that each man should take great care in providing in advance for the wise and efficient administration of his affairs after his death. The idea of establishing a foundation was suggested to Mott by a General Motors attorney who had drawn up the necessary documentation to set up a foundation for the owner of a group of cigar stores. Here was an engineer's kind of planning for the future, a way of organizing his help to the community and making it business-like—taking as much care in the spending of his money as he had devoted to earning it.

The very real encouragement offered by the income tax laws also indicated to Mott that the Government encouraged private giving—and, with his strong sense of responsible and personal administration of any business, he has always felt that he could make sure of getting the greatest value for people by carrying out his own program of help to the community.

Mott had already, over a period of years, demonstrated his strong desire to help others; he had given an important

97

building to Flint's Hurley Hospital, a farm for the use of the children of Flint, land across from his home for use as a park. He had been a major factor in the establishment and success of the YMCA and the Boy Scouts in Flint. His efforts and funds, with the help of Dr. DeKleine and the Flint School Board had initiated a dental and medical clinic for Flint school children. He had contributed generously and regularly to other community endeavors, and had taken special interest in boys' club work and the Kiwanis Health Camp while in Detroit. Actually, his services as mayor were another kind of gift to the community. An item from the diary Mott has maintained for a number of years gives a clear and simple statement of the origin of the Foundation:

> As the years went on, with less demand for time from business, and with greater realization of my responsibilities to society, and observing how many well-intended ideas and plans went astray after a man's death, when he provided funds in his will and left the execution of same to trustees, untrained and unfamiliar with his policies, I caused to be incorporated in 1926 under the laws of the State of Michigan, the Charles Stewart Mott Foundation, with a broad charter to carry on philanthropic, charitable, and educational work, with six Trustees, the principal one of which was my old and trusted friend Roy E. Brownell whose ideals were identical with my own.
>
> The idea was to get started and in operation worthy projects and the Trustees familiar with the work during my lifetime, instead of leaving funds and hoping that satisfactory results might be forthcoming after my passing—a hope which was not forthcoming in many instances I had observed in the case of those who left the job to be started after death.

The original trustees, in addition to Mott himself, were his three children, Aimee Mott Butler, Elsa B. Mott, C. S. Harding Mott—along with Roy E. Brownell, Mott's attorney as well as his close friend for many years, and Edward E. MacCrone of Detroit. The first officers were: president and treasurer, C. S. Mott; vice-president, Elsa B. Mott; secretary, Roy E. Brownell.

Mott's initial gift to the Foundation was 2,000 shares of General Motors stock, valued at $160 a share at that time. Since then its assets have increased steadily through annual gifts from Mott and the members of his family.

Thus, in terms of funds, the power plant was being built— but not for nine years was it to be hitched to the great vehicle for which it has since become internationally known. For the first few years after 1926, the Foundation furnished financial support to a number of projects including: The Flint Rotary Club's Crippled Children's Program, Kiwanis Health Camp, Lions Club Sight-Saving Program, Flint Community Fund, United Service Organizations, America Red Cross, Flint Institute of Arts, an underprivileged boys' camp near Flint, various local churches, and several colleges and universities. The Foundation did not in itself undertake any single major project or program during this period. But as the depression settled over Flint, with spreading waves of social disintegration, Mott became increasingly interested in the problems of children and young people of Flint. And in 1935, the engine and the vehicle were to be joined to become the Mott Foundation Program the world knows about today.

TEN

It was in 1929 that Mott's banking activities proved rather expensive to him. Mott had been president of Union Industrial Bank, then had become chairman of the board of directors. Less than a year after the Union Industrial Bank had become part of the Guardian Group, it was discovered that a group of employees of the bank had been playing the market and had embezzled some $3,593,000 from the bank. Mott recalls:

> I was in Detroit and was called on the phone in the after-
> noon and told that there had been some financial trouble in
> the Union Industrial Bank, and that there had been an em-
> bezzlement by some of the employees. I had to get in my car
> and hustle up to Flint, getting there in the early evening. I
> remember that there was a meeting of the directors which
> lasted until about four or five o'clock in the morning. The
> stock in the bank was then owned by the Guardian Group,
> and at the invitation of the directors and managers of the
> Guardian Group, I put up securities of about a million dollars
> to make a loan to make good on the embezzlement—and that
> continued from time to time and increased until it got to be
> over three million dollars. In the final analysis about two mil-
> lion dollars was lost. There were a number of other stock-
> holders who had a meeting, and they undertook to make
> pledges to pay a certain amount depending on the stock they
> had—but I had first to loan, next the directors helped me out.
> Then they had a meeting of the stockholders and they helped
> the others out. When the whole thing sifted out, I think it cost
> me about one and a quarter million dollars.

Newspapers all around the country carried the story—and amazement seemed to be about equally divided between the size of the embezzlement (said to be the largest in the history

100

of the country)—and the fact that one man, Mott, had provided funds to cover the loss.

It was, of course, the market crash which had brought the loss to light—since the bank employees were notably unsuccessful in their stock speculations with the bank's money. The *Literary Digest* of December 7, 1929, carried the story of the affair, quoting various newspapers and presenting a picture of Mott. The Detroit *News* said, "Out of the strange situation at Flint, Mr. Mott emerges as a hero."

Later one stockholder brought suit against Mott, the Guardian Detroit Union Group, Inc., the Guardian National Bank of Commerce, and the Union Industrial Trust and Savings Bank—to recover some $27,000 which the stockholder had paid as an assessment on stock owned. The claim was that Mott should have been able to detect or forestall the defalcations if he had attended the directors meetings regularly. The case was dismissed, and Mott was absolved of blame—the point being made by the court that the directors who had attended the meetings regularly were unable to forestall the defalcations, and that the bank examiners could not discover them.

General Motors and Flint shared the accelerated production of 1928 and 1929. In those two years together, General Motors sold some 10 million units for more than $7 billion. Chevrolet alone produced 1⅓ million cars and trucks in 1929. And then, of course, came the difficult times. The depression was devastating everywhere but perhaps most painful of all in such cities as Flint, which had almost always been known for its prosperity. To the people who had come from everywhere for Flint's big wages, it was as if golden streets had turned to lead. These workers with such diverse backgrounds had possessed nothing in common except their source of income; when that failed, only their differences remained.

For Mott, the career of William S. Knudsen increasingly gave reason for pride in having hired him. First as vice-president of Chevrolet and then—from January 24, 1924—as president Knudsen made tremendous contributions in the expansion and development of the Chevrolet Division to its leading position as the volume manufacturer of cars. Beginning April 1, 1932, Knudsen was also in charge of Pontiac production. On February 23, 1932, Knudsen wired Mott at Jack Van Ryder's, Camp Verde, Arizona:

TEN YEARS AGO TODAY DUE TO YOUR KIND OFFICES I WENT TO WORK FOR THE CORPORATION. WILL YOU PERMIT ME TO THANK YOU AGAIN FOR YOUR KINDNESS?

WILLIAM S. KNUDSEN

On October 16, 1933, Knudsen was made an executive vice-president of General Motors as general supervisor of car and body manufacturing. This brought an even closer relationship between him and Mott.

Although the strong development of Knudsen fitted in with Mott's principle to "organize himself out of a job" by helping bring up strong leadership within General Motors, Mott still carried vital responsibilities in 1934, and still spent a good portion of the week at the General Motors Building in Detroit, remaining a vice-president until 1937.

Among Mott's consistent loyalties has been that toward public service, both through an active interest in public and political affairs, and through agencies devoted to social service. Through backing boys' club work in Detroit, Mott had purchased and established a summer camp for underprivileged boys at Pero Lake, northeast of Flint. At first this camp was operated by the Vortex Club of Detroit; later, Floyd Adams operated the camp as a Mott Foundation activity.

The 185-acre farm south of Flint that Mott had originally purchased to be operated by a church men's club as a summer camp for Flint children later reverted to Mott, and he gave it, along with additionally purchased land, to the Flint YMCA, as Camp Copneconic.

A year of vital transition in Mott's life was 1934. By that time, his three children were married and away from home.

Mott continued at Applewood, and had an active circle of friends with whom he spent much time in Flint: Roy Brownell, the William Masons, Mrs. Nell Medberry, Taine McDougal, Willis Thorne, the H. H. Curtice family, the James Burroughs family, and others. Tennis had become an almost daily activity in good weather, and there were the grounds and the livestock at Applewood to hold his interest.

From the time of the Union Industrial Bank difficulties in 1929, Mott had been involved in a number of legal actions. One included appearing in 1934 before a Washington investigating committee concerned with the affairs of the Guardian Group. His attorney and friend, Roy Brownell, accompanied Mott on the trip to Washington. Ferdinand Pecora was conducting the questioning. Mott's diary, under date of January 17, 1934, notes: "After being sworn in by Senator Fletcher, I was asked by Pecora what my principal business was. I established it as, 'defendant of law suits, etc.' Then he questioned me regarding sale of a large block of Guardian Group stock to Harry Covington, and I gave full reasons and explanation of the transaction—bringing in the excellent work done by Covington and his advancement in the organization."

The next day, Mott was recalled for another hour and a half. He notes in his diary for January 18:

I was not badly treated but was asked many leading and searching questions regarding sale of stock to Covington, and some other matters relating to Group, and also re: Union Industrial Bank defalcation and payments thereon. I probably overlooked some opportunities for making record, but did inject some things that were not intended by Pecora. It was somewhat difficult at times, but I was not razzed and did not feel nervous, and I think the record is all right, though of course future events may prove to the contrary.

While he was in Washington, Mott visited the Senate, House of Representatives, and Supreme Court. Just as he was checking out at his hotel, ready to return to Flint, he encountered Pecora in the hotel lobby. Mott told Pecora he had nothing of which to complain. Pecora grinned, shook hands, and wished Mott a pleasant journey. In the following weeks, Mott was widely congratulated in Detroit and Flint for his statements before the investigating committee.

Returning to Applewood, Mott was taken aback by the amount of paperwork awaiting him in connection with other legal actions, tax matters, and similar affairs. He notes in his diary for January 20, 1934:

> No end of work to be done. Of all the damn-fool footless things—with lawsuits, attacks, hearings, reports, etc., the amount of work to be done is terrific, and it has to be done if I am to get a show for my white alley. And when it's all done, it is simply to keep me from "paying through the nose," being mulcted, going to jail, or what not. It doesn't put me ahead a foot but just wears me out and makes me ill-tempered and damning everything in general—especially an army of sharpers and shysters in the Government and out. If I have left a particle of faith in humanity, patriotism, or public spirit, it will be a miracle. As soon as I can get things off my neck and postponed for a few months, I'll try to go West, for the benefit of my friends in the East if for no other reason.

On the next day, Sunday, January 21, 1934, his diary notations include: "Walked around the place for an hour. The horses seemed glad to see me, but that was because they expected sugar, which I brought them." (This may very well be the most cynical recorded statement of a man who has been anything but cynical in his attitudes.)

The next day, Mott's diary notes, ". . . it was quite apparent that local Income Tax Inspector and Reviewer were determined to make life a nightmare to me. Among other things, they were going to annihilate my Foundation." Mott presented full facts and figures, asking no favors, but determined to secure justice "based on the law."

A day later, January 23, 1934, the diary notes include:

> . . . stopped in to see Ket and ask him regarding progress on Diesel engines for ships, boats, locomotives, individual

railway cars, trucks, and aircraft; also, developments of anti-knock fuel, variable transmissions, automobile springing, aerodynamic designs, and other things, and never before has it appeared that there was any greater opportunity for tremendous changes, developments, and improvements (all of which are in progress at the Research Laboratory) than at this moment. The amount of confidence in the future of General Motors gained by such a conversation with Ket is almost beyond comprehension and, as you know, I am not much given to exaggeration.

From the middle of February until the first of May, Mott made one of the Western trips he enjoyed so much, including some rough-country travel. He also visited the home of a cousin, Sarah Mott Rawlings, wife of Dr. Junius A. Rawlings, of El Paso, Texas. Enjoying his stay with the family, Mott found himself particularly happy in the company of one of the daughters, Ruth Rawlings, whom he mentioned more and more frequently in his daily journal.

On October 13, 1934, Charles Stewart Mott and Ruth Rawlings were married in St. Clement's Church Chapel in El Paso, Texas. Mott reported the happy wedding day very fully in his diary in such terms as this: "The Bride was on the arm of her father, and as she came down the aisle, tall and stately and like the Elsa of *Lohengrin,* the waiting Bridegroom turned toward her, and she looked at him, and he was nearly overcome with emotion."

After a leisurely and greatly enjoyed trip to Hawaii, the Motts returned to El Paso November 15, and to Flint November 27. Mrs. Mott shared her husband's wide-ranging interests, and brought new enthusiasms of her own—and Applewood blossomed afresh in hospitality and happy life.

Mott still carried his responsibilities as General Motors vice-president, along with a diversified program of interests—including his banking activities, his investments in the sugar industry, and his other industrial occupations. His own personal staff at this time included Roy Brownell as attorney,

John Getz as a financial secretary, Miss Ruth Dill as secretary in Detroit, and Miss Ellen Rubel as secretary in Flint. In addition to handling his own affairs and those associated with the Mott Foundation, Mott acted as financial advisor and agent for his children and their families as well as for his sister and her children. Each of Mott's three children had presented him with grandchildren—and the first child of his son, C. S. Harding Mott, was also named Charles Stewart—so that Mott referred to him frequently and affectionately in his diary as "III."

Mott has always had a tremendous zest for living, and in 1935 it was intensified to new levels as he introduced Mrs. Mott to his far-flung world of interests. Her delight with everything, and the evident approval with which she was accepted by his friends and associates, were additional elements of pleasure and pride to Mott. Mrs. Mott had been active in Junior League work for years, and she took an enthusiastic interest in the workings of the Mott Foundation—as she did in all the varied fields with which Mott was concerned.

The Motts took a Western trip in the spring of 1935, and Mott gave his wife an introduction to the Arizona country he had come to enjoy so much. Back home in Flint early in May, Mott resumed his busy round of activities in Detroit and Flint. His diary for May 16, 1935 (in which Mrs. Mott is mentioned as "C.R.") indicates his great interest in the camp for boys:

> Roy Brownell arrived for lunch and immediately afterwards, he, C.R., and I drove over to Mott Camp for Boys, on Pero Lake 18 miles from here, where we looked over progress of work in preparation for our summer camp. The kitchen has been moved to its new site; new dining hall–auditorium is nearly completed, with fine chimney and fireplace. A new well has been put in about 220 feet deep and will be operated by electric automatic Delco pump. Wires for electricity are being run from main line a few hundred yards away, so there will be electricity not only for pumping, but for electric ice boxes and lights.
>
> We have delivery of a fine new Chevrolet truck with C.C.C.

steel body, which is just a dandy thing for our work, not only during construction but also to carry supplies. It also has seats for bringing the boys over from town. Garages are being built under the dining room. We are putting up another building with three small hospital rooms for our camp Doctor. Later we may put up another small building in suitable location, which we will call the Administration Building, for the camp Director, from which point he can keep an eye on all of the activities. These are the only buildings that will be used. The boys will be housed two in a tent which will have wooden floors and cots, which experience has proved the most satisfactory arrangement, both for the boys and for operation.

We are also changing the landscape slightly by removing the knob of one hill, filling in and leveling a large athletic field where the boys will have their sports. We are also developing a fine swimming dock, providing ample safety and supervision for the youngsters. Altogether, the place is showing a lot of activity and improvement.

We have had a list of some 800 suitable boys prepared by the city school principals. These boys are from 10 to 14 years of age, and from families which are utterly unable to bear any expense or provide such outings for the boys. As it looks now, we expect to be able to take care of between 400 and 500 of these boys this summer. There will be about 80 boys at a time in camp covering two-week periods. Our personnel organization is all arranged for, and it looks as though the project will go through in good shape.

Roy Brownell, one of our Trustees, is very much interested, and puts a lot of time and thought on it. C.R. is very enthusiastic and expects to make frequent trips out to see the camp this summer.

There are many other references to the camp in subsequent diary entries; capacity was increased to over 100 boys instead of 80 in each group before the season began. Floyd Adams, who was operating the camp for Mott, worked very hard perfecting the establishment. On his sixtieth birthday, June 2, 1935, Mott visited the camp; his diary for that day reflects pleasure and pride in the many improvements.

On June 21, 1935, Mott's diary records his attending a

Rotary Club meeting at which Frank J. Manley, supervisor of physical education for Flint public schools, was the speaker. Four days later Mott reports a visit from Manley—which ended in a tennis game with Mott and Manley playing against Mr. and Mrs. James Burroughs. Thereafter, Manley's name is found frequently in Mott's 1935 diary. A long July 25 entry demonstrates the personal interest and concern Mott felt for the boys attending Mott Camp:

At 5:00, Floyd Adams picked me up and took me out to the Boys' Camp. We made inspection of the place. At 6:00, bugle sounded for assembly and the boys assembled in groups of their tribes around the base of the hill on which the flags were located. The staff were on the hill in front of the administration building. The boys were called to attention and the leaders checked them in their tribes, examined their hands for cleanliness; later each leader reported members of tribe all present and accounted for, and the boys were called to raise their hands in salute to the flag while Colors were being blown on the bugle and all the flags in the camp were simultaneously lowered. When this ceremony was over, the boys marched up to the mess hall for supper.

I was called on for a little talk, and afterwards I think every boy in the place came up and shook hands with me. They seemed to be a mighty nice lot of kids and extremely appreciative. This is rather noteworthy in view of the fact that the families from which these boys come are probably below average, the parents being least educated and informed, uncultured and ignorant, not giving their children proper training nor care. In fact, sometimes we think the parents of these boys need training more than the boys do. These boys are not at all used to restraint or control. In a camp of over 100 boys it is necessary to have control for their own welfare and safety, and this is not accomplished by strict discipline or punishment but entirely by leadership and confidence in the leaders engendered in the boys. I think a good job of this is being done. . . .

Of course this is the first year that we have operated this large camp, which is running about 115 boys. Our organization, staff, etc., is more or less newly put together. . . . Next year we hope to have the whole proposition running like clockwork. I forgot to say that when I made my talk to the boys, I told them that C.R. was very regretful that she could not have been present, and that she had sent best wishes and kind regards to all of the boys, and especially to those whom she had met in their homes. . . .

Often in his diary, Mott expresses his enthusiastic approval of Harlow H. Curtice both as a friend and as an executive. The September 25, 1935, entry records Mott's attending a Buick appreciation banquet given in honor of Curtice that evening, at which speakers included Sloan, Knudsen, and other major figures in General Motors—with that automotive pioneer, A. B. C. Hardy, as chairman of the affair, and Flint *Journal* editor, Michael Gorman, as toastmaster. Mott's diary notes, "My personal feeling is that Curtice and his associates have done a marvelous job, and no honor or recognition can be in excess of what they deserve." The next day, Mott felt that the tributes to Curtice "did not quite ring the bell, due to absence of a strong and direct statement," so he undertook to write such a statement—and showed it to Gorman. Gorman asked Mott for a copy, and on September 27, 1935, the following story appeared in the *Journal* along with pictures of Curtice and Mott.

TRIBUTE PAID CURTICE IN SPEECH THAT WASN'T MADE

So enthusiastic was the spirit of Wednesday night's appreciation dinner for Buick and the crowd included so many the audience would have been glad to hear, that no doubt a very interesting volume would be a collection of speeches which might have been made.

Charles S. Mott, vice-president of General Motors, a director and member of the Finance Committee, was confronted with this thought and "the speech I might have made" was obtained from him. "I would have directed my remarks to Harlow H. Curtice, President of Buick, and it would have been something like this," he said:

"We, your friends and neighbors, as citizens of Flint are

gathered here tonight to honor you and through you your organization who have done so much for us.

"This hall is large and it is filled. It would have to be many times as large to hold all of your admirers and those whom you have benefited.

"Some of us are stockholders of General Motors, some are merchants, professionals, and others of all walks of life. But all of us are your friends and all of us are benefited directly or indirectly by your excellent management of the Buick Division and your interest and participation in matters of civic interest.

"And we are here to acknowledge that debt and to express to you our gratitude.

"We have listened with interest to Mr. Sloan who says we are now out of the depression and on our way to prosperity. We sincerely hope he is right and know you are doing your best to make this a fact.

"We are always glad to hear from Mr. Knudsen—than whom the working man has no more sincere a friend—his attitude towards labor and a fair deal is an inspiration to us all. And we know of no one who will work harder to put his ideas into effect than yourself.

"You have just completed the presentation of your new line of Buicks, which carry all of the merits of past years plus. These new cars have the maximum beauty, performance, and satisfaction that has ever been put into a line of automobiles, and the only persons who will suffer thereby are your competitors and Buick service men.

"We know that you could not have done this alone. We know that you have had to have the earnest assistance and co-operation of your associates, engineering and manufacturing departments and Fisher organization, and we want them to know that we understand and appreciate it. But every business has to have a head, to sort the wheat from the chaff, to hold up a standard to work to, and to make decisions of prime importance. You are head of the Buick and you have done all three things, and we are here to tell you of our appreciation and friendship. We are glad to be your friends."

C. S. Mott

Thus Mott gave public affirmation of his respect and admiration for Curtice—and showed once more his abiding loyalty to Sloan and Knudsen also, and to General Motors. There are many definitions of the functions of the head of a business —but perhaps none was ever simpler, clearer, or more genuinely inclusive than Mott's ". . . to sort the wheat from the chaff, to hold up a standard to work to, and to make decisions of prime importance." Over the years, at Buick and as president of General Motors, Curtice continued to hold Mott's respect, admiration, and friendship. Mott once mentioned Nash and Curtice as the two men with the greatest gift for common sense he had ever known.

While Mott's interests and activities in behalf of Flint were broadening and intensifying, his personal plans widened also. After he and Mrs. Mott had visited Bermuda in January, they had decided to buy Parapet, a 9-acre Bermuda estate with a fine house and two smaller dwellings. The estate includes about 1,000 feet on Hamilton Harbor. The Motts spent the last days of October, all of November, and the first few days of December, 1935, at Parapet—enjoying everything hugely.

Mott immediately undertook many repairs and improvements for Parapet—correcting some faulty electrical wiring himself, and engaging carpenters, plumbers, gardeners, electricians, and an architect to follow out his plans. There were tennis, bicycling, and pleasant times with Mott's sister, Edith, and her husband, Herbert Davis, living not far away.

Returning to Flint early in December, Mott plunged immediately into the complex patterns of interests and activities in Detroit and Flint. His diary for Monday, December 16, 1935, notes: "Frank Manley came up and made a very complete report on his recreational work, on which he is doing a magnificent job." This concerns aspects of Mott's 1935 activities not yet detailed, and which deserve being set forth here in closer view and from another perspective in the pages to follow.

ELEVEN

To quote from the introduction of this book: "When a man believes that nothing else is important, really, except people, how can he implement his belief effectively?"

In a broad sense, the deeply satisfying answer to that question was demonstrated to Mott by one man, Frank J. Manley, whose life has been dedicated to the ideal of giving men, women, and children the greatest possible opportunity to develop. This ideal was identical with Mott's own; the difference was that Manley—bruising his head against official obstacles, and his heart against human suffering, during Flint's depression years—had worked out a definite means of carrying the ideal into actual practice. His impulsive trial-and-error experience in attempting to help young people in those difficult times had given Manley a blueprint for action. But action on a scale large enough to be truly helpful to the obvious needs of the community called for funds far beyond any Manley had been able to secure. When Mott found that he and Manley shared a common ideal, and that Manley had a practical plan of attack on the devastating waste of human lives characteristic of depression living, the Mott Foundation in its present form had its real beginning.

Like Mott, Manley came to Flint from New York State, but his early years and his path to Flint were very different from Mott's. Manley grew up in Herkimer, New York—and the automobile affected his family's income situation adversely. Manley has made references to his early days, and his first years in Flint, in the course of various talks he has made and in written notes. From these sources, in Manley's own words, is drawn the following account of the background and the factors which lead to the Mott-Manley combination that created the Mott Foundation as we know it today.

My father had a livery stable. Automobiles were coming into being more and more, and the livery stable business was going out. We couldn't hire any help in this livery stable, so I stayed at the barn and hung around there driving hacks during the first influenza epidemic in World War I. I started skipping school, and my father didn't care a whole lot. He didn't seem to care too much about formal education anyway. My mother had died years before, when I was ten.

In the ninth grade, I quit school altogether. I didn't get much urging to finish school except from my sisters, who were a little older than I was—and from the fellows at the pool-room. So it was the boys at the poolroom who were my educational counselors and vocational guidance directors. They wanted to have a good football team—and I played a pretty rugged brand of ball in those days—so they got me to go back to school.

I went back to school to play football—and, after that, basketball and baseball. I had to keep up passing grades in my school subjects to be eligible for sports. After four years of keeping eligible in order to play, they stopped my high school athletic career by graduating me. With that experience, it's no wonder I picked up the idea that participation in athletics was not only the way to keep out of trouble, but also the motive for getting an education.

In fact, I believed that athletic participation was a sort of saving grace for all mankind. Athletics beckoned me on to college, too—and I came to Michigan State Normal College in Ypsilanti, where I continued with sports and physical education.

From 1923 to 1927, I had the privilege of learning from Professor Wilbur P. Bowen, the greatest physical educator I've ever known. He not only believed in the importance of athletics and group recreation—he believed that they provided the key to good living, and that all community facilities should be made available for people to use for such activities. He felt that when people have a chance to express themselves in athletics and recreation, their tendency to do the right thing is improved for their whole lives. He was preaching a doctrine that my own experience verified, and I was—and still am—

inspired by his ideas. One of his specific ideas was keeping school buildings open around the clock, around the year, for public use in recreation programs open to everyone.

And, from Professor Charles M. Elliot, head of the Special Education Department at Michigan State Normal College, I derived another fundamental idea: every person is an individual and is to be treated as such. This includes the fact that you don't treat anyone as being a Catholic, or Jew, or Gentile, or Negro, or capitalist, or laborer—but only as a separate, individual human being to be respected and valued for himself.

After being graduated from college in 1927, I came to Flint as a physical education instructor in the fall—and the most important things I brought with me were those two beliefs. I came to Flint with the idea of practicing those two things: treating everyone as an individual, and using all the resources of the community for the people through recreation and athletics. At least I knew exactly what I wanted to do.

I had enthusiasm and energy. I was teaching at Central and at Whittier, and directing the physical education program in the elementary schools. In 1928, I became supervisor of physical education for all Flint Public Schools.

One day, the principal at Martin School told me they were having trouble with a group of boys who were skipping classes and accomplishing nothing when they did come to class. I said, "Let's form a Sportsmen's Club. I'll come out noon hours." We started with fifteen boys, and the group built up to thirty. I'd go out three noon hours a week and put on a basketball suit, and those kids would maul the daylights out of me. Then we'd have a business meeting, which consisted of my saying, "Give me the reports from your teachers. I want to know how you're doing." The reports got better all the time—and so did the boys. Some of those boys had already been in trouble with the courts—but they all turned out mighty well. I wasn't a social worker; I just knew that if you paid some attention to them—and gave them a chance at athletics —it would straighten them out. Later I came to understand that it wasn't athletics as such—but the personal attention that really mattered. I started two other Sportsmen's Clubs at other schools, and wanted to spread this kind of plan all over

Flint—but the Board of Education could find no money for it.

All those fine school buildings—which, after all, belonged to the people—were closed in the afternoon at 4 o'clock, and no efforts of mine could get them opened for use after that hour. All the people in authority listened to my story, but there was always a reason they couldn't do anything about it.

I started trying in 1927, in the boom days, and kept right on trying into the depression days when things were mighty rough in Flint. People were shaking their heads about the ever-increasing juvenile delinquency.

We had all kinds of traffic accidents, too, especially involving children, for lack of sufficient playgrounds and playground supervision. We had many drownings in the Flint River and other local swimming places as kids found their own recreation. I saw all these things happening—and, believing in athletics as I did, and the use of community buildings and resources for public participation, I thought I had the answers to all this tragic waste of human life, but I couldn't seem to convince anyone in a position of authority.

I went out on calls with members of the Flint Police Department. I saw what life was like on the wrong side of the tracks in Flint. I couldn't help feeling most people would do the right things instead of the wrong things if they had a chance; I wanted to give them that chance, but I couldn't make any headway. It seemed to me that the men in charge of things were wearing blinders, or didn't really want to see what life was like for most folks in Flint. They'd listen while I talked, but it seemed they didn't really hear what I said because they didn't do anything about it.

I went to probate court every Saturday morning, and before long I had a list of ninety fellows on probation to me—boys who were really in trouble, and who otherwise would have been sentenced to the Boys' Vocational School at Lansing. I'm not sure I knew what I was doing, but I was trying. I worked with those kids. Maybe I learned a lot more from them than they learned from me. I found that a little love— a little personal attention—and really treating them as individuals went a long way with those boys. I tried to get them organized into a club, and got a few other fellows who felt as I did to take an interest in them. But as far as making progress with my major idea of public recreation and athletic programs using public facilities, I still was getting nowhere.

Chris Addison, who was in charge of traffic safety for the Flint Police Department, teamed up with me to see if we could do something about safety and juvenile delinquency, working through the PTAs and Child Study Clubs. Chris gave more than 1,400 talks in one year, speaking in every schoolroom in Flint. I don't know how many groups I spoke to. We would try to get to these people with actual cases—not naming names, but telling the real circumstances of juvenile crime, drownings, traffic accidents, and the other ills threatening Flint's young people. We did strike sparks of response among these groups, and win loyal friends for what we were trying to accomplish.

Flint's PTAs were strong and active even in those days, and they were deeply interested in the problems, and possible solutions to those problems, which we presented as dramatically as we could to their groups—but even their interest did not make the schools available for use to the public.

A Recreation Council was formed, with all Flint agencies concerned with recreation represented: the City Recreation Department, Junior League, YMCA, YWCA, Boy Scouts, Girl Scouts, Industrial Mutual Association, and others. I was named first chairman of this council, and each agency was to make what contribution it could, within its appropriate area of service, to a co-ordinated recreation program for Flint. This Recreation Council sponsored our first leadership training institute, meeting twice a week, with volunteer adults training high school students in arts and crafts, group games, and techniques of organizing and supervising groups of small children.

At this time, we had also initiated an intramural sports program in the schools for greater participation than the "varsity" sports permitted, and had expanded the Sportsmen's Clubs.

At last, with the backing of Parent-Teacher groups and other agencies, we looked forward to a real summer playground and recreation program in 1933.

Our summer program was successful within its limitations,

but when school opened again I still had the sense of failure. The school doors were still locked at 4 o'clock, shutting away those rooms, gymnasiums, shops, and other facilities from the public that needed them so greatly.

By the summer of 1934, there was help from a new source —the Federal Emergency Relief Administration, Works Progress Administration, and National Youth Administration.

In the summer of 1934, Flint had forty backyard playgrounds, twenty-four school playgrounds, and fifteen City Park and Recreation Department playgrounds in operation. Children took full and happy advantage of these playgrounds, and the accident figures for children dropped to half the 1933 figure. Hundreds of softball teams were organized. That 1934 program demonstrated the greatness of Flint's need, and the good response people would make to such a program when given the opportunity. We planned an even bigger program for the summer of 1935.

Such a demonstration was proof of the need for a year-around program, open to everyone, utilizing the school buildings and facilities. I continued my speaking campaign, talking to every group that would listen to me.

In June, 1935, I got myself invited to speak at the Rotary Club, along with the other luncheon clubs. By that time, it seemed to me that I had been running on a treadmill for eight years for all the progress I had made. It seemed to me that the very people who could do something about Flint's problems were exactly the ones who couldn't be made to see, to understand, to feel, and to act. I didn't know many members of the Rotary Club I spoke to that day, but to me they symbolized exactly the people I hadn't been able to reach. I am sure I was rude, and that my bitterness about the inaction of Flint's men of influence—including the men in that room— was more than evident. I ridiculed those men for sitting so comfortably and complacently in their club meetings, while all Flint's social ills continued unabated. Looking back, it seems clear that I could have made only a very bad impression —but at least I *did* make an impression.

One of the men who came up and talked with me a minute or two afterwards was C. S. Mott. I had never met him before.

He said something about having a backyard playground of his own, and invited me to come over and see it.

Of course, I had heard many things about Mr. Mott—some of them right, but most of them wrong. I had heard that he had a large fortune but that his Scotch qualities made it unlikely that he would spend any of it. I did not know what to expect, but thought that he would not be inviting me to come to see him if something in my talk had not impressed him to the point where he was considering doing something to help.

I visited Mr. Mott's home, Applewood, then a sixty-four-acre farm-estate just four blocks from the center of Flint. When Mr. Mott found I liked tennis, we played a few games. Mr. Mott was sixty years old that June of 1935, but still a fierce competitor. He didn't mention my Rotary Club talk, but invited me back for more tennis.

About the middle of August, when I was figuring that all I was going to get out of the summer was some exercise, I mentioned to Mr. Mott that I was going back to Herkimer, New York, for a couple weeks vacation before school started. We were taking a breather between games on the tennis court at the moment.

Then, out of a clear sky, Mr. Mott lobbed this question across the tennis net: "What do you think of a boys' club here in Flint?"

He caught me off guard, but I managed a return. I said, "I think the boys' clubs are wonderful; it's just too bad we can't open the forty boys' clubs we have here in Flint."

He said, "What do you mean?"

I pointed to Central High School, visible from Mr. Mott's tennis courts. "There's one," I said. "It's closed down at 4 o'clock, when a boys' club should open. It's complete with two gymnasiums, a swimming pool, a cafeteria, shops—everything you would want in a boys' club, along with what you'd want for girls' club, mothers' club, family club, a complete community center. Only we can't use it. And that's just one. There are forty such schools in Flint—one within half a mile of every man, woman, and child in town. They all stand idle after 4 o'clock every day, because the Board of Education has no money to keep them open."

Mr. Mott heard me. After eight years, someone really *heard* what I was saying—someone who could do something about it. "Well, how could we go about trying it?" he asked.

I answered, "I suggest you put it up to the Board of Education. It won't be too difficult to work out a basis of starting such a plan in ten schools to begin with."

Mr. Mott thought that five schools would be enough to handle for a beginning, and he was right. Before we quit the tennis court that mid-August day in 1935, we had agreed that Mr. Mott would put the idea up to the Board of Education.

When he did so, the members of the board thought it was a wonderful idea. I learned another big lesson. There is always a *best* person to present any idea—usually the one who can do most toward making that idea into a fact. They could *hear* that idea from Mr. Mott, because they knew he had the means to translate it from a mere idea into a wonderful reality. I saw that it was much more important to get a good idea accepted than it was to get the credit for it—and that's another lesson I have tried to remember ever since.

It was agreed that Mr. Mott would furnish $6,000 for the school year, for supervision in those five schools, while the Board of Education would assume any additional cost of heat, light, and janitor service. That was the real beginning of the Charles Stewart Mott Foundation Program of the Flint Board of Education as we know it today, the beginning of Flint's community school concept, the first step from which all the many subsequent developments of the Foundation were to proceed. It was, above all else, the moment when the *needs of Flint's people* began to assume paramount importance in community thinking.

I have realized since that the eight years spent trying to overcome obstacles before 1935 served many good purposes. We had not only tilled the soil, preparing for acceptance of the ideas; we had also, in our informal surveys, and through our contacts with so many groups throughout Flint, obtained a real sense of the community needs as the community itself

119

expressed those needs. And, perhaps most important of all, we had developed a group of trained, capable, loyal, hardworking leaders—people dedicated to the same concept of community ideals which had kept me trying against all obstacles through the years. Without the able, devoted services of those leaders, the subsequent accomplishments of the Mott Foundation would not have been possible.

Thus, from the special view of Frank J. Manley, director of the Mott Foundation from those days in 1935, we have the story of how this tremendous program began—utilizing funds set aside by Charles Stewart Mott and his family for the Foundation, following methods developed by Manley, and working toward the common ideal shared by Mott and Manley to give people a chance to improve their lives and to make Flint a better place to live for all its people.

Manley's concern with using publicly owned facilities—the schools—as community centers for community activities, suggested the partnership with the Flint Board of Education. Mott had already worked out one such cooperative arrangement with the board in 1918, and late in 1935 he also agreed to contribute $6,000 to supplement the board's health program with the understanding that the board would not reduce the $24,000 budget already allotted as the maximum available. Mott had initiated this gift after finding that many boys selected by the schools to send to Mott Camp showed serious need of medical and dental care.

TWELVE

It would have been simpler and easier to build an impressive boys' club building and set up an endowment than to operate the Mott Foundation actively and personally. But Mott has always given the same interest, imagination, and ability to the task of spending his money well that he devoted to earning it in the first place. With thousands of foundations in the United States—more than two hundred of them in Michigan—very few actually operate their own programs on a direct working basis. And no other foundation is known to work with and through a local board of education in the way the Mott Foundation has operated since 1935.

A program for conserving, enriching, and improving human lives can be developed effectively with business methods, common sense, the techniques of good administration, research and pilot-project experimentation, and sound organization to avoid waste. That is exactly what the Mott Foundation has done. The use of the forty existing school buildings in Flint for a program to improve the lives of the people who owned those buildings appealed to Mott's common sense and practical judgment. He felt that he could do much more good with the Foundation's funds in this way—get more human value for Flint people with the dollars spent. It would have been wasteful to him to duplicate already-existing buildings—buildings which could be made available and admirably serve community recreation and education purposes.

The board of education, in 1935 and after, has been most happy to have funds made available for good programs that lacked public funds. In effect, the board has sponsored most aspects of Mott Foundation activities, and it has requested Foundation funds to carry on programs for which there was a demonstrated community need. In addition, the Foundation has carried out many projects with other community agencies.

Mott has often described the function of the Foundation as, "greasing the wheels of already-existing machinery," and he has spoken of "not spending money for bricks and mortar to put up buildings" but "utilizing existing facilities and spending our funds for supervision and instruction to bring people the most good." But these principles have not stopped the Foundation from meeting a demonstrated community need. If a new building has been shown to be necessary to carry out needed work, the new building has been constructed.

When the board of education formally accepted Mott's contribution of $6,000 for supervision and equipment to be used in a recreation program to be conducted at five schools, the money was deposited to its account for disbursement only by the board's business manager, as authorized. In general, this same arrangement has prevailed ever since in administering the board of education–Mott Foundation activities.

In this pilot project, five Flint schoolhouses were lighted up that fall of 1935. Public response was so overwhelming as to make Manley glad they had not tried to begin with ten schools. Enrollment was about three times greater than Manley's most optimistic expectation. Manley was delighted—but he needed more supervisors and teachers, and it was clear that the $6,000 would not cover the whole year as expected.

After Mott's return from Bermuda in December, 1935, Manley wanted to request additional funds which obviously would be needed for the program—but he still felt unsure of Mott, and was afraid that Mott might not welcome such a request.

Manley was rehearsing over and over again in his mind just what he would say to Mott to tell him that the program had succeeded so well that it was rapidly running out of money. Before he had worked up his presentation to a point of usefulness, Mott called and asked Manley to come over. We return to Manley's notes for his account of that crucial interview.

122

I picked up every scrapbook I had, and a complete record of every penny spent, and just what it had been spent for. Mr. Mott welcomed me into his living room (which I always think of as a shade smaller than a standard basketball court). I talked, and showed the multitude of clippings—an amazing array of favorable publicity and commentary from the Flint *Journal* in particular. There were stories about the classes, stories about the leaders, stories and more stories about the crowds of people taking advantage of this new opportunity for recreation and education. I talked, and showed the figures —exactly what we had spent, and what the money had brought us. I talked about how we could cut down delinquency and crime. I talked, and kept on talking. Mr. Mott listened, and twiddled a pencil. It seemed to me that I didn't dare stop talking, because I had already made it evident that the money was not going to last out the year. And when I stopped talking about what we were doing, I would have to come to the point of asking for more money to continue—or the whole program would have to be dropped. I never talked so hard in my life. Mr. Mott listened, and did not say anything. I realized afterwards that he would have had to interrupt me to say anything at all, because I was talking on a marathon basis. We were sitting at one end of that enormous living room. Maybe, in my talking, I had come to the point of repeating what I had said earlier; I am not sure. Anyway, Mr. Mott got up out of his chair and walked to the other end of the room and turned off a small lamp bulb burning there. I thought that perhaps this was his way of showing me that—since he couldn't afford to leave the light bulb burning—he certainly couldn't afford to contribute extra thousands of dollars to the program I was describing. Prejudices imparted to me by others flooded over my mind once more; I felt hopeless and defeated.

Mr. Mott sat down in his chair again. "What you have reported sounds very good," he said. "If you need any more money, speak up."

For all my talking up to that point, I couldn't "speak up," although he had opened the door wide to just the request I had come to make. The shock was too great. His words were so far from what I had expected him to say that it stopped me cold; I just couldn't shift gears that fast. It was like a perfect placement in tennis; he had made his point, and I was so far from being in position for it that I couldn't even wave my racquet at it. Somehow, I managed to answer, "I'll have to think it over—figure out how much more we will need. I'll see you tomorrow or the next day, and we'll figure it out."

I understood at last that hatred of waste on the one hand went right along with appreciation of value on the other with Mr. Mott. When he noticed an unnecessary light burning, he turned it off. When he saw that our five-school experimental program was proving successful far beyond our expectations in terms of human values, he was volunteering additional funds for it without my even asking. I realized that this was the turning point for the program—the moment of its transition from an experimental pilot project into a going, growing, established concern.

Still somewhat in a daze from the unexpected turn of events, I went out of Mr. Mott's great house and climbed in my five-year-old second-hand Chevrolet. I know the motor was not hitting very smoothly, yet I rode home on a cloud— as happy as a young man could possibly be. I knew that Mr. Mott really understood, appreciated, and believed in the program—and would back it to whatever extent necessary to produce the good human results we were both concerned to achieve. When I got home and went in the house—every light was on, and my wife and the children were in bed asleep. I thought, "There's the difference between the Motts and the Manleys—the haves and the have-nots. We will probably never learn to conserve the pennies and make dollars out of them—but at least we can share the human ideal of helping to illuminate the lives of others, and make our own contribution to carrying out the ideal in reality."

In the course of the next few days, Manley worked out a plan for continuing the program through the remainder of the school year and through the summer, and Mott provided the additional funds necessary. From that day on, the Mott Foundation program has expanded every year to a current budget of $1.5 million.

Manley and others had made the most of funds available through the Emergency Relief, Works Progress Administration, and National Youth Administration, to restore opportunity to Flint. But it was the opening of the school doors—the inauguration of a plan not limited by the restrictions hemming in Governmental agencies—that gave Flint a real open door to opportunity again.

While the beginning of the plan had been keyed to establishing boys' clubs in the schools, there were requests for similar activities for girls and adults. The people themselves were moving toward the community-school concept naturally and spontaneously. The program was diversified and expanded to meet the demonstrated interest and need.

The leaders—originally one man and one woman at each of the five schools—were given an intensive special training course covering the philosophy of the program, organization of clubs, athletics, dramatics, games, library facilities, story telling, psychology of handling various age groups, and the relationship of the program to the problems of juvenile delinquency. Experts in these special fields were called in to give concentrated instruction to the leaders.

A Flint *Journal* story, covering the new program in detail, noted:

> There will be no standardized type of program. Each community center will establish the programs desired by the individual groups, so that every boy and girl in the city will be given an opportunity to enjoy a wholesome type of recreation. There will be no fee of any kind, and all the boys and girls in Flint are invited to enroll at their own community centers. The project will be carried on from 6:30 to 9:30 o'clock every night excepting Saturday. It is planned to utilize the entire day each Saturday for programs more comprehensive than can be carried out during the three-hour periods each night.
>
> To finance the huge recreational program, the Mott Foundation has provided $6,000 for the season, of which $5,000 will be required for the full time services of the community

center leaders; $500 for athletic and miscellaneous equipment, and $500 for medals and expenses for a proposed decathlon.

Frank Manley, physical and recreational director of the Flint public schools, is the active manager of the project.

The general committee in charge includes Circuit Judge James S. Parker, president; Probate Judge Frank McAvinchey, treasurer; Frank Farry, Boy Scout leader, secretary; Leland H. Lamb, superintendent of schools; Dr. A. J. Wildanger, Dr. Henry Cook, Dr. Lafon Jones, Floyd Adams, C. S. Mott, Roy E. Brownell, and Mr. Manley.

The article continued with the names of the leaders for each of the five schools, and emphasis on the point that each community would choose its own types of recreational activities, in terms of the interests and needs of the people attending. The story continued:

The types of activities to be conducted in the community centers include:

Physical

Gymnastics, basketball, indoor baseball, volley ball, indoor track, wrestling, boxing, swimming, skating, and hockey.

Social

Checkers, dominoes, cards, modern and old-time dancing, game nights, social mixers, parties, and picnics.

Auditorium

Chorus, community singing, orchestra, band.

Dramatics

Pantomime, minstrels, plays, stunt clubs.

Community Nights

Speakers, movies, lantern slides, home talent nights, concerts.

Class Rooms

Sketch club, art classes, sewing groups, hobby clubs, airplane clubs.

The efforts of the community center leaders and supervisors will be supplemented by the services of those who can help with various projects, such as dramatics, handicraft, and marionette shows.

Orchestras will be available for dancing; pianists will be provided for tap dancing classes; musical directors will be available to teach glee club and other choral work, and others whose talents will assist the general program will contribute their share.

With such a list of possibilities to start from, it is no wonder that opportunity-hungry Flint responded. Even before the first evening of actual operation of the five centers, preliminary meetings with coordinating committees representing each school and surrounding neighborhood had already required rearrangement and enlargement of tentative plans. The first regular evening schedule included gymnasium classes for elementary boys, junior high boys, senior high boys, young men, and married men; girls' tumbling; mothers' knitting class; dramatics; boxing; wrestling; ping-pong; girls' handicrafts; general games; story telling; knitting and sewing for girls ten to eighteen. On the second evening, junior and senior basketball leagues were organized, and several other activities were initiated, including a married women's gymnasium class, a fathers' club, and a women's chorus. (It might be noted that the number and variety of activities presented through the Mott Foundation has been expanding ever since.)

The five schools chosen for the recreational program— Martin, Lowell, McKinley, Zimmerman, and Homedale—included in their areas some of Flint's highest-juvenile-delinquency sections. The idea that the recreational and athletic program—substituting wholesome for unwholesome activities —was the answer to juvenile delinquency was very much in the minds of those backing the endeavor. A distinguished visitor in November, 1935, had the same idea.

Mrs. Franklin D. Roosevelt visited Flint and reported her findings in her syndicated column appearing in many papers throughout the country. Her comments included these:

They have done a remarkable job of co-ordinating in Flint. Their community plan co-ordinates all the various community forces—industrial, social, philanthropic, recreational, and educational. So it seems natural that the Youth Administration, and the WPA, and all other government agencies have done a co-operative job here with the city. The outstanding factor in their programs is the use of schools. Instead of closing them at 4 o'clock, they remain open and become community centers. Classes of every description go on just as they do all day and recreational programs are carried out. They are trying to provide out-of-door recreation for every child in the city. They showed me a park that had been made from a dump. A public-spirited citizen had contributed some very good tennis courts which are going to be sprayed and used as a skating rink this winter. Someone else has donated the money to put up a building where they will have showers, toilets, a game room, and a stage where they can rehearse their plays. There is to be an outdoor theatre in the park next summer and some stone fireplaces are to be built for picnics. Another public-spirited citizen has paid the teachers who stay overtime to teach in the schools. Last summer everyone who had a backyard vacant lot or field which could be used as a playground, was asked to fix it up and open it for the neighborhood children. The result is that the Boy Scouts and Girl Scouts are putting a course of training as leaders in these playgrounds into their program this year. The city has become so much interested and recognizes so well the value of this entire program that it would probably go on without any Federal aid. What the community is spending in prevention of crime will probably be amply covered by the reduction in young gangsters and hoodlums who manage to destroy a good deal of property.

A full page of pictures of Mott recreation activities in the December 22, 1935, Flint *Journal* showed a boys' harmonica group, archery in the game room, a girls' gymnasium class, a beauty-culture class, a tap-dancing class, a girls' basketball game, boys in a woodworking class, younger children playing games, and young women knitting. Publicity of this kind made its own real contribution to swelling the attendance.

Although there had been some woodworking activities in the first months of the program, it was not until February, 1936, that regular industrial-arts courses assumed major importance —with the contribution of salvage materials from Flint industries, and instruction from regular teachers in the school workshops. Before the winter program was over, it required almost a full newspaper column each day to list that evening's activities at the five schools.

During the last week of the evening schedules for that first year, the Flint *Journal* noted:

> The greatest recreational program ever provided for the youth of Flint will bring its winter schedule to a close this week after having served more than 120,000 young people.
>
> Designed to provide wholesome recreation adapted to the needs of every section of the city, the winter program of the Charles Stewart Mott recreation project will conclude Friday night after having recorded a community achievement without parallel in the nation.
>
> Utilizing school buildings as community centers, the Mott project has proved successful far beyond the original hopes of its sponsors.
>
> Figures compiled today show that the project has served 120,032 young people with an average attendance each week of 5,456. Of this total, 76,516 were boys and 43,516 girls. The average weekly attendance of boys was 3,478 and that of girls was 1,978. In addition to these totals, thousands of adult spectators were cared for.
>
> This does not include the closing event of the city-wide program which will culminate in a decathlon and pentathlon at Dort Field on May 23, with nearly 12,000 boys and girls competing for bronze medals and honor ribbons. . . .
>
> Not only has the project reduced juvenile delinquency, but it has also been a material factor in carrying on the child safety program, which, combined with the back yard

playground movement, has given Flint the enviable record of not having had a child killed by traffic while playing in the streets for more than one year. ...

The article concluded:

> One of the cardinal factors in the success of the Mott program is recognition of Jefferson's philosophy that the schools are built for all the people. The project takes advantage of facilities that have been available for years, but which the average community always has neglected.
>
> It is based on the fact that school buildings stand idle the greater part of the time and that these buildings can be made into community centers where the wholesome recreational activities are provided for otherwise idle hands. ...

Thus one of the continuing objectives of the Mott Foundation was recognized in the first year of operation: serving as an exemplar pilot project for other communities. The community-school concept emerged clearly—as did the Foundation's unique partnership with the board of education. Also evident from the nature of the program was the emphasis on opportunity. Another principle demonstrated in the first year, and followed consistently ever since, is adapting the program to specific needs of the people themselves. No cut-and-dried program was handed to the people; each section of the community determined its own activities by its declared interests and needs. The use of qualified personnel—chiefly teachers—for instruction, leadership, and training in their own fields was also evident in the first year's operations. Above all, the genuine American democracy of the program was made clear: the true respect for people as individuals with abilities, needs, and capacity for growth and development when opportunity exists. The Mott Foundation program is a demonstration of democracy, recognizing that real equality is not a matter of hereditary endowments, but of opportunity for each person to develop his own highest possibilities.

THIRTEEN

A great happiness came to the Motts with the birth of their daughter, Susan Elizabeth, at El Paso, Texas, on February 13, 1936. Mrs. Mott's father, Dr. Junius A. Rawlings, attended at the delivery of his granddaughter. Only weeks later, tragedy shadowed the new happiness of the family with the illness and death of Dr. Rawlings. Mott noted in his diary for March 25, 1936 (the day of the funeral of Dr. Rawlings):

> Regarding Dr. Junius Rawlings' place in the hearts of the people of El Paso, I am sure that no other man in the city was regarded with so much love and affection as he. . . . He was the most kindly man I have ever known, thought no evil of anyone. . . . He spent endless time working for the poor and needy without financial remuneration and without regard to hours or care of himself. . . . His was a life of self-sacrifice. . . . He will be terribly missed by his family, his friends, and his beneficiaries, but as an example of a fine life he made a record that his family may justly be proud of.

Back in Flint by early June, Mott spent a good part of his days at his office in the General Motors building in Detroit. The man who had invited Mott to Flint in 1905, W. C. Durant, had come to one of the bitter valleys of his incredible career. His Durant Motors had abandoned Flint operations in 1926, and then transferred to New Jersey, but by 1928 it had fallen by the wayside. Durant himself had tried other ventures, but the Midas touch appeared to have been lost. In 1936, pressure from creditors forced him to file a voluntary petition in bankruptcy. He listed almost a million dollars in debts, and had only his clothes, valued at $250, to offer as assets.

A small group of men long associated with Durant quietly contributed a sum of money for the fallen giant of the automobile industry. Those men, whom Durant called his real friends, included Mott, Chrysler, Sloan, R. S. McLaughlin, A. G. Bishop, and Dr. Campbell (Durant's son-in-law). Durant was most grateful for this help in a cruel hour; he wrote his thanks to Mott, and mentioned that he proposed to dedicate his memoirs to these real friends. Unhappily his autobiography was not completed at the time of his death, and the full story of this "larger-than-life" figure in American industry and finance has never been made public.

The "real friends" of Durant who contributed the fund for him at the time of his bankruptcy were well aware that— despite differences most of them had had with Durant at one time or another—he was the Titan, the Founder of the Feast, the opportunity-maker. As long as boldness, daring imagination, dramatic action, and infinite enterprise were required to shape an empire out of a vision, Durant was the indispensable man. But when caution, retrenchment, and conservation were essential, Durant was out of his element. Looking back, it is easy to wonder why he did not keep just *one* of those 90 millions of his personal fortune he poured into the market in 1920 to support the falling price of General Motors stock. The same character qualities which had led him to accumulate that fortune prevented him from salvaging any substantial portion of it. Fortunately for the Titan, some of the Olympians remembered and honored him. Mott has always made it a point to credit Durant for the greatness of his founding contribution and the gigantic momentum he imparted to General Motors in the early years. To those who know and appreciate the unique qualities of Durant, nothing in the failures of his later years can take away from the amazing roster of his successful accomplishments.

The depression was still the depression and Flint had many more bitter days ahead, particularly during the sit-down strikes of the first weeks of 1937. Social, economic, and political forces of more than local magnitude came to grips in that long-closed chapter of Flint's history. On February 11, 1937, an agreement ended the strikes—and mutual understanding and constructive working together have been typical of the years since. Throughout the strikes, Mott Foundation programs continued uninterrupted, except that some activities requiring use of the gymnasiums in some schools had to be suspended for a short time because the gymnasiums were utilized temporarily as quarters for the National Guard.

Just as it is the mutual conviction of Mott and Manley that only people are important, the Foundation itself demonstrated repeatedly that the most essential building block in a community program is leadership by people who care about people. Given a nucleus of such leaders, all else may follow. Without such leadership, the individual and community objectives seem at an impossible distance. Manley, in his years of trial and error, had found among his school associates a small but effective group that shared his vision and had the background, experience, and skills to build that vision into a practical reality.

To understand the response to the Foundation's program, it is both necessary and appropriate to note some of those leaders who put the program into practice. Outstanding among these are Myrtle Black, Alton R. Patterson, Harold D. Bacon, and William F. Minardo.

It is impossible to measure the special contribution of Mrs. Black to the total development of the Foundation program— not only in her special field, adult education, but in her relationship to the evolution of the total concept, and in her intensely loyal assistance to Manley whenever and wherever required.

Graduated from the University of Chicago in 1922 with the degree Ph.B., she received her M.A. and Ph.D. from the University of Michigan, in 1942 and 1952 respectively— thereby exemplifying the value of adult education in her own life. Wife of a Presbyterian minister, Mrs. Black had exceptionally heavy financial responsibilities to her invalid mother, and had taught school for four years while the family lived at Kinde, Mich. Coming to Flint, Mrs. Black was unable to secure employment in teaching other than as a substitute because of a depression ruling against hiring married teachers.

In 1933, the F.E.R.A. announced possible part-time work for unemployed teachers, and Mrs. Black along with hundreds of other Flint-area teachers-without-a-school went to see about it. Frank Manley, Phil Vercoe, and John Wellwood of the Flint public schools had been delegated to handle the applicants under this special program. When Mrs. Black arrived, she found Manley, Vercoe, and Wellwood inundated with crowds of applicants. She volunteered as a secretary-helper to assist in registering applicants, and Manley hired her then and there. Mrs. Black worked for one agency after another, but since Manley remained in charge of liaison between the public schools and the Federal agencies, she was always working with him to some extent. Thus it can be said that she, like Manley, was already in motion with the objectives of the Foundation even before Mott and Manley had instituted the formal program in the fall of 1935. Since that time, it would be difficult to say whether Mrs. Black has grown more with the Foundation, or the Foundation has grown more with Mrs. Black. She is now well-known in adult education circles throughout the United States for her work through the Foundation.

Alton R. Patterson had been Manley's best friend and roommate at college, and they had come to Flint together after graduation from Michigan State Normal in 1927—each to his first job as a physical education instructor. Patterson shared Manley's belief in the social value of sound recreation, and worked closely with Manley in the formative days of the Mott Foundation as supervisor of recreational activities in the schools in the north part of Flint. Later he widened his activities and became assistant director of the Mott Foundation program as well as director of pupil personnel, attendance, and child accounting for the schools. Loyal, intelligent, and purposeful, Patterson made an important contribution to the development of the Foundation program—and his death in 1951 was a serious loss to the leadership.

134

C. S. Mott in 1898,
Gunners Mate 1st Class

In 1902: C. S. Mott drives his first car, a 1901 Remington

(*Bottom*) View of downtown Flint in 1905

(*Top right*) Officers and supervisors of Weston-Mott Company pose with C. S. Mott (front row, fourth from left) after move to Flint in 1907

(*Bottom right*) C. S. Mott at the wheel of his third car—a 1907 Stevens Duryea, made in Chicopee Falls, Massachusetts. With him in the front seat is Mrs. Mott. In the back seat are his mother, Mrs. John Coon Mott, and Hubert Dalton

Weston Mott Offices, on left, beside the Buick plant at the corner of Industrial and Hamilton Avenues, 1910

Four early leaders of America's automobile industry: Alfred P. Sloan, Jr., C. S. Mott, C. W. Nash, and H. H. Bassett, at Nash's Kenosha (Wis.) plant in 1916.

(Left) "Desert Dick"—C. S. Mott in Arizona, 1932 *(Right)* With wife and children on his seventy-fifth birthday on June 2, 1950: (top) Mr. and Mrs. C. S. Mott, (middle) Harding Mott, Elsa Mott (Mrs. Kenneth Ives), Aimee Mott (Mrs. Patrick Butler), (bottom) Stuart Mott, Maryanne Mott, Susan Mott (Mrs. Sherill Dansby)

President Eisenhower congratulates Mr. Mott on receiving the 1954 Big Brother of the Year Award

(Above) In 1958, laying the cornerstone of the Charles Stewart Mott Building of the University of Chicago: (front) Chancellor Lawrence Kimpton, C. S. Mott, Dr. Robert Burns, (back) Mrs. C. S. Mott, Harding Mott, Aimee Mott Butler, trustees of the Mott Foundation

(Top right) At dedication in 1957 of the Mott Memorial Building for use by the Flint College of the University of Michigan: Dr. Alexander Ruthven, President Emeritus; Dr. Harlan H. Hatcher, President; Dr. David French, Dean of Flint College; C. S. Mott; Walter E. Scott, President, Flint Board of Education

(Right) The foundation of the Foundation

Frank J. Manley, Director, Mott Foundation

Harold D. Bacon is another of the original little group of exceptional leaders with both the heart and the skill to make the original Mott Foundation idea work out in fact. A graduate of Western State Teachers College (now Western Michigan University), Bacon had come to Flint as a physical education instructor in 1928, and his qualifications were admirably adapted to the needs of the Foundation plan. In 1934, he became assistant supervisor of physical education for the schools—and later was made supervisor. He first directed the Foundation recreational activities in the west part of Flint, and later became supervisor of recreation for the Foundation. He has earned a national reputation as a caller of square dances, and has woven a wide range of activities into a recreation program of impressive versatility.

William F. Minardo is the fourth of that original group of closest associates of Manley. Having graduated from Notre Dame in 1932 with a B.S. in physical education, Minardo became a physical education instructor in the Flint schools in 1934. With the inception of the Mott program in 1935, he became supervisor of recreational activities in schools on the east side of Flint. Above all, Minardo brought unflagging enthusiasm and wholehearted good feeling toward people to the program—which made him the ideal man to become the first community-school services director in 1951. With part-time helpers, Minardo also assumed responsibility for directing community services at other community schools. In more recent years, he has been acting as consultant and general problem-solver for the directors of community services in all Flint schools. In 1957, he received his M.A. in Community Education at Michigan State Normal, Ypsilanti. Endless energy, warmth of heart, and genuine concern for people are among Minardo's exceptional contributions to the development of the program.

There have been hundreds of others in the course of twenty-seven years, many of whom have enhanced the Foundation program with abiding enthusiasm and special abilities, but these four were among the very first—and three of them are still devoting their skills and energies to carrying on the Foundation's work.

The national publicity received by the program in 1936 included an article in the New York *Times*, a Christian Science *Monitor* story with pictures, and stories in *Newsweek*, *The Commonweal*, and many large newspapers. The Flint *Journal*, by the end of 1936, had distributed some eight hundred copies of its booklet, "The Flint Plan of Recreation," in response to inquiries from other communities.

The fall, 1936, recreation program, opened in fifteen schools and drew wider and more enthusiastic participation than the previous year's; over 4,000 people enrolled the very first evening. An important development was a group of shop classes in both wood- and metalwork, supervised by Harry Burnham, in which fathers and sons, mothers and daughters, could learn manual skills, use of tools, and methods of making and repairing many household items. Constant addition of new types of classes, as interest in different fields developed, kept bringing more and more variety to the program.

Beginning in January, 1937, the Mott Foundation held a series of public-forum meetings, with prominent speakers leading discussions on topics of current interest.

It was in 1937 that Mott ceased to be a vice-president of General Motors, although remaining a director. He retained his office in the General Motors building in Detroit, and continued to spend considerable time there. In May, 1937, the advancement of the man Mott had hired for General Motors fifteen years earlier, William S. Knudsen, to the presidency of the corporation, along with the election of Floyd Tanner, one of the many men who started with the Weston-Mott Company and continued their progress with General Motors, as a vice-president, caused Mott to write letters of congratulation to both these friends. Tanner had started with Weston-Mott Company over 25 years earlier as workman and had advanced steadily.

College commencement in 1937 brought special honors to

136

both Mott and Manley. The honorary degree, doctor of engineering, was conferred upon Mott by Stevens Institute of Technology. At a dinner held by the trustees of Stevens, Mott was called upon for a brief talk. His diary entry includes these remarks:

> A number of years ago I used to go cruising with a couple of highbrow engineers and their wives, and when an auspicious moment arrived I would innocently ask whether or not the world was more civilized now than a hundred years ago. Apparently, this is a most controversial question, and it never failed to start a long and heated argument which usually ended up with, "Well, what do you mean by civilization?" If the war in Spain, the conquest of Abyssinia, the Soviet government, the conditions in France, Germany, and Austria are to be considered—it is a question.
>
> I live for four months each year in Bermuda, where, thank heaven, automobiles are not allowed on the public roads and transportation is principally by horse-drawn vehicles and bicycles. My wife is praying for a horse and buggy—which seems "logical and according to the American Constitution" (at least one man said that). At any rate we are much more primitive than here in the United States and perhaps more civilized in our relations with other people.
>
> Here in this country corporations and individuals are spending immense sums of money every year in research, the prosecution of which is one of the most interesting subjects that I know of, and the results produced change almost every condition in life—tremendously beneficial in many ways but causing social problems no end.
>
> These problems will have to be solved and when they are solved with fairness to all, I think we may say that we have advanced in civilization.

Michigan State Normal College conferred the honorary degree of master of education on Frank J. Manley, in recognition of his outstanding work in physcial education and recreation. Newspaper reports of the award pointed out that it was rarely made, and that Manley was the first to receive it from

137

Michigan State Normal (since renamed Eastern Michigan University). This recognition was particularly gratifying to Manley because he had taken so much of his inspiration from his instructors at the college.

A diary entry of July 23, 1937, demonstrates both Mott's continued activity in General Motors and the interest he has always maintained in every type of new development—whether in sciences, arts, or humanities.

> Back to office I 'phoned Kettering and found that he could see me so went over to the research laboratory and he explained a lot of things that he and the laboratory are working on. Regarding Diesels—I saw a lot of new stuff on the drawing boards, and I saw some of the engines and blocks. He also showed me their very marvelous fuel injector. . . . I also saw new developments in automobile engines, chassis, spring construction, and bodies. I asked about fuel. Ket has for years wanted to develop and produce fuels with higher octane and anti-knocking qualities. . . . When Ket first started his experiments which resulted in Ethyl gasoline, the automobile engine was up against the fact that there was no standardized fuel. Different oil companies produced gasoline with tremendous variations of purity and anti-knocking qualities—some very good and some very bad. The results of the perfection of tetra-ethyl lead and Ethyl gasoline has been standardized production of regular gasoline.
>
> Now, what Ket wants to do is to produce a fuel with a very much higher octane or anti-knock rating than Ethyl gasoline—either by new and improved oil cracking processes, or addition of tetra-ethyl lead or other ingredients. If that can be accomplished, a much higher compression engine can be used, with much higher efficiency and more miles per gallon. . . .

Two days later, July 25, 1937, Mott's diary notes: "Mr. W. C. Durant 'phoned me and came up and spent an hour, telling me what he is busy with at present. He has gone into the oil business, especially in Louisiana, and is spending a lot of time down there. I expect he is 72 years old, but seems to be as healthy and lively as ever. He is well-steeped in the oil proposition. . . . I will say that he did not try to sell me anything. . . ."

An August 15, 1937, Flint *Journal* article headed, "Flint Plan of Recreation Becomes a National Affair," emphasized the rising interest of other communities in finding out what Flint was doing. Three thousand copies of the booklet, "The Flint Plan of Recreation," had already been sent by the *Journal* in response to inquiries originating in forty states and four foreign countries—and 500 more requests had come in since the last printing of the booklet was exhausted. Throughout these beginning years of Foundation activities, the consistent friendliness and helpfulness of the Flint *Journal* in publicizing Foundation activities with both stories and pictures—from marble-shooting, Golden Gloves boxing, safety playgrounds, and softball leagues, to classroom activities, public forums, musical programs, and a host of other events—were important factors in keeping the Flint-area public informed about opportunities offered.

FOURTEEN

In September, 1937, the Mott Foundation increased its contribution to the next season's recreation program to $31,400, more than 50 per cent over the previous year's funds. With fifteen schools open throughout the 1936–1937 season, 12,641 persons had enrolled in a wide variety of activities. The 1937 summer program had seen more than 3,000 back-yard safety playgrounds in operation—with over a million child-days of attendance at these playgrounds during the summer.

Five schools had been opened for the recreation program in 1935; fifteen schools had participated in 1936; twenty-two schools were opened in 1937. A twenty-five-week winter program was planned, to extend from November to the next May. It was still viewed as a recreation program, but the adult education aspect was beginning to emerge increasingly, as the desires and needs of mothers and fathers were made evident. The announced schedule of activities offered included: airplane clubs, art, band, basketball, beauty culture, boxing, citizenship, common branches of education, cooking, dramatics, English, fencing, game rooms, gymnasium, handicraft, harmonica, hobby clubs, home nursing, knitting, library, history, nature study, orchestra, ping-pong, puppets, sewing, shops, shower clubs, singing, social dancing, stamp clubs, tap dancing, fly tying, bait casting, commercial law, pottery, funny-paper room, stoic clubs, newspaper work, public forum, toe dancing, ballet dancing, court procedure, archery, and badminton. This list was expanded as other interests and needs were expressed by those attending. About four newspaper columns were required to list a week's scheduled activities at the schools; the lighted schoolhouse was very much a going concern in Flint.

On December 4, 1937, a son, Stewart Rawlings, was born to

the Motts—"a fine, well-formed boy, weighing ten pounds," as Mott notes in his dairy for the day.

A new Mott-Foundation-backed plan to improve child health in Flint was announced late in 1937. Called the Mott Health Achievement Program, it was designed to interest both children and parents in the correction of physical defects and control of communicable diseases. The school health department, with Dr. James A. Olson as director, had worked out the plan with the city health department, headed by Dr. George Hays.

Dr. Olson stated the objective of the program as an endeavor "to eradicate the physical defects that now exist in school children, and that are handicapping these children in their learning abilities and social relationships," and to impress upon parents, children, and teachers the fact that, "the child's health, more than any other factor, determines his regularity of attendance, his behavior and his ability to cope successfully with problems with which he is confronted."

During the first months of the program, some 20,000 children in 28 public and 4 parochial schools participated. Physical examinations were given to the children, only 5 per cent of whom were found to be free of any defect worthy of attention. The others averaged three defects each—a total of more than 60,000 correctable health defects among the children examined. Parents were urged to have family physician and dentist correct the defects, and by April, 1938, 20,000 such corrections had been made. The children who passed the physical examination at the end of the year's program received "Flint Health-Guarded Child" awards from the Mott Foundation—each in the form of a medal with the child's name inscribed on it.

In the summer of 1938, the Mott Foundation assisted in a basic reorganization of Flint's health services. This involved a consolidation of the school and city health departments into a community health service program. Methods of conducting the Mott Health Achievement Program were altered, but the objectives remained the same, and nursing service in community health education was intensified.

There was also a decided shift of emphasis within the Foundation program toward enlarged opportunities in adult-education classes. A correspondence-school program was developed in association with the extension service of the University of Michigan, offering both high school and college subjects for credit—so that those whose education had been interrupted could resume it and work toward diplomas and degrees. Four centers were established for these courses, in addition to the wide range of other classes in adult education offered by the Foundation. The only charge to the student for the correspondence courses was $1 per subject per semester for the cost of materials and mailing the lesson units.

Still another major change in the Foundation program in 1938 had to do with the employment of six visiting teachers. The background of this new Foundation activity dramatizes the underlying pattern of the evolution of the whole program. It has been sketched by Manley in these words:

> When I first told Mr. Mott we could reduce delinquency and develop a strong program that would prevent crime, nobody in the world believed it more than I did. My only thought was that if we could give everybody a chance to have—as I had had—an opportunity to participate in athletics, that was all there was to it. Sadly, this proved to be simply not true. We opened up the schools, the gymnasiums, the shops; we provided recreation of many types, under fine leadership; we had worlds of participation. The buildings were jammed with people taking part in increasing varieties of activities.
>
> But the sad fact was that we had as many juvenile delinquents as ever. We could have cheated the facts by a little wishful juggling of statistics—because there happened to be a change in handling juvenile cases in Flint at that time, and many more were put on probation instead of being sentenced to institutions. What we considered to be a wise and humane policy on the part of Judge John Baker resulted in only one-third as many sentences to State Training Schools

as in the past. It was almost too much of a temptation for us to claim reduction of juvenile crime by two-thirds with this circumstance to back us up. But we decided we did not want to fool either ourselves or the public. The actual number of cases coming to the courts, and the relative magnitude of the charges, did not seem to have been materially altered.

After gathering the facts, I was so astounded that the program wasn't having more tangible effect that I decided we must find out the underlying causes. As a result, we instituted the visiting-teacher program. We wanted them to find out, above all else, what made kids act the way they did. Here, at last, after a drought of recreational opportunity, young people had a highly varied choice of recreational and educational activities available, under enjoyable circumstances, with the best of friendly leadership. Young people participated in even greater numbers than we had dared to hope—yet juvenile delinquency went on apparently unabated. We had to know why this was so. The visiting teachers were to find out, so that we could direct the program to solve the big problem with which we had started.

While we didn't realize it at the time, all the future developments of the Foundation, and the many-sided attacks we were to mount against the factors preventing socially sound life for boys and girls, were to be based on the findings of those six ladies who were going into the homes of Flint's children.

Thus, the six visiting teachers began, in the fall of 1938, to work with teachers, nurses, attendance officers, and social-service centers to get at the problems of children who appeared to be under exceptional stresses. The visiting teachers—also designated as home counselors—were given training and assigned to districts. They had various types of social-service-work backgrounds.

It was announced to school staffs that, "Whenever home or family problems, either directly or indirectly, seriously affect the behavior of school children, the visiting teacher may be called in to assist the school in adjusting the case with the co-operation, if necessary, of such other agencies as are interested and active in these problems."

The Mott Foundation had been aware that a child with one or more health problems does not have an equal opportunity; from 1935, a health program had been developed, intensified by the health-achievement approach in 1937. From the work of the visiting teachers, it became evident that home patterns were firmly imposed upon children—so that to help the child get his equal chance, it was necesary to help the parents and the home reach a sound level. In this way, adult education may be seen as a definite approach to one aspect of juvenile delinquency. Similarly, the many other fields in which the Mott Foundation has worked to meet demonstrated community needs are related to the original central problem.

Still another 1938 development was the initiation of the Stepping Stone Program for girls. The plan is basically an educational endeavor cultivating attitudes and attributes conducive to development of personal charm, self-improvement, and moral responsibility for the individual, and orderliness and harmony for the home. It is a practical training program in personality and character building, involving specific skill, knowledge, and pride in planning and maintaining a fine home —from meal preparation, sewing, maintaining health, to gracious human relationships. A pilot Stepping Stone Club in 1938 showed the very great need for such a program, and a very real value to be achieved. A little history of the Stepping Stone Clubs by Mrs. Milton Pollock, director of the Stepping Stone Program from its inception, begins: "The idea for organizing Stepping Stone Clubs for girls was born of a consciousness that every girl has a hope and a desire to make something fine of her life, and needs only an inspiration and a design for living to help her make a reality of her dreams."

By 1942, twenty-three Stepping Stone Clubs of eighteen members each had been organized in the Flint schools, with members from fifth grade through senior high school. In 1943, Michael Hamady of Flint gave a large home and fifteen-acre estate to the Mott Foundation for use in carrying out a training program in home and family living for the Stepping Stone girls.

144

To develop this training program, a house mother, a home economist, activities supervisor, cook, and caretaker were engaged under supervision of the director—and a year-around program is conducted dedicated to the ideals of individual development centered in the concept that a fine home is the matrix of good life. In 1962, more than 600 girls were members of the 31 Stepping Stone Clubs—the age range being ten to eighteen years. The clubs meet once a week after class hours at school, and spend a two-week period each year in residence at Hamady House for special concentrated training in the most fundamental of human arts, getting along with people, particularly at home.

In June, 1939, the Mott Foundation aimed toward establishment of a clinic in which physical defects could be corrected. The plan received the approval of the medical and dental societies during the summer, and Hurley Hospital offered space and facilities on a reasonable basis. As these arrangements were being made, Mott also became concerned about the problems of treatment of crippled children. The Flint Rotary Club had been active in this field, devoting about $4,000 a year to investigation of the needs of crippled children in Genesee County, transporting the children who needed care to University Hospital, Ann Arbor, and otherwise facilitating treatment for children most urgently in need of it. The state appropriation to pay for such care was reduced by half at this time, and the Rotary Club felt hopeless about getting the whole job done with only 50 per cent of the usual funds from the state for medical expenses.

There were special problems which made it impossible to do the work required for Genesee County children in Flint—and Mott began attempting to find a solution to these problems. After many meetings with members of the State Crippled Children's Commission, the Governor, University of Michigan officials, and others, Mott was able to note in his diary a plan by which care for crippled children could be provided in Flint at much less cost than had been involved in taking each child to Ann Arbor, with the Foundation contributing up to $13,500 toward care and treatment for one year and thus compensating for the reduced state appropriation.

September 26, 1939, a civic appreciation dinner produced a remarkable group of tributes to Mott and his accomplishments. The dinner was held at the Durant Hotel, and was sponsored by the Junior Chamber of Commerce of Flint, with more than 550 attending. Mayor Harry M. Commins, speaking for the community, began the tributes in generous terms, saying that Flint was "glad and proud" to name Mott "as her first citizen." Flint's superintendent of schools, Leland H. Lamb, expressed special gratitude for Mott's "personal touch" throughout the Foundation's activities. William S. Knudsen, president of General Motors, spoke of Mott as a friend, noting his helpfulness both as a business asociate and as an inspiration in his personal life. Arthur H. Sarvis, president of Flint's park and recreation board, said of Mott, "His philosophy is to conserve human values." Harlow H. Curtice, president of Buick, called Mott's services "so great it is impossible for anyone to measure them." F. A. Bower, president of Flint's community fund, said of Mott, "He has had a very vital part to play in every agency in our association." The president of the Flint Junior Chamber of Commerce, E. D. Potter, presented a scroll recognizing Mott for "enriching the lives and broadening the opportunities of thousands of our youth."

In responding to the tribute, Mott expressed his gratitude for the dinner and the kind words, explaining some of the rewards he found in the activities of the Foundation:

> An avocation has become larger than a vocation for me. Probably I have more fun than the people do. . . . This event is going to spur me on to try to merit new confidence. . . . This is an opportunity to get something off my chest I've wanted to say for a long time. This work that has been attributed to me is something I have participated in in only a small measure compared with others. A lot of it was chance and good luck. Frank Manley was playing tennis with me and we got to talking about boys' work in Detroit

and I told Frank I was interested. . . . we discussed a plan for using school buildings. The board of education was quite skeptical, but willing to try it out.

I miss my guess if the people in this room have any idea of how good the board of education is. Without their co-operation, this program would never have got to first base.

Regarding Frank Manley, I think we could hunt all over the country and I don't know where we would find a man who approached him in ability and tenacity. He actually puts over the program in such a big way and makes a success of it.

When we were starting, we found lots of youngsters who needed attention, and "the old judge" (Roy E. Brownell) does more work than I do by a lot. I'm away, and he stays home and stands the gaff.

Mr. Lamb is another one of those regular guys . . . Jim Olson (school health officer and head of the Mott health program) is another brick, another one of the best. What we want is health-corrected children.

And I want people to know the amount of work done by these people—Dr. Fred Miner and the Kiwanis health camp, the Rotary Club with crippled children; Judge Frank L. McAvinchey of the Lions Club in furnishing glasses—he's shooting down our alley, too, and is entitled to a lot of credit; to Bill Knudsen here, in his Clara Elizabeth Fund; Mr. William S. Ballenger who has provided and developed that wonderful park on the west side; to Floyd Adams of Detroit for starting our boys' camp idea, which was one of the early things we had; and to Frank Farry, present Mott camp director—the boys think he's the salt of the earth and he's certainly doing a marvelous job.

All of these people have done things for which speakers have given me credit, but it's those whose names I've mentioned who are entitled to the real tribute.

Many additional telegrams and letters added to the tributes. A wire from Sloan said, "I am happy today to join the citizens of Flint in extending to my old friend C. S. Mott all the best wishes and recognition which he so richly deserves. We are all indebted to him for having made Flint a better city in which to live." A communication from Sen. A. H. Vandenberg said of Mott, "He is a great American in his citizenship and his humanities. He is great in his achievements for the common good. He is loyal to his country, his conscience, and his friends. I send him my sincerest greetings."

There were many other tributes, and a Flint *Journal* editorial the following day summed up the appreciation aptly:

> Seldom, if ever, has a heartier tribute been paid to a man whose good works his friends and his community wished to honor then when 550 men and women, all who could be accommodated, gathered Tuesday night for an appreciation dinner to Charles Stewart Mott. . . .
>
> The evening will be a memorable one for all who attended, as well as to Mr. and Mrs. Mott. The presence of each who attended was an indication of personal feeling, and, in the aggregate an expression in a rather official way of the community's thanks for the generosity, leadership, and kindly interest which the Motts have shown Flint and its people. . . .

In his diary for the day, Mott notes,

> I was extremely glad to have an opportunity to make a number of remarks regarding the efforts and ability and successful accomplishments of those who have co-operated in making our program possible and who are working our side of the street. I have from time to time tried to indicate my feeling and regard for the above-mentioned, but there never was or will be as good a chance to make the remarks that I wanted to make regarding them as when I had such public and undivided attention.

In the fall of 1939, the Mott Foundation Children's Health Center at Hurley Hospital was able to implement the health-achievement program by a plan providing essential medical and dental care "for children of borderline indigent families." The purpose was to bridge the rather large economic gap between families eligible for medical care as part of public relief programs and families able to pay for medical attention for their children. All full-time medical personnel were to be pediatricians; the staff also included a part-time pediatrician, examining general medical man, otologist, opthamologist, consulting orthopedist, two full-time dentists, two dental hygienists, nurse, dental assistant, audiometer technician, medical social worker, and clerk. Children were considered for care as referred by public health nurses, Mott Foundation visiting teachers, high school principals, Mother Superiors of parochial schools, private physicians, and various social agencies. Each child referred received a complete physical examination; if care of any magnitude was indicated, the economic status of the family was investigated through the medical social worker to determine eligibility.

The integration of the functions of the health center with the health-achievement program has provided a persistent and well-rounded attack on the ills, defects, and threats to the health of Flint children. The working budget of the Mott Foundation Health Center has increased to an annual figure exceeding $100,000—and there is no real way of assessing the total value of the services provided to the children in Flint over the years.

For a publication of the Michigan Association for Health, Physical Education, and Recreation, Manley summarized the Mott Foundation program as it stood in 1939 in these words:

The Mott Foundation program has four essential parts: recreation, adult education, camp for underprivileged boys, and a clinic for children who need some corrective work but whose parents are unable to finance the work.

Mr. C. S. Mott, who is president and founder of the Mott Foundation, believes in using all the natural resources available in the city. This means not only the physical equipment, such as school buildings and vacant lots, but also the latent leadership which is to be found in every community among the service clubs, chambers of commerce, and women's groups. . . .

The Foundation is able to conduct, promote, and develop a well rounded program in health, physical education, recreation, and safety by using all the resources possible in the city of Flint.

At this writing there are seventy different activities being offered and practically everyone who wants to participate in some constructive leisure time program has an opportunity to do so.

There were 25,000 different participants who took part in the program last winter. A good many more thousands enjoyed a well rounded program of summer activities in the city and some four hundred boys were sent to camp.

Through the four divisions of the Foundation there is an unusual opportunity to put into practice the theories that we, as health educators, have had for some time.

The Foundation began 1940 with another new approach to community service: a plan whereby the courts would turn certain probation cases over to the Mott Foundation visiting teachers for investigation—with the thought that "through the existing Mott program of education and recreation, many probationers would be encouraged to find interests and outlets for their ambitions." Still another new activity was a series of programs devoted to planning a new home—covering everything from selection of a site to financing arrangements.

The March, 1940, issue of *GM Folks,* the magazine about General Motors people everywhere, featured the Mott Foundation with a cover picture—and thirty-six additional pictures along with text to make up a dramatic story. Walter E. Scott, a Flint reporter who had covered the very first Mott Foundation activities, was managing editor of *GM Folks* and he took special pride in this full-scale presentation of the Mott Foundation's developments and objectives. In 1963, as a member of Flint's board of education, Scott is still justly proud of the 1940 story in General Motors' national magazine, as he is of subsequent Mott program developments.

In 1940, Mott arranged for the building of the Dr. J. A. Rawlings Health Center in El Paso, honoring Mrs. Mott's father, who had long provided medical attention for families in need. The J. A. Rawlings Health Center building was dedicated August 11, with Mrs. Mott, and her mother, Mrs. J. A. Rawlings, present at the ceremonies opening this most appropriate memorial.

FIFTEEN

With the beginning of 1941, Flint was already changing over to defense production. Even earlier, Knudsen had been called from General Motors to the Government to help production on a national scale. At a tribute dinner in Knudsen's honor, Mott had been pleased to be selected to make the presentation of gifts from Knudsen's General Motors associates.

Mott took a great interest in the transition to manufacture of armaments in the General Motors plants, and kept himself informed on the progress of developments. His diary notes a visit to AC Spark Plug Division—then producing Browning machine guns, on which they made delivery of the first thousand almost a year ahead of schedule. Mott was also highly active in United China Relief campaigns, in the course of which Henry R. Luce, of *Time, Life,* and *Fortune,* visited Flint as a guest at Applewood. Luce spoke at a United China Relief program, and Mott matched each dollar contributed by those attending.

In December, 1941, just two days before Pearl Harbor, Mott accepted an Office of Production Management assignment to help locate people with specialized experience and ability to assist the national defense production program. While in Washington, he visited Knudsen and observed, "He says he is quite well and looks so, though his 19 months show somewhat in his face."

With the acceleration of war production, 1942 was a busy year in Flint, although some temporary unemployment accompanied the big changeover. Increasingly, the Mott Foundation adapted activities to the changing situation.

Mott took the initiative and called a meeting of prominent and active Flint citizens, resulting in the organization of a War

151

Chest Board—reported to have been the first organized in the United States—to handle financing of defense and war-connected activities. F. A. Bower, the former Weston-Mott engineer who had gone on to become chief engineer of Buick, was appointed chairman, with Mott as chairman of the executive committee. Mott was appointed by Flint's mayor, Osmund Kelly, to the Flint Civilian Defense Council, which first faced the task of enrolling, classifying, and training civilian-defense volunteers.

At the annual Applewood dinner for the Flint Board of Education, the adaptation of the Foundation–board of education activities to civilian-defense needs was discussed. Mott's diary for February 9, 1942, reflects typical evening Foundation activities in a Flint school:

> At Central High School I found a tremendous amount of activity in education program, largely on matters approved by the Office of Civilian Defense. Large classes of mechanical drawing, blueprint reading, shop work, and typewriting—about 120 in a salesmanship class. The gym is in constant use in physical training, etc. As a matter of fact, there is not an hour in the day or evening when gymnasiums are not in constant use. The swimming pool, of course, is in full operation. Another group of men were training in singing, and in the auditorium an entire cast for Civic Grand Opera. On other evenings the program varies, including radio, electricity, organic chemistry, etc. There was one room in which were located the counselors on job placement. There is an income tax class, a French class, and a Spanish class. I am sure that I have overlooked mentioning some that I saw, besides some that I probably didn't see. Of course something similar, or different, is going on in all our large school buildings.

An immediate civilian-defense need was 250 cots for use in Flint hospitals in case of emergencies, and Mott financed the cost of the cots, working closely with Dr. Gordon Bahlman, in charge of the civilian-defense medical program.

152

On February 13, 1942, Susan Mott was six years old—and on February 27, Susan and her brother Stewart, born December 4, 1937, welcomed a new baby sister, Maryanne Turnbull Mott—to the great happiness of the whole family.

Mott Foundation personnel helped in every aspect of civilian-defense and war-preparedness activities, from assisting in the complex registration of volunteers to arranging and conducting a multitude of training programs both for civilian defense and for employment in war production. The emphasis on Americanization accelerated Foundation activities in citizenship training, in which many aliens were assisted toward their naturalization. The Foundation's counseling, training, and placement service interviewed thousands of young people, helping many of them to find jobs. The interest of both Mott and Manley in physical fitness was also reflected in training activities related to the war; it became self-evident to many people that physical fitness was the necessary basis of usefulness, and there was a marked increase in the Foundation's enrollment in this field. Specific classes in shop skills—blueprint reading, machine shop, drafting, and other similar courses—were very popular.

Manley was appointed Chief of Volunteer Participation, the aspect of civilian defense related to community organization, training, and morale. City Manager George Gundry headed the protective services, including air raid wardens and related emergency groups making up the rest of the civilian-defense program, with City Planner George C. Hayward as executive director for the whole organization, reporting to the Flint Council of Defense. Quite naturally, the facilities, experience, and organization of the Foundation adapted ideally to civilian-defense training.

A 1942 Foundation development of importance was extension of the adult education program to include college-level classes for credit.

In the fall of 1942, the Bureau of Government of the University of Michigan published a brief study of the Mott Foundation in its series of Michigan Pamphlets, under the title: *An Ex-*

periment in Community Improvement. This twenty-nine page booklet, written by Robert S. Ford, director of the bureau of government, and Frances H. Miner, reviewed and appraised the Foundation's activities. It concludes with an excellent thumbnail-sketch of the Foundation in 1942.

The program now being carried on in Flint is unique in several respects, of which the following are perhaps the most important. First, it developed in response to definite needs of the city and expanded only when it became evident that new activities could be administered in an effective and efficient manner. Second, the organization and administration of the Mott program and of various community agencies have been co-ordinated in such a manner as to achieve the greatest efficiency in operation. For example, the director of the Mott recreational program is also the supervisor of physical education in the school system. The director of the Mott Children's Health Center is director of health in the public schools. The health achievement program in the public schools is supervised by the director of health of the public schools and the director of nursing for the city Health Department. The Mott visiting teachers co-operate closely with the city and country public health nurses. An important person in the administration of all aspects of the program is the superintendent of schools. Other illustrations could be mentioned, but these will suffice to show the type of community co-operation and centralized administration that is necessary to carry out a comprehensive program. Third, the use of existing facilities in the community, both material and organizational, reduces the cost and increases the effectiveness of the program. Being tax-supported, the schools are the common property of the people of the city, and they have the additional advantage of being natural locations for community centers. Finally, the Mott program shows the possibility of co-operation between private and public agencies, of private funds superimposed upon and partly administered by municipal organizations, and its object is not only to accomplish results in Flint, but to serve as an example for other communities by showing how an improvement of community life may be effected. In general, this program emphasizes the importance of health, education, wholesome activity, good citizenship, and the kind of democracy that comes from the intermingling of many kinds of people in their leisure time.

When there are added to this review the special emphasis of the Foundation on civilian defense, Americanization, and other developments heightened by the war—and the opening of a college division—the result is an accurate picture of the Mott Foundation as it entered 1943 with a $140,000 budget for the year's operations.

Flint's war-connected activities were accelerated through the Foundation's program in 1943—particularly in the varied fields of civilian backing for the war effort through Flint's Neighborhood War Clubs, a remarkable accomplishment in community organization as part of civilian defense. F. A. Bower was chairman of this project, and the Mott Foundation made many essential contributions to its success. Typical of the Foundation's help was sponsorship of classes and demonstrations in canning foods. The block-sized clubs throughout all parts of Flint—along with the completely democratic organization and training of air raid wardens and other protective-service groups of civilian defense—gave a quality of mutuality and unity to Flint's war effort which could scarcely have been achieved otherwise.

The death, on June 20, 1943, of Frank G. Farry, Mott Camp Director, was a serious loss to the Foundation program. A man genuinely dedicated to boys' work, Farry had been effective beyond the power of most men in influencing the lives of many thousands of boys constructively. Joseph Grady became Director of Mott Camp, and the work continued.

In the spring of 1943, Lieutenant-General Knudsen visited Flint to present the commencement speech to General Motors Institute graduates. General and Mrs. Knudsen were house guests at Applewood while in Flint, and Mott notes in his diary that General Knudsen's address was "one of the best I ever heard him give."

155

Mott has never been more active than during these war years—and his diary reflects the amazing scope of his activities in the Foundation, civilian defense, war chest, and in his widening industrial and business interests. His diaries include discussions of the progress of the war, many references to the progress of industry in war production, and continuing concern with Flint's social problems. Through all this multitude of activities, Mott's concern for all members of his family is also reflected in every page of his diary—which is, in effect, a remarkable kind of newsletter written for the benefit of his children and other members of his family and his closest friends. On June 20, 1943, for example, Mott records the christening of daughter Maryanne.

Reverend Jackson took Maryanne in his arms, dipped his hand in the fount three times and anointed her head and made the sign of the Cross on her forehead. Then Maryanne decided to take part in the proceedings and stretched out to dip her own hand in the fount, which Reverend Jackson permitted her to do, and she anointed her own head, repeating this operation twice, rather to the entertainment of the onlookers. It was undoubtedly very unusual and it was a lot better than having her howling and protesting—as a matter of fact she made quite a hit.

A few days later, there is a detailed report of visits to Mott Camp and to Hamady House. Another of Mott's special characteristics emerging clearly from the pages of the diary is his consistent fondness for animals. Perhaps the most amazing features of all in his diaries are the conversations reported there —because Mott has always been discussing an infinite variety of subjects with the people around him, and reports of many of those conversations find their way into the diary. Most of all, the diaries are evidence of the myriads of friends Mott has made everywhere; they remember him, and he remembers them.

Among those friends, none has been closer than Roy Brownell—and when Mott is in Flint, there is seldom a day's diary report without a reference to time spent with Brownell. Conferences with Manley are almost as frequently reported. The diary also recounts the details of daily life—the many activities of Mrs. Mott, including her participation in Red Cross, child welfare board, Junior League, and other civic organizations—and the doings of the three younger children—along with letters from the older children—reflecting Mott's pride and pleasure in his family. Any single year's diary would constitute a volume at least half the size of this one.

As Flint industry increased war production, there were more and more jobs. Many women went to work in the shops, and new juvenile-delinquency problems were created. The problem became increasingly acute, with so many unsupervised children throughout the city. The Foundation assisted in the development of nursery schools to care for small children whose mothers were employed.

Victory gardens, nutrition, rationing, salvage, child care, physical fitness, and allied efforts were approached through the neighborhood war clubs and the Mott Foundation in a city-wide cooperative endeavor. The Mott Foundation precedents were of inestimable value in trail-blazing for the block-plan clubs, and the backing of the Foundation was a major factor in the development of these neighborhood meeting groups—one of the truly democratic dividends of the war effort, as Flint neighbors learned to know each other and to work together for common purposes.

The board of education and the Foundation undertook to organize boys' clubs in a number of areas in the city. For girls, the Stepping Stone program was expanded. Practical nursing courses, and the opportunities offered by the college division of the Foundation, were other comparatively new programs that received wide acceptance in late 1943. In the college division, the second semester, opening January 10, 1944, added ten more instructors and seventeen additional courses, making the total number of courses forty.

In April, 1944, the Mott Foundation purchased "Flint's

Skyscraper"—the sixteen-story Union Industrial Building—in pursuance of a policy of investing in income-producing properties to assure the continuing endowment of the Foundation. Mott and Brownell represented the Foundation in this purchase from the Flint Depositors Corporation. The building —which had been built in 1929 at a reported cost of $1.7 million—was purchased for $525,000; it was bringing in $33,000 annual income.

Father Flanagan, of Boys Town, visited Flint in the spring of 1944; he praised the efforts of the city and the Mott Foundation, noting that ". . . all cities are not as blessed with civic consciousness as this one with its Mayor Kelly and Mr. C. S. Mott." Local youth agency leaders discussed Flint's problems with Father Flanagan, and as a result, the Mott Foundation, Probate Court, YMCA, Flint Guidance Center, schools, Junior Chamber of Commerce, and Flint Optimist Club began planning for a Flint version of the Big Brother movement for Flint. As a result of the conference with Father Flanagan, the Mott Foundation worked with other Flint agencies in establishment of the Flint Youth Bureau, and Joseph T. Ryder was employed as director. In addition to the efforts of the Foundation in this field for a number of years, the Junior Chamber of Commerce and the Optimist Club had been working in the same direction. Mott, who introduced Father Flanagan at a chamber-of-commerce luncheon, indicated the full cooperation of the Foundation in implementing a program for Flint boys.

Another 1944 development was the institution of a pilot project at Martin School, with additional teachers to bring the pupil-teacher ratio down to an approved figure, and the use of complete testing and individualized instruction methods as recommended by educators. Foundation funds made possible the additional teacher personnel for this "model school" demonstration.

At the end of the 1943–1944 health-achievement program, 8,571 or 48.2 per cent of the 17,782 children participating were found to be free of dental defects, as announced by Miss

Cornelia Mulder, school health coordinator. Miss Mulder, a dental hygienist with the health achievement program from the beginning, has been a directing force in the whole health program. The 1944 health-guarded child figure was 5,785—or 30.08 per cent of those participating—free of correctable physical defects. In addition, 2,129 free miniature X rays had been provided for high school students in the year, in cooperation with the Genesee County Tuberculosis Association.

Mott had been interested in the activities of Goodwill Industries, providing employment for handicapped people, for some time, and early in 1944 he planned with Brownell and the local Goodwill Industries manager to improve the organization's operations in Flint. Mott was also concerned with the problem of returning veterans, and conferred with Russel V. Somes, supervisor of the Industrial Mutual Association's Veterans Service Department in working out cooperative arrangements for rehabilitation, training, and education for veterans in which the Foundation could be of assistance. Mott also invited President Ruthven of the University of Michigan to Flint to discuss such plans.

Increasingly, Mott felt that employment of mothers of young children often left the children without proper care or supervision—and, in effect, created the kind of basic situation leading to juvenile delinquency. It was clear to him that this policy on the part of industry was at cross-purposes with the efforts of such a community as Flint to improve home conditions for children and reduce the causes of delinquency. He wrote a letter, on June 5, 1944, to the board of directors of General Motors Corporation. The letter states, in part:

Re: Working mothers of children
under fourteen years of age

Gentlemen:

Due to hiring of the above without investigation of home conditions and results produced, juvenile delinquency, neglect, and distress of children affected have increased intolerably all over the country.

Through Mr. Frank Manley of the Mott Foundation and Flint School System, we have, during the past year, investigated many homes of delinquent and maladjusted children. Out of a group of one hundred—65 boys and 35 girls—we found that fifty-one cases came from broken homes. In fifty-five cases both parents were working outside the homes. Only seventeen indicated any affiliation with any church. We have detailed case history of all of them. . . .

I am not asking that you refuse to employ any of these women, nor do I ask the Corporation to go to the trouble or expense of making home investigations. But—I do suggest that you adopt a policy of refusing to employ any of them who do not bring with them a proper certificate, signed by a proper social agency, to the effect that the hiring of this woman will not seriously harm her children. In Flint, such social agencies are already in existence and undoubtedly most of the families in question are already on file.

If you don't care to adopt the above policy at once, I ask that you refer the matter to your Management with request that complete Study and Report be made to Directors at early date.

Subsequently, General Motors adopted such a plan in Flint, and later the Administration Committee of General Motors Corporation unanimously resolved, "that Vice-President H. W. Anderson is requested to contact all divisions of the corporation and explain the plan which is now in operation in the Flint area in regard to the employment of mothers having children under fourteen years of age, and advise the divisions that it is the wish of this committee that similar action be taken by them."

On November 2, 1944, Mott attended a banquet sponsored by the Flint Chamber of Commerce to honor the establishment in Flint of a University of Michigan Extension Center. University of Michigan President Alexander Ruthven—a man Mott has always admired greatly—was the principal speaker. The printed program for the evening was headed: "With the advent of the University of Michigan Extension Center combined with

the College Division of the Mott Foundation already in existence, Flint's educational opportunities have been broadened to
meet the requirements of all adults in the community." Gyles
Merrill reported to the group Mott's interest, activity, and
support of the University of Michigan Extension Center, and
presented a handsome plaque honoring Mott for "significant
contributions to our community life. . . ."

Mott responded to this completely unexpected tribute by
explaining that the Foundation's activities in adult education,
health, and recreation were an expression of his concern for
the city where he had spent thirty-eight years of his life. He
spoke, also, of his friendship for President Ruthven, and others
of the University of Michigan staff, and of the gratification
provided by the University's establishment of these new adult
education facilities. Mott said in simple terms that he got more
real pleasure from his participation in the whole program than
from anything he did in business or personal recreation.

The Flint *Journal* of November 9, 1944, noted that the
Mott Foundation was providing $17,500 to the Flint Board
of Education to buy the old post office building in downtown
Flint at Kearsley and Harrison Streets as a permanent headquarters for social agencies and perhaps one or more school
offices. The other building purchased earlier in the same year
by the Mott Foundation—the former Union Industrial Building
—was renamed the Mott Foundation Building effective January 1, 1945.

SIXTEEN

June 2, 1945, was Mott's seventieth birthday. He received con-
gratulatory messages from near and far. In his diary for the
day, Mott comments, "Having now reached the mature age of
three score and ten I suppose I am expected to be put up on
the shelf, but I have many friends from 10 to 25 years older
than I am who are still hustling around, so I don't expect there
is much chance for me to quit."

During 1945, Frank Manley compiled a comprehensive review of the Mott Foundation after ten years of operation. This
study is much more fully developed than the University of
Michigan booklet of 1942, and it includes more of the underlying factors leading to the initiation and evolution of the many
aspects of Foundation activities. The introduction to the study
presents the important social problems the Foundation was
created to meet. Other sections of the report cover recreation
and child welfare, adult education, guidance and counseling,
child health, camping and club programs—and it concludes
with a summary and a look ahead. A few quotations demonstrate the clear vision and deep feeling Manley has always had
toward improvement of opportunity for people of every age,
and in every situation—with particular concern for the young.

> This study will trace the community needs which the Mott
> Foundation program in Flint has been attempting to meet,
> the adjustments in thinking, planning, and executing of plans
> to meet emerging and changing needs, the progressive de-
> velopment of the program, its objectives and philosophy, its
> expanding scope, and the policies and procedures used in
> carrying it out. . . .
> Juvenile delinquency and other forces making for social
> disintegration—highlighted and intensified because of war—
> are causing increasing concern. Much study is currently being

given to the problem of what shall be our dynamic philosophy of education. Questions such as these are being asked: should the schools assume social leadership and share with parents, social workers, and citizens in general the responsibility for a constructive reorganization of forces—an effective concentration of community resources upon problems of children, youth, and adults? Can the public school—that most American of all institutions—make any progress in restoring to our complex lives something of the community interest, the neighborly spirit, and the democracy of a more rural day? Can the public school—utilized as a real community center —serve as a focal point from which influence and leadership can radiate for community good, and through which the efforts of other public and private agencies can be integrated —thus helping to neutralize the disintegrating forces of modern urban life?

... by studying the development and pattern of one ten-year experiment it is hoped significant trends, strengths, and limitations may be revealed. Through the generosity and vision of a local citizen, Mr. Charles Stewart Mott, the schools of Flint have had a unique opportunity for a demonstration of the effective use of existing school and community facilities. ...

... leaders in the field of education are more and more emphatically proclaiming that we cannot separate the welfare and social integration of the child from the welfare and social integration of the various members of the home, of the individual adult in his environment, and of the family with the community at large. ... To achieve the goal of social planning in a democracy—building a community in which every individual, regardless of race or creed or color, may enjoy equal opportunity for fullest self-development—democracy has always put its trust primarily in three institutions: the home, the school, and the church. ... What is the responsibility and opportunity of the school in integrating, coordinating, and interpreting the social and educational resources of a community to those who need these services—in short, in acting as a *bridge* between those who have needs and those agencies and individuals who wish to serve?

163

Manley outlines the social history of Flint, and describes the circumstances leading to the establishment of the first Mott Foundation recreational activities in 1935. He points out that the Foundation had adapted with ready flexibility through three periods: the depression, the conversion to wartime living, and the postwar readjustment—always working with, and through, the other institutions and agencies of the community. As to the appropriate role of the school, Manley remarks that the Mott Foundation is unique among foundations as "the only one which actually underwrites the public school in its effort to provide a wider scope of service for all children, youth and adults in the community."

The study continues with a detailed report of the origin, evolution, and (as of 1945) current status of each division of the Foundation program—demonstrating the fact that "shifting of emphasis to meet changing needs has been a definite basic principle of operation throughout." Another fact demonstrated is that "the general method of operation sometimes involves plans to finance a total program, sometimes to finance part of a program, and sometimes to fill in the gap where there is a specific need and later to withdraw support when the job has been completed or is being accomplished by another group." Illustrations are offered in which, after the Foundation had shown the value of a program, other agencies or institutions have carried on the work. Manley comments, "The Foundation feels it has been most successful when this sort of thing happens." He also states, "Clearly, the Mott program tries to show the possibility of co-operation between private and public agencies and of the use of private funds administered by a municipal organization; namely, the public schools. Its primary object is not only to accomplish results in Flint, but to serve as an example for other communities by showing how an improvement in community life may be co-operatively effected."

The Foundation's annual budget had increased from a comparatively small figure in 1935 to $200,000. Other 1945 Foundation developments included the opening of the Flint Interracial Community Center, with this stated objective: "The purpose of the Center shall be to work toward the improvement of better living, working, and playing conditions in the city of Flint, Michigan, between the races, in the fields of recreation, social, moral, and civic affairs by co-ordinating and supplementing such services to provide the best possible services to the community regardless of race, creed, color, or religious affiliations."

There was also a marked expansion of the health-education and services program, a veterans' educational-counseling service established at Flint Junior College, and initiation of a junior high school sports program.

Early in 1946, Harding Mott—promoted to major in the Army Air Force shortly before termination of his military services—began devoting much of his time to Foundation activities, along with assisting his father in widely varied business interests. In January, 1946, the Foundation received an award of meritorious service from Donald S. Leonard, state director of civilian defense, "in recognition of extraordinary and outstanding service in Civilian Defense during World War II."

The February, 1946, issue of the *Michigan Education Journal* printed a six-page report of the success of the Mott Foundation project at Flint's Martin Elementary School. The report noted that after two years—with two additional teachers and a full-time clerk provided by the Mott Foundation—the school "advanced in educational achievement, from twenty-second place to sixth place among Flint's twenty-six elementary schools." The primary factor had been reduction of the pupil-teacher ratio to 30–1. In addition, the report points out, teachers changed as much as the pupils, feeling renewed dedication to the opportunity to do a better job with smaller classes. L. A. Lundburg, assistant superintendent in charge of research and statistics, is quoted as saying, "Teachers certainly responded to the program, doing many things they felt they had wanted to do but had been prevented from doing by the serious pupil overload." The Martin 6A class—after two years of the demonstration of "reasonable" conditions—tied for the first place among all Flint elementary schools, showing in sixteen school months progress equivalent to that normally expected in twenty-seven months.

This demonstration is typical of one of the directions Mott Foundation activities were to take in the next period of years— pilot projects in improved educational methods, development of the school as the heart of effective community integration.

On August 29, 1946, Mott joined a great many old friends in celebrating C. F. Kettering's seventieth birthday at Kettering's birthplace farm, a few miles from Loudenville, Ohio. Mott made the journey with one of his closest friends, H. H. Curtice. The celebration is reported in detail in Mott's diary.

> This farm is where Kettering's parents lived and where Kettering was born. He still owns the property and has it operated. They had originally expected 50 or 100 people, but the party at the farm grew to 500. We found Ket receiving guests in the barn where he had worked as a youngster. . . .
>
> We had a very nice country dinner. Afterwards there was some talking from the top of a farm wagon where there was also a small piano, and Ket and three of his high school classmates sang their class song. . . . In the course of time we were taken in to Loudenville where in the large public park there was a stage set up, a band, and a large number of seats for the audience. A number of us from out of town sat on the platform for a while during which Col. E. A. Deeds introduced us and told something of Ket's history. Then we moved down to the lower level. . . . A pageant was given on the stage depicting the conditions during Ket's youth. . . .
>
> At 4:00 o'clock there was more speech making, but everything was in the clear at 4:30 when broadcaster Tom Manning took over for a so-called national hookup on the air, describing what was going on, and then introducing Ket, who made a remarkable talk about conditions in general.
>
> Then came a parade, passing between the first row of the band, of real old fashioned carriages, wagons, and equestrians. Then the early hand-cranked automobiles the last of which

was the single-cylinder Cadillac. And then a parade of the very latest models, 1946. . . .

Among those present was Col. E. A. Deeds—he is about 72 years old and is Chairman of the Board of the National Cash Register Company. I knew him during World War One, and ever since, and he is extremely friendly with me. He and Ket started the Delco some 40 years ago, and the starter and lighting system were first invented and first produced in Deeds' barn. . . . I also met Orville Wright, whom I have known for a long time. He celebrated his 75th birthday last week, I believe. He is the surviving brother of the Wrights who flew the first plane at Kitty Hawk.

In the presence of Wright and others I told the following story. Some ten or fifteen years ago I was attending a large gathering, when suddenly I was surrounded by six or eight very charming and effusive young women who showered every attention upon me. My chest and head began to swell, and I was wondering how I had acquired this wonderful appeal and power over women, when one of them made a remark to me including the name of Mr. Wright. I very foolishly said, "But I am not Mr. Wright; my name is Mott," and the speed with which those girls deserted me in search of the right Mr. Wright completely dissipated my illusion.

My old friend Lt. General Bill Knudsen was there, now in civilian clothes, and I had a nice talk with him. . . . He told me now he has 11 grandchildren. . . .

Other Foundation developments in 1946–1947 included in-service training of teachers, for a new approach to the work of health education and of the visiting teachers. A special home-making program was instituted to assist war brides—and enlarged programs in English and civics were established to help displaced persons and war brides. A basketball program for all junior high school boys was organized, and a demonstration physical education program for elementary schools was begun. A special lecture series, "Building Your Marriage," was jointly sponsored by the Mott Foundation, the Clara Elizabeth Fund, the Flint Council of Churches, and the YWCA. Another experimental course, "The Charming Woman," presented discussions and demonstrations in the elements of charm—styling, walking, comportment, speech, dieting, hygiene.

A grant of $2,400 was made by the Mott Foundation to the University of Michigan to support a graduate program in the Department of Pediatrics for a physician who could serve in the Flint school health program after two years of study. An audiometer technician was added to the staff at the Mott Foundation Children's Health Center. Mott recreation supervisor, Harold Bacon, was invited to visit Brazil on a good-will tour, demonstrating Foundation recreational and physical education techniques. This 1946–1947 program worked on a $214,304 budget, exploring new areas of services as needs emerged. With the Flint Institute of Arts, the Foundation sponsored lecture courses on art for appreciation, understanding, and enjoyment of both classic and modern painting. The first annual inter-cultural banquet was held at the Flint Inter-racial Community Center, with Dr. Gilbert Jones, of Wilberforce University, as the speaker.

In 1947, Mott was awarded the Stevens Institute of Technology Alumni Award Medallion; the presentation was made by alumni president Herman K. Interman. Stevens' President Harvey N. Davis was the principal speaker; Mott was recognized for his loyalty and devotion, and for his helpful guidance and enthusiastic support of the college. Several months later, Mott attended the fiftieth anniversary dinner of the Stevens Class of '97. He dedicated the new Charles Stewart Mott Field House which the Mott Foundation had contributed to Stevens Institute.

Less than a month later, Mott received the Forney W. Clement Memorial Award by Kiwanis, "In recognition of outstanding service." Mott notes in his diary for the day:

> Of course I had to say something in acceptance, and so I said that I assumed that the award had something to do with the activities of our Foundation, and I compared the program to a motor truck of which the Board of Education was the body and Frank Manley was the engine which did all

of the work, and the Foundation simply furnished the gasoline; therefore, Frank Manley, who is the hardest working chap in the community on things for the general good, was really entitled to the award, and that in accepting it I took it for the work that he had accomplished.

Another 1947 diary entry indicates the admiration of Mott for Charles Wetherald, who had been made manager of U.S. Sugar Company.

Our new manager, Charles Wetherald, who until a couple of years ago was Production Manager of Chevrolet, producing a billion dollars worth of war materials per annum during the war, and over a million cars per annum pre-war, is an expert in agriculture, cattle raising, and factory management. He has already greatly improved operations and reduced costs, and this year our sugar production will be greater than we ever produced, probably 100,000 tons.

The fall of 1947 brought additional Foundation activities—expansion of evening classes, organization of a Stepping Stone Mothers Club at Lincoln School, and the beginning of a Fairview School pilot project. The genuineness of community need and interest was demonstrated by ever-increasing enrollments and requests for new courses. Other parts of the program were continuing with wider and wider acceptance and participation. Adult education and recreation . . . summer recreation and safety activities . . . athletic programs for boys and girls . . . the college division . . . practical nurses' training . . . vocational guidance and job placement . . . citizenship and naturalization classes . . . veterans' institute for education and counseling . . . the visiting teachers . . . the Flint Youth Bureau . . . the experimental education demonstration at Martin School . . . an experimental study conducted at McKinley Elementary and Junior High School to consider the needs of boys and girls from kindergarten through the ninth grade, with possible curriculum changes or adjustments . . . Hamady House homemaking demonstrations and Stepping Stone Club program . . . Mott Camp

... health guidance and protection ... special education classes ... and other activities.

The 1948 winter term adult education courses—including the college division, high school division, and general courses—covered a wide scope of interests. There were courses in economics, accounting, political science, psychology, mental hygiene, child development, food preparation, sewing, beautifying the home, money management for the family, problems of international relations, music appreciation, effective speaking, correct English, Spanish, photography, creative writing, crafts workshop, water color painting, Braille reading and writing—plus vocational and business courses.

Mott's diary, his personal "five-foot book-shelf," continues in great detail, demonstrating Mott's amazing interest in every aspect of the world around him. There are countless stories of the doings of the three younger children—and reports of the activities of the three older children and other family members and friends. There is constant evidence of Mott's kind of responsible personal management; he believes in employing the finest of specialized management for his interests, and he also believes in and practices complete personal participation in those interests himself; this applies equally to the operation of the Foundation, and the water companies, sugar company, department stores, bank, and other business interests. He has always accepted very seriously his responsibilities as a director of General Motors, along with other assignments he has carried out for that corporation. Such personal management does not mean taking responsibility and decision away from the executives employed; it does mean that, in the director function at the policy-making level, Mott believes in getting all the facts for himself in order best to direct and advise the major policies of operation so that executives have fully informed and intelligent backing.

Nothing has delighted Mott more than finding and developing able executives. His appreciation of Wetherald has been noted. He found another such excellent executive, Victor Weir, as chief engineer of one of the water companies, and broadened Weir's responsibilities to include a strong hand in the direction of all the water companies. Mott's fact gathering, and attendance at directors' meetings of all these interests have always involved a great deal of travel—and while traveling, Mott engages in conversations with many people, often reporting the incidents in his diary. There are also forceful expressions of Mott's own beliefs on national and international affairs, economics, physical fitness, behavior, science, and industry. He has lived up to that obligation of the civilized man to know something about everything, and to have a point of view toward everything. At the same time, he has always had an acute sense of the congruities, and there are many jokes and anecdotes in the diary reflecting a highly active sense of humor.

In September, 1948, the former old post office building was formally opened as the Flint Community Service Center—housing a number of Flint Community Chest agencies. Mott had provided the funds with which the Flint Board of Education had purchased the building, and the dedication ceremonies included presentation of a portrait of Mott (arranged for by a group of his friends) to be displayed in the building. When Mott saw the portrait, he announced that he would "have to go to the art institute and have the artist paint me up so I would look as good as the picture."

A December diary entry mentions a discussion of some thirty acres of Mott's estate fronting on Court Street:

I was very busy and almost forgot a luncheon date with Harding to meet Superintendent of Schools Mark Bills, Manley, and the School Board Committee at noon at the City Club. . . . I told the school folks that if they would put up a modern school there, I would give them the property. . . . The school must be rather different from schools built in the past. In other words, it must be functional in every respect and not an architectural, unfunctional monstrosity. The size of the grounds will permit plenty of athletic fields, parking facilities, etc. I wouldn't be at all surprised in the far distant future if the entire balance of our Applewood property found its way into the hands of the Board of Education—when the Mott family no longer cares to use it for themselves.

This vision of the functional school, coupled with another exploratory program then being conducted by the Foundation at Fairview School, suggests the larger community-school concept toward which the Foundation and Flint were moving.

The comprehensive annual report of Mott Foundation activities for 1947–1948 devotes thirteen pages to the Fairview pilot project. School and Foundation resources were concentrated on this elementary school in a highly industrialized section of Flint bounded on the west and south by the Buick Motor Division and on the east by the Flint River. Housing conditions were crowded, and there were few play areas and wholesome recreational centers. Of the 393 children in the school 92 per cent were Negro. A few quotations from the report present a glimpse of the tremendous undertaking proposed.

> In the Fairview District, the serious-minded parents who want better things for their children find life a continual struggle to combat destructive influences. Children whose parents have long since bowed to prevailing conditions come to school in a poor state of nutrition and health, with serious behavior problems and little hope for the fuure.
>
> The principal, staff, and consultants ... decided upon six areas of special need and proposed to do whatever they could during the year to:
>
> Survey the community needs and then attempt to meet them ... interest community members in greater co-operation ... re-evaluate the curriculum and make necessary changes ... improve health conditions ... provide activities that would lessen frustration and aggression and substitute accomplishments, satisfaction, and happiness ... work toward better understanding of children.
>
> Home calls were made to discover housing, types of employment, family income, educational and social backgrounds, religion, attitudes, diets, adult education interest. ... Above

172

all, the teachers of Fairview School have a feeling of great kindness for humanity. . . . They attempt at all times to create a warm "class room climate" where there is good rapport among all individuals, where there is mutual respect and understanding. . . . During the year many consultants have given generously of time, interest, and special skills. . . . Fairview staff members spent much time on curriculum study . . . developing a curriculum to fit community needs. . . .

Every effort has been made through the year to improve the health of the children. . . . The number of "Health-Guarded" children at Fairview has increased dramatically as the result of the concentrated efforts of all concerned. The highest previous percentage was 11.5%. This year it was 57.5%. . . . During the winter season, Fairview children purchased 533 bottles of milk, and 2,747 were distributed free through the co-operation of the Community Fund. . . .

During the year, twenty clubs have been organized as extra-curricular programs to furnish wholesome leisure time activities and more constructive experience in the hope of lessening frustration. . . . Visiting teacher services to Fairview School have been carried on in two ways: personal service to children, and teacher in-service training. . . . The adult education program was available for any possible service to the parents of the neighborhood. Planning meetings with various groups of mothers were held at the beginning of the year to plan a study and service program which they felt might be most helpful to them. Objectives were sociability, friendship, understanding. . . . A table cloth and tea set were provided for use at meetings, with different mothers acting as hostesses. . . . There were service programs—a sewing day to help remodel, alter, and repair children's clothes, assistance with the costumes for the Christmas play, the Tuberculosis Chest X-ray program, the Health Achievement program, etc. . . .

These excerpts give only a partial reflection of the total effort at Fairview to make the school the true center of a community which had had no meaningful relationship to the school—or to any real community center—before.

The Mott Foundation's educational explorations were breaking down the wall between the home and the school. The Fairview project was one of several special educational attempts to relate the school and the community in the most effective fashion; re-evaluation of school curriculum was one such area of consideration, so that what the school would teach would be truly relevant to the needs of the people being taught.

In March, 1949, thirty-nine educators from colleges visited Flint to review the Mott Foundation program, and reported something like amazement at the scope and down-to-earth effectiveness of the activities. Mott outlined the Foundation's basic purposes to the visitors at Hamady Clubhouse, and they had an opportunity to observe the Stepping Stone program for girls. They visited Fairview School, and learned something about the project there from Miss Josephine McDougall, the principal. Cooperation between the Foundation and the schools in the health program was explained by Miss Cornelia Mulder, coordinator of health education. Dr. Arthur L. Tuuri, director of the Mott Foundation Children's Health Center, outlined the several aspects of the health program. Joseph T. Ryder told the visiting educators about the Flint Youth Bureau, and Walter S. Holmlund detailed the operation of the visiting teachers' work. The educators—who had come from five state colleges and educational agencies—also visited the Interracial Community Center and adult education classes at several schools. They heard about the Mott Camp, and the boys' baseball program—and some of them attended a recreation square dancing class.

This tour by a fairly large group, coming to Flint to learn ways and means of improving educational methods, was the forerunner of increasing numbers of visitors from almost everywhere who have wanted to see the many-sided Foundation program in action.

SEVENTEEN

June 1, 1950, on the eve of Charles Stewart Mott's seventy-fifth birthday, Flint held a birthday party in his honor at the Industrial Mutual Association auditorium. The Flint Board of Education was the official sponsor of this diamond jubilee birthday party—but it was community-wide in participation: everyone was invited to attend, and more than 5,000 people did so. A pageant presented scenes from Mott's life, under the title, "Portrait of an American," with text read by the author, Miss Ola Hiller, to a background of music. Mott was shown as a schoolboy, as a sailor, as mayor of Flint, as an industrialist—and in relation to a cluster of Foundation activities. Then Mott was presented with a portrait of himself surrounded by a montage of typical Foundation scenes—a picture painted by Al Washington, who had received his early art training in the Foundation program.

In response, Mott read a brief statement he had prepared in advance—because, as he notes in his diary, "I would have been too dizzy to make these remarks extemporaneously, and I had a definite message I wanted to put across, so I wrote it out and read it."

> This is a wonderful party and I wish to express my thanks and appreciation to everyone who has had a part in it, and also Frank Manley and his staff and the Flint Board of Education and Co-ordinating Committee without whose activity and co-operation the so-called Mott program could not have existed.
>
> While not wanting to depreciate your compliment to me, I cannot but feel that this is a great moment in the life of Flint when the attention of Flint folks is directed to what can be accomplished here by a Board of Education, and a model

furnished which can be copied by other community organizations.

Through the School Board's activities Flint has been supplied with a health program for children, and recreational and educational facilities for adults as well as children, including post-graduate courses through co-operation of the University of Michigan.

Now comes Flint's great opportunity to approve a Bond Issue to build more and needed educational buildings, including a couple of modern and functional elementary schools, and improvement of Junior College.

A study of Flint's Social Science Research shows that in Genesee County there are a couple of thousand young folk who desire the elements of a college education, but because of economic conditions cannot afford to stand the expense of living out of their homes.

It has shown the great desirability of the establishment here in Flint of a Four Year Community College or branch of the University, and I have been authorized by our Trustees to say that if you will approve the proposed bond issue and if such college facilities can be provided, our Foundation will be delighted to contribute land and/or funds to the amount of a million dollars, and it is our very great ambition that you will do this.

We note that a fine new library is proposed which we hope will be located on your new Civic Center.

This wonderful night and the work that has been done is the result of hard work and intensive effort on the part of hundreds of individuals in Mr. Manley's organization, and I can't close without expressing to them my heartfelt appreciation.

Again I thank you all for this wonderful celebration and hope that, with your co-operation, Flint will become the real Model City to be copied by others.

Flint was challenged to rise to the concept of having four years of college available locally. This idea had interested Mott for several years, since President Ruthven of the University of Michigan had indicated that the possibility of establishing a branch of the university at Flint might receive serious consideration by those authorized to make such decisions. Mott had made the provision of a million dollars in money or land, or a combination of both, contingent upon approval of a school bond issue by Flint voters.

A Flint *Journal* editorial of June 7, 1950, reports the results of Flint's vote on the bond issue in glowing terms.

THINGS ARE GOING FLINT'S WAY; IT'S A GREAT YEAR!

Flint can feel a bit proud of itself today! Tuesday its citizens voted overwhelmingly in favor of the two measures which will mean more and better schools for the City's children.

As a result of that election, Flint will get four new elementary schools, additions to several existing schools, a new library, a school administration building, and a new college which, if certain problems can be worked out, may embrace a four-year curriculum. . . .

The little folk of this community are the principal beneficiaries of the enlightened balloting which approved this step by a margin of almost 4 to 1.

But the adults of the community will benefit too. Their children and their neighbors' children have been guaranteed a better opportunity for a better education. Better education means better citizens. Better citizens means a better community. Better communities mean a better Nation, and a better democracy.

Everybody wins. . . .

The emphatic approval by voters of a $7-million bond issue was the subject of general elation throughout Flint; no new schools had been built for twenty years. General Motors and the UAW–CIO had recently signed a five-year contract, and Flint once more felt the surge of progress; the difference was that now Flint looked toward a significant part of that progress in the educational-cultural field, improving opportunities and the quality of living for its people. It is not possible, of course, to know exactly the extent to which the fifteen years of Mott Foundation activities—and Mott's personal example—had contributed to this raised level of community vision, but certainly Mott and the Foundation had provided the original impetus toward Flint's new respect for human values.

On Wednesday, June 8, 1950, President Ruthven—meeting with the Flint Advisory Board of the university's Social Science Research Project—commented on the action of Flint voters, "Adoption of the bond issue by Flint citizens means more than just making available more funds for education. It means a revised and enlarged educational program." Ruthven also noted that it would be difficult "to estimate how much not only Flint and the State of Michigan but education everywhere owes to Mr. Mott." Mott was then asked to comment at the meeting. He pointed out the demonstrated desire of Flint people to take advantage of additional educational opportunities, as shown by ever-increasing enrollment in Foundation classes and University of Michigan extension courses.

> But a lot of young people in Flint who would like a regular college education do not have the funds to live away from home. We of the Foundation thought it would be a fine thing to round out Flint's school system by adding two years to our Junior College. . . .
>
> On my return from Bermuda recently, I learned that the people of Flint would consider a school bond issue. Because of the good feeling created by the signing of the five-year contract between General Motors and the UAW-CIO, it looked as if the bond issue would readily pass. In that proposal was $1,600,000 for rebuilding Junior College. I thought it was a corking good time to throw in my bit toward a four-year college. . . .
>
> I won't be losing a million dollars as someone told me. I, as will the entire community, will gain much through this expansion of education. The endeavor can furnish an example to other communities, and we hope some of them will copy it.

The university's research project in the Flint area (to which the Foundation had contributed support) had found that from 2,000 to 3,000 Flint-area young people would attend a four-year college if one were locally available. Mentioning this report, Mott added, "Even if only half the number of estimated students were to enroll, it would be worthwhile to provide a college education for those wanting one but who couldn't go away from home to get it."

With the tremendous accomplishment of Flint in the field of educational-cultural development since 1950, it is perhaps not too much to say that Flint is still celebrating Mott's seventy-fifth birthday party in the ways that mean most to him.

All in all, Mott received a remarkable recognition from his friends, neighbors, and the whole community . . . recognition of the growing fifteen-year contribution of the Foundation to community life . . . recognition of the promise of a finer Flint inherent in the Foundation's continued efforts and in Mott's offer of $1 million toward a four-year college. Perhaps the vote of Flint people in favor of the school bond issue was the greatest recognition of all.

The Mott program showed changes and developments during 1950, as every year. The top 20 members of Stepping Stone Clubs were given a three-day visit to Michael Hamady's estate on Mackinac Island in August. Mott Camp, with Lester Ehrbright as director, became a year-around resource, with Flint Youth Bureau outdoor excursions planned there after the regular camping season. In-service training for teachers— widening the scope of the visiting-teacher program, under direction of Walter S. Holmlund, received national recognition.

Registration for the fall term of Mott Foundation adult education classes exceeded all previous records—with 2,200 people enrolling on the first of four evenings. Mott visited the registration center at Central High School the evening of September 18, 1950. His diary for the day notes:

> The enrollment was being held in the two gymnasiums on second floor, and the queue of those waiting to be registered was a file of four wide, and reached as far as front door. And the gymnasiums were chuck full of folks. Around the edges of the gymnasiums were tables with teachers and volunteers making the enrollments in various classes. I found not only

Miss Dill there, but also Miss Wood from our office and Miss Hubner from Building office, a lot of teachers and staff whom I already knew, plus a lot more whom I met. The whole thing was most inspiring because of the interest and enthusiasm of those entering these classes.

We have been doing this same sort of thing for some years past, but this year the enrollment is greater than ever before. Tonight was simply the first of four nights for enrollment. It doesn't seem possible that there could be as many desiring to enroll during the next three nights. . . .

On October 3, 1950, Mott was asked to make a recording of a memory of the old days for a Chevrolet meeting which was to be held after he would have left for Bermuda. This is the text of the recording:

NARRATOR: There are some in this room who remember when Chevrolet was a sickly child of only nine years, when W. C. Durant felt the stock market crash about his ears for the second time, and the presidency of General Motors passed from Durant to Pierre S. du Pont, who decided to take inventory of all GM Divisions. Mr. C. S. Mott has been a Director of GM since 1913, and was at this time Director of Advisory Staff and Supervising Vice President of Car and Truck Divisions of General Motors. Isn't that when the experts wanted to close down Chevrolet, Mr. Mott?

MOTT: Yes, 1920 and 1921 were heartbreaking times. And it looked tough for Chevrolet. Ford was outproducing Chevrolet ten-to-one, and although Chevrolet sales reached 15,000 in 1920 the plants in Flint were practically idle by October. In 1921, Chevrolet sales were cut almost in half. Apparently Mr. du Pont employed a firm of consulting engineers to analyze all divisions. In their report they said Chevrolet could not hope "to compete with the market," meaning Ford. They recommended Chevrolet be closed out, but Mr. Alfred P. Sloan, Jr., urged that Chevrolet be given another chance. On February 23, 1922, I hired William S. Knudsen as my assistant, and on March 25, 1922, he was made Production Vice President of Chevrolet. It was the turning point. Two years later Chevrolet showed a profit of five million dollars.

It was also in 1950 that Mott, with some pangs of nostalgic regret, approved the sale of the farm horses with which his 64 acres in the middle of Flint had, until then, been worked.

At the Automobile Old Timers eleventh anniversary dinner at the Waldorf, in New York City, October 18, Mott was cited for his "long and varied contributions to the automobile industry and to General Motors Corporation." Mott met many old friends at the meeting, including J. Frank Duryea who was, Mott notes in his diary, "Chief Engineer of Stevens Duryea Auto Company of Chicopee Falls to whom we furnished bevel drive axles back in the early days—1904 on. He is credited with building first commercial gasoline cars around 1895, and won Chicago auto race back then."

Mott was first of six to be awarded the Distinguished Service Citation. Bill Holler was Master of Ceremonies—a man Mott has always been proud to have hired for General Motors—and Mott was asked to speak. He began:

> Fellow Old Timers and Guests, I had not expected to be called upon, but fearing that I might be I brought along a few notes in the way of stories regarding a number of real old timers who have passed on to their reward. My first subject is William C. Durant, without whom there never would have been a General Motors.

Mott told them about Durant, the master salesman . . . Louis Chevrolet . . . Walter Chrysler . . . and Alec Hardy . . . with stories that were much appreciated by his audience. Speaking after Mott was his good friend, C. F. Kettering.

The catalog for the January, 1951, registration for Mott adult education classes listed 266 courses, held at school buildings throughout Flint; enrollments continued to break previous records. The board of education's study and research committee continued to explore ways and means of developing four years of college in Flint, conferring with University of Michigan officials about the possibility of a branch of the university.

In May, 1951, Joseph A. Anderson, chairman of the committee, reported a recommendation to the board that it suggest

181

immediate construction of a new Flint Junior College, at an estimated cost of $2.8 million—with the expectation of expansion to four years of college later at an additional cost estimated at $1.2 million. It was also suggested that the University of Michigan be asked to operate the third and fourth years of the college.

The death of William S. Ballenger, one of the pioneers of the automobile industry, cost Flint one of its finest friends of recreation and civic enterprise. Ballenger Park, established by Mr. and Mrs. Ballenger in 1935, has been a much enjoyed recreation center ever since. His will set up trust funds to maintain the park, and to set up another park. Other funds were set aside to build a field house on the campus of the new college being planned for Flint. After other specific bequests, the substantial remainder of his estate was bequeathed to Flint Junior College. The Mott Foundation had worked cooperatively with Mr. Ballenger ever since the early recreation programs of 1935—and the trust funds set up by the Ballenger will gave further impetus to Flint's developing plans for educational, cultural, and recreational development.

The health-achievement program in the schools showed great advancement in 1951, with more than half the children in the health-guarded category for the first time. The Foundation began operating the Tot Lot program as a separate division in 1951, with advisory committees in the area around each of the seventeen Tot Lot locations.

A teen-age safe-driving program was another important 1951 development; a number of community agencies cooperated in developing the plan, with Dr. Myrtle Black, Mott Foundation adult education supervisor, as chairman of the committee. A parent-child program was initiated, sponsored by the Foundation and the schools, with the backing of community organizations. The first class was attended by almost a thousand parents and teen-age children; four classes were held, with increasing attendance. Plans were made to continue the program with small classes, and a practice driving area, in the fall.

The Foundation's budget for the 1951–1952 year was $300,000, of which almost one-third was for the health work. The adult education program enrolled 11,577 persons in the 1950–1951 season, and plans were made to accommodate even more in the next year, with about 300 courses offered in 20 centers throughout Flint.

The death of Alton R. Patterson, assistant director of the Mott Foundation program, and director of pupil personnel and attendance and child accounting for the Flint public schools, was a serious loss to the community. A strong force in the complex and arduous work of developing and carrying out the Foundation program from its very first days, Patterson was one of those quiet, effective men of exceptional ability, judgment, and loyalty, and real dedication to his work.

In Flint, the event of the year for Mott, Manley, the board of education, the Foundation staff—and the public—was the opening of the Ralph M. Freeman Elementary School, Flint's first community school. The concept had been growing for many years; part of it was in Manley's convictions when he came to Flint; part of it was in Mott's belief in the fullest use of available resources; an aspect of it had been demonstrated with the first after-hours utilization of school buildings in Flint in 1935; step after step had been taken in the same direction; the Fairview School pilot project had taken an unlikely and difficult district and turned it into an effective center of community development. Now, with the Freeman School—Flint's first new school since 1929—a school had been *designed* functionally as a community school.

President George V. Gundry of the board of education greeted the audience at the dedication ceremony, describing the new school as

> ... an investment in the American way of life ... Flint's first true community-type school and its first new school in more than twenty years. With the help of the Mott Foundation, we have shown enviable leadership in the use of schools by the whole community. And there is every reason that the whole community should use the schools. The community

builds and furnishes the buildings. It even provides the children to fill them.

In this building you will have a headquarters for community education, where children will come for an education second to none, and for training in citizenship.

Here you will come for education yourselves, and see fine plays, hear fine music, and relax in a world that is too full of hurry.

Mott was called upon to speak. He said:

I am glad to be present at the dedication of this new school building, and to congratulate all concerned. ... First, the school board ... second, the public ... third, the children who will come here ... and finally, myself for the realization of what has been my dream for many years. To my mind this building embodies the best ideas devised by experience and ability, and results in a highly functional and 100 per cent efficient center for both education and community use. I shall not attempt to enumerate all of the details, other than to say that all of the facilities may be used separately, in units, or together. I hope you will make a close inspection. This is the first completed of four school buildings planned, and I am sure that hereafter all schools in Flint will embody this idea, and that many other cities will copy us.

Ralph M. Freeman, for whom the school was named, had served on the Flint board of education from 1935 to 1949. A Flint attorney, known as a community leader, he was happy to be present at the ceremony dedicating the school.

Thus, the new Freeman Community School demonstrated its added facilities on the evening of its dedication. The differences in the design, construction, and use of Freeman School are described in *Flint School Review* for December, 1951.

The building includes eight classrooms, two kindergartens, a gymnasium, auditorium, arts and crafts room, a community conference room, hallways, lavatories, a health room, teachers rest room, storage rooms, offices, and a power plant.

Such statistics are not remarkable in themselves. What is

remarkable is that this floor space was planned for multi-purpose use to meet the varied needs of the community. The people who built this school—the taxpayers—will receive almost twice the value from the building and its rooms, largely because of planning for its maximum use as both an ideal elementary classroom building and a community center.

Freeman School can be used the day-round and the year-round. The building was so designed that it can accommodate large or small groups. By cutting off corridors with accordion-like wall gates, just the library, just the auditorium, just the community conference or arts and crafts rooms, or just the gymnasium can be used—all without opening up other parts of the building. The building is expansible—so planned that other classrooms, recreational facilities, or even a swimming pool can be added.

The gymnasium is suitable for groups of all sizes. It can be used for dancing and social recreation, for festivals, exhibits, games for small children, as well as for the customary gymnasium athletics—basketball, volleyball, tennis, badminton, shuffleboard. It has five badminton courts.

The auditorium seats 300 on a sloping floor. The seats bordering the aisles are of different widths—18, 19, and 20 inches—so that along the rows no seat will be directly in front of another to obstruct the view of the stage. Both children and grown-ups who will use the stage for plays, assemblies, movies, and forums, will have access to a workroom, dressing and prep rooms.

The school has a community room which during the school day is used as an audio-visual room. It has stoves, cupboards, a refrigerator, and comfortable furniture which make PTA meetings, Child Study Club gatherings, teacher and parent teas, and neighborhood conferences pleasurable and friendly affairs. The arts and crafts room is supplied for use by both children and adults in painting, ceramics, leatherwork, sewing, woodcarving, and other hobbies and crafts.

Kindergarten rooms open to a play area restricted for small children. Here their play is not interrupted or hampered by older children.

Each classroom is self-contained. Each has its own washroom and lavatory for both boys and for girls. This innovation in school planning does not cost any more than the customary "down the hall" lavatory. There are no lockers in the hallways since each classroom has its own such facilities. Each room has bi-lateral lighting—lighting directly or indirectly from the outside through low windows and glass blocks on the upper outside walls. This natural lighting is augmented by well-placed fluorescent ceiling light fixtures. Rooms and hallway ceilings are of acoustical tile. Classroom and corridor drinking fountains are recessed.

This, then, is the physical plant of a community school. In order to make it function effectively as a real community center, William F. Minardo, a member of the Foundation staff from its first days, was appointed director of the school-community program, a position commonly known in the years to come as "building director." Actually, the community-school building director was to become the key to the community-center functions of the community schools—coordinating, leading, helping in a thousand ways to develop the community participation in activities.

Organization of the Mott Foundation program was changing through these years, as experience showed better ways of accomplishment. Coordinators of various parts of the program were named to assure responsible direction of each aspect of the work. Community-school developments were instituted at Parkland and Roosevelt schools. At Parkland, the interest of the community was in a health and homemaking project comparable to the one which had wrought so great a change for the better in the Fairview School community. Buick assisted in development of a large park area for community recreational purposes at Roosevelt School. Through the youth bureau—with its ever present evidences of the effects of alcoholism on sound family life—a beginning was made in a program to assist in prevention and cure of alcoholism.

With regard to the four-years-of-college idea—which Mott had been pursuing vigorously since Ruthven's mention in 1946 that the university might consider branches in other cities—Mott wondered whether the retirement of Ruthven might raise a new problem. In May, 1952, a group of Flint men—including George V. Gundry, Joseph A. Anderson, Dr. W. Fred Totten, S. S. Stewart, Jr., Dr. Mark W. Bills, John M. Barrett, Frank J. Manley, and Harding Mott—met with the new president of the university, Dr. Harlan H. Hatcher, and members of his staff. The university agreed to present a plan for operation of a four-year college in Flint. Mott had already made available 32 acres of his property—valued at $132,000—as a site. This land was part of his home-estate, with large frontage on Court Street, and adjoining the Oak Grove campus of the old Flint Junior College. The board of education found that sharply increasing construction costs threatened the completion of the building program planned when the voters of Flint had approved the $7-million bond issue in 1950—but the idea of having a full four years of college in Flint never lost momentum. The board decided to proceed with junior college construction; under the terms of the Ballenger will, funds had been made available for building a field house, and Mott agreed to make available the million dollars he had pledged so that a science building could be constructed.

In July, 1952, Dr. Hatcher consulted Mott on a proposal the university was considering submitting to Flint with regard to conditions of affiliation to provide four years of college. Mott felt that some of the elements of the proposal were rather unreasonable—particularly in relation to arrangements on land which Mott had agreed to deed to the Flint Board of Education "with provision that they cannot dispose of it otherwise than back to the Foundation." Also, Mott felt some provisions of the proposal would conflict with terms of the Ballenger will to the disadvantage of the college development. Mott told Hatcher that the committee named by the board of education had decided to make a return proposal to the university, embodying suggested means of proceeding with the college plans. Mott notes in his diary: "We had a very pleasant talk and I am quite

187

sure that Dr. Hatcher took no offense at what I said, and, as a matter of fact, I think he agreed with me."

On July 29, 1952, Mott deeded the 32 acres of his land to the Foundation, and then, acting for the Foundation, "gave and conveyed this property to the Flint Board of Education with the provision that it shall be used only for educational purposes and not otherwise disposed of."

Just when the Mott program adult education classes were opening in 1952, *Time* magazine printed an article about Mott and the Foundation, calling Mott, "Mr. Flint," and beginning with a 1952 incident:

> ... two small boys invaded Mott's office to complain that the Park Department could not afford to keep the city swimming pools open in August. Mott immediately decided to foot the bill. "We are," says he, "a last-resort organization."
>
> Today, with more than $20 million in stocks and real estate (the Foundation owns at least one bank and four department stores), the Foundation can afford to do quite a bit of last-resorting. But that is only the start of its work. By its alliance with the Board of Education, the Foundation has turned the schools into neighborhood centers, given hundreds of teachers a chance to earn extra money, and made Flint more community-conscious than ever before.
>
> At 77, Charles Mott, a director of General Motors since 1913, chairman of the board of U.S. Sugar Corp., and member of innumerable organizations (e.g., American Legion, United Spanish War Veterans, Royal Bermuda Yacht Club, Elks, Moose, Masons), still works hard at his goal. He pops into his paneled office every working day, keeps it filled with fresh flowers and humming with fresh ideas. ... "We must build back to community activities," says Mott, "to get people to know their neighbors and bring about a wholesome, small-town atmosphere in a big city."

When plans for the junior college science building were drawn up, the estimated cost was $1,557,000. Mott agreed to increase his original gift of a million dollars by the additional $557,000 rather than to have the plans reduced to a less adequate building. The board of education announced that the name of the new building would be the Charles Stewart Mott Community Center of Science and Arts.

Two other new community schools were dedicated in 1952: the John L. Pierce School and the Ernest W. Potter School—both built with the same concept as the Freeman School to be real centers of community life. Dr. Spencer W. Myers, Flint's new superintendent of schools, took part in the dedication ceremonies of the new schools, expressing his increasing pride in association with Flint schools. At the Potter School ceremony, he said, "The building will never be anything but concrete and mortar, but it is the reflection of the dream of Thomas Jefferson and Alexander Hamilton that men should be free to develop to their own greatest capacity and that this can best be accomplished through public education."

On December 4, 1952, Mott and a group of other Flint men met with Dr. Hatcher and other University of Michigan representatives. Mott pointed out that the junior college was well under way, and that he had not lost interest in an additional last two years of college by the university, and that "we were prepared to help finance any additional buildings in case they were needed and the School Board unable to do the financing . . . that we thought well of higher education, and what we are most tremendously interested in was the upgrading of Flint folks—call it education or anything else you want. We do not argue about that, but we propose to give Flint folks an opportunity to learn various trades, professions, etc., along any lines they want as long as it enables them to live happier and more prosperous lives." President Hatcher assured Mott of the university's continued interest in the possibilities of a branch in Flint.

A December 22, 1952, entry in Mott's diary has a title line:

SHIRT SLEEVE ECONOMICS, OR SHOULD I SAY SHIRT TAIL

Some months ago our husky fourteen-year-old son, Stewart, bigger, taller, and heavier than his father, asserting his strength on the mixing valve in his bathroom, broke the handle off. Local plumber was unable to get it replaced and make repairs, and finally was instructed to put in a new mixing valve, and I have just received the bill for same. The valve alone cost $22.50, and the cost of installation, etc., at $4.00 per hour, brought the cost up to $100.00.

Now, the economic question which I bring to your attention is as follows:

I pay tax of 90% on my income, thus in order to acquire $100 with which to pay this particular plumber's bill, I have to receive from General Motors $1,000.00 (on which I pay tax of $900.00, leaving $100.00 with which to pay the bill).

Furthermore, in order to pay me $1,000 in dividends, General Motors has to earn $4,000.00 before they pay income tax. As check on this let me say that G.M.'s earnings before income tax equals 19.90% of sales, and G.M. Dividends for 1951 equalled 6.75% of sales, which is practically ¼ of the 19.90.

From this you will note that liquidation of expense caused by Stewart's breaking the handle off the mixing valve required an earning of $4,000 before taxes by G.M., which should be a lesson in economics and a warning against using too much strength on plumbing fixtures.

This particular item from Mott's diary was utilized in *Newsweek* by Henry Hazlitt (for whom Mott has always had high regard).

The Mott family's 1952 Christmas cards must have been mailed early, because Pierre S. du Pont wrote Mott a letter of acknowledgment eight days before Christmas. On November 30, 1920, du Pont had somewhat reluctantly accepted the presidency of General Motors to lend the prestige and conservative strength of his name, character, and experience to the corporation in those troubled times when the whole structure was threatened. By mid-1922, the financial position of General Motors had been improved vastly, and an internal reorganization had improved operations to a remarkable degree. With the restoration of confidence, stability, and an advantageous financial position for General Motors accomplished, Pierre S. du Pont retired as president May 10, 1923, to be succeeded by Alfred P. Sloan, Jr.

The letter which Pierre S. du Pont wrote to Mott just before Christmas in 1952 gives a glimpse of those dramatic events thirty years before, and a suggestion of the importance of Mott's part in them.

December 17, 1952

Mr. Charles S. Mott,
    500 Mott Foundation Bldg.,
        Flint, Michigan
Dear Stewart:

Your Christmas cards are always a source of enjoyment, as they give some news of you and your surroundings. Since you sent your first card, the children have changed much. They are a fine trio but they may be disappointed to learn that I do not share their love for dogs. Those in the picture seem well placed and happy.

I have thought of you a great deal during recent weeks on account of the Du Pont lawsuit, which started trial in Chicago in November. The recount of historical events in General Motors brought you frequently to mind—my mind. You were a tower of strength during the Durant debacle. Without you, Sloan, and Bassett, the company could not have pulled through. Your energy and sincere belief in the company did much to win over the bankers, who held the reins but were glad to give way to those worthy of handling them. I wish that you and Sloan would write up General Motors in the early days. The Du Pont side of the case has been pretty well covered during the lawsuit to which it has been subjected. Perhaps the writing has not been very readable but very many cold, hard facts have been set forth which all redound to your credit.

My best wishes for a happy Christmas to you and to your wife and family.

Sincerely yours,
Pierre S. du Pont

On January 13, 1953, Mott replied to du Pont's letter. Mott's consistent loyalty to General Motors, his concern for better methods and products, and his care to disclaim any credit he felt he did not entirely deserve, are particularly evident in his reply.

January 12, 1953

Mr. Pierre S. du Pont
Wilmington, Delaware
Dear Pierre:

Your kind letter of December 17th was duly received, and we are complimented by your interest in our cards and family.

Regarding Chicago lawsuit, it was a great surprise to me, for though I occupied an important executive position in the '20's, I was not aware of any so-called "pressure." Certainly the du Ponts never even asked my help.

I personally "pressured" Buick and Cadillac, and secured an executive wire from Sloan to Cadillac ordering them to comply with dealers' orders when the dealers specified Duco, and Hannum and I put up a job whereby we could get Fisher to two-tone Duco Oakland closed cars. This pressure did not come from du Pont Company, but from car dealers who were disgusted with the terribly bad paint and varnish finish.

Although I have always had and will continue to have the most kindly feelings toward the du Pont family, who have done so much to help General Motors Corporation and its personnel, my efforts on Duco were self-started by me for the benefit of General Motors product. I should have been ungrateful if I refused to help my friends, but such was never asked of me, and was not the reason for my condemning paint and varnish in favor of Duco. The difference in the results spoke for itself.

Originally the Fishers opposed Duco, and it was by above method that we got it across, and a few years ago one of the Fishers said to me, "C.S., our use of Duco was one of the greatest things that ever happened to General Motors," and he was right.

Together with my late friend George Hannum I will accept responsibility of above.

As to other matters which you mention, you overcompliment me. I did what I could in the '20's when our various divisions were not co-operative, and at times without good leadership. Fortunately, with Sloan's patient leadership and organizing ability, there came through a group of young and able men to take over what the older men, of whom I was one, were glad to give up. Today we have a wealth of competent men in General Motors—a lot of them whose ability is enough for any job in General Motors or elsewhere. How they acquired all of this ability staggers me, but they have it, and you and I feel very happy that what the du Ponts put their shoulder to is now the healthiest outfit in the country.

I have carefully inspected the new models, and am sure that you will be proud of their acceptance by the public.

Again let me thank you for your letter, and tell you how happy I am to have your friendship and that of the du Ponts.

With best wishes,

Sincerely,
C. S. Mott

EIGHTEEN

All the regular Mott Foundation activities kept growing, and there were always new developments . . . teen clubs . . . children's drama classes . . . a program for older people . . . the driver-training program. Manley, in speaking to a Foundation staff meeting, reaffirmed basic principles, and emphasized the tradition of continuous adaptability of the Foundation—reminding everyone that "Everything the program is doing or has done is the result of a specific thing that needed to be done. If any organization in Flint can take over what we are doing, we'll get right out of it and put our efforts to new tasks."

On March 31, Mott turned the first sod on his former Court Street property in a ground-breaking ceremony to mark the beginning of construction of the new Mott Science Building. A Freeman School "open house" in April demonstrated to all Flint how a community school was actually being used by the families of the area surrounding it. Some 2,500 persons were already active there in more than twenty-five groups and organizations . . . Brownies, Cubs, Scouts, PTA, Freeman Men's Class, Mott Foundation classes, basketball leagues, Flint Community Players, square dancing groups, teen-age clubs, and others.

In addition to being Mott's seventy-eighth birthday, June 2, 1953, was voting day in Flint—and Flint citizens approved an additional tax of 5 mills for school purposes for ten years, estimated to raise about $20 million, permitting construction of more community schools and taking care of operational costs. The vote was about 68 per cent in favor of the increase. Two days later, the Flint *Journal* announced:

> The community-center program now financed largely by the Mott Foundation in Flint's three new school buildings will be extended into every area of the City.

C. S. Mott, originator and president of the Foundation, has informed the Board of Education that every school becoming a community-center type building—either a new one to be built or an old one to be remodeled—will be offered a community-school program.

Mr. Mott predicted "a great future for Flint" on the heels of passage by the voters Tuesday of a $20,000,000 tax levy for the City's schools.

And the Foundation, Mr. Mott said, expects to assume its full share of responsibility in providing financial resources for development.

The Foundation is spending $370,000 for education, recreation, health, and character-building through the schools in the current year. This is besides capital gifts. While the Mott program expansion undoubtedly will be keyed to the school expansion now permitted by the tax increase, some informed persons see its annual cost as reaching $500,000 soon. . . .

With funds available to the school board through the new tax source, four to six new schools will be built and existing ones remodeled, enlarged, or facilities improved. The Foundation does not yet know how many additional community-center programs will be set up, but enough are being planned in old as well as new sections so that they will be in reach of all Flint residents.

What program will be offered at those strategically located buildings will be determined largely by requests of persons in the areas. Teen-age clubs, athletic programs for young and old, dramatics, adult education, crafts, and family events have proven popular in the Freeman, Potter, and Pierce neighborhoods.

Because of overwhelming support in these areas for the tax levy, the community center programs were seen to be one of the deciding factors in Tuesday's election. Flint has been cited far and wide for its new-type schools and programs.

Mr. Mott said Tuesday's vote was "a vote of confidence in the present school board. The people showed they approved of the board and what it has done. They also put the board under an obligation to carry out what the people have voted for."

The new community-center programs and whatever other projects may be developed and to which the Foundation gives support will be formulated by the Co-ordinating Committee of the Board of Education and the Mott Foundation. Members of the committee are appointed by the board. The committee is constituted of board members and persons selected from the community.

"The Foundation's budget has increased each year," Mr. Mott said. "We never have yet turned down a budget proposed by the Co-ordinating Committee."

On June 8, 1953, a devastating tornado struck Flint, causing many deaths and injuries, and destruction of many homes. Mott's daughter Susan happened to be in the tornado area at the time, and had a narrow escape. Dr. Tuuri, of the Mott Children's Health Center, devoted countless hours to the care of children injured in the tornado, and the whole community rallied to assist stricken neighbors. A little later, a movement was instituted to help rebuild homes destroyed in the tornado, and Saturday and Sunday, August 29 and 30 were set for Flint's community good turn, "Operation Tornado." An entry from Mott's diary for August 29, 1953, follows.

I drove up to the North End to Coldwater Road, which is about six miles North of the City Hall, and one mile beyond City Limits. There, in accordance with instructions received, I drove East on Coldwater Road to 1189 and joined Project No. 6 of "Operation Tornado," and got started on the work at one o'clock. I was given an official tag and an A. F. of L. Federation card and immediately started in nailing sheathing on the newly erected uprights of a house that had been pretty much destroyed by the tornado. I was equipped with a carpenter's apron with pockets for 8 and 10 penny nails, and as requested had brought my hammer with me, and for three hours I worked on sheathing the back and side of house. Believe me, the weather was hot. At the end of three hours, the handle of the hammer had somewhat loosened the skin on my right hand, but had not yet come to a blister, and after three hours without sitting down, I realized there was a lot of difference in my general physical condition at 78 from what it was 20 years ago when Harding and I worked for three weeks, sun-up to sun-down, at Camp Verde on both masonry and carpentry on a ranch house. However, four o'clock was official quitting time and I had just enough strength left to drive home where I had a bath, a big orange-lemon drink, and an hour's rest.

Much was made of this incident in the way of national publicity, and there may very well have been skeptical souls who considered Mott's work on "Operation Tornado" as a gesture. It was a taken-for-granted act of good-neighborliness to help where help was needed; Mott has always felt a personal responsibility to have a literal hand in what needs to be done, and if the hand has been somewhat blistered in the process he has accepted that, too. His work in "Operation Tornado" was not a stunt but a self-imposed obligation fulfilled—just as the work of his son, Harding, and grandson, Harding, Jr., on the same project on the following day was taken for granted by these younger Motts.

In September, 1953, the Mott Foundation financed and gave to the Flint Board of Education a new voice to reach the community—its own FM radio station, WFBE, with an excellent staff directed by Miss Ola Hiller. Enrollment for adult education and recreation classes broke all previous records. Parent-teacher association membership also reached an impressive high of 16,835—suggesting the increased sense of community participation awakened in Flint. The eighth Annual Flint Folk Festival at the IMA Auditorium—a widely enjoyed extravaganza of square dancing with Harold Bacon as master of ceremonies—drew tremendous interest, and a crowd of 3,500.

In December, a new pilot project was announced by the board of education—in which an attempt would be made to meet the problem of "ninth-grade dropout" from school by combining practical work experience with academic training for boys attracted more to building-trades than to regular high school studies.

Volume of adult evening school class registrations increased so greatly that 398 courses were offered for the winter term beginning February 1, 1954, in 33 centers throughout Flint. Twenty-five of the courses were new—including a thirteen-week course called, "The United Nations—What's In It For Me?" presented to the whole community over a local radio station, WFDF, with supplementary printed materials furnished to those who registered. The course received an impressive enrollment by mail, and was spoken of with some enthusiasm by Mrs. Franklin D. Roosevelt in her daily newspaper column.

Flint's fourth community school, the Gyles E. Merrill School, was dedicated February 3, 1954. A few days later Mott received a distinguished service award from the Michigan Congress of Parents and Teachers. He also received a salute from the student body of Flint Junior College as part of the first honors convocation on the new campus and a few days later he received a Saginaw County distinguished service award from the Saginaw County Board of Supervisors, "for generous contributions to Saginaw County Hospital for research in the field of tuberculosis."

In 1954, Manley set forth an evaluation of Mott Foundation work in accordance with a policy of periodic examination of the program, plans, and operations to determine how well they measured up by the best available yardsticks. Manley's report begins:

1. Has the Mott Foundation Program helped the City of Flint to become a better community, with better and happier homes and better and happier children and adults? Has the Foundation in any way relieved or excused the community from making every effort to "pull itself up by its own bootstraps" or, on the contrary, has it "primed the pump" to release individual and community energies, abilities, and good will for the benefit of all?

2. How does the Mott Foundation Program, in its philosophy, purposes, plans, and operations measure up to the recommendations of the country's leading authorities in the field?

To establish a background for answering the questions, Manley reviews the social history of Flint up to the beginnings of the Foundation program in 1935. He illustrates the pump-priming function of the Foundation's work by showing the tremendous increases both in funds for civic and educational accomplishment and in membership in such community agencies as the Girl Scouts, Boy Scouts, and YMCA.

For measurement against established educational yardsticks, Manley matches specific Foundation policies, functions, and activities against recommendations of the recognized authorities in the field. He is able to demonstrate how the Foundation meets each recommendation. Not only is the Foundation a stimulus to other community improvement 'evelopments, but it places emphasis on prevention and education . . . ventures into new and exploratory fields, taking the initiative rather than merely applying patching plaster . . . provides capital for experiments which cannot currently be financed by public funds . . . actually gets things done in everyday, down-to-earth practice . . . concentrates on selection of personnel with dedication, creative initiative, and human warmth as well as outstanding excellence in knowledge and techniques . . . makes provision for wise and responsible administration . . . does its work in its own community . . . makes use of existing facilities . . . adapts programs to what people really want and need. Each of these things the Foundation does is in accordance with the recommendations of those whose opinions are most respected in the field of theory and practice in the operation of foundations. Exactly *how* the Foundation fulfills these recommendations is well-documented in Manley's thorough review and evaluation of the work of the program from 1935 to 1954.

In July, 1954, Mott was pleased to be able to honor Manley by presenting to the board of education a check for $188,810 for construction of an indoor swimming pool at Northern

High School, the pool to be named for Frank J. Manley. The Mott Foundation Co-ordinating Committee had recommended the construction of the pool, reporting, "There is general agreement that all physically fit young people should have an opportunity to learn to swim and become acquainted with water safety."

When he received the recommendation, Mott replied,

For a number of years Frank Manley has talked to us, off and on, about the great need for such a facility—not simply on the basis of pleasure or sports, but to teach a lot more folks to swim.

Our daily papers contain a list of too many people who have drowned due to not knowing how to swim when a little training would have saved their lives. We were told that of the young men entering the United States Navy during the last war only 15 per cent knew how to swim. That was a very poor record.

Each year at Mott Camp at least 650 boys partake of swimming instruction. The experience has been that all but about 1 per cent of those attending are able to swim before leaving camp. This is a dividend they receive in addition to healthy exercise, sport, and pleasure.

The Mott Foundation is glad to be able to grant your request; and because the idea of the project originated with Frank J. Manley, and in further recognition of his many other unselfish contributions to the advancement and welfare of the citizens of Flint, we desire that this pool bear his name.

With adult education classes beginning in late September, 494 classes were offered; advanced registration totaled more than 10,000. The Foundation budget for 1954–1955 exceeded $500,000.

November 23, 1954, was a day of celebration in Flint—in honor of the production of the 50 millionth General Motors automobile. As part of the day's ceremonies, the new Harlow H. Curtice Community College Building was dedicated at the Junior College. In the course of a speech, Curtice announced that General Motors would contribute $3 million toward Flint's college and cultural development. He identified the contribution as a Flint centennial project, in honor of the coming year, when Flint would celebrate its hundredth anniversary as a city. Among other things that Curtice said were the following:

> The science and arts building, now nearing completion, will be dedicated to Charles Stewart Mott. This very campus you owe to his generosity. The Mott Foundation has a nationwide reputation for its accomplishments.
>
> One of the pioneers of our industry, Stewart Mott was long active in the management of General Motors and is the oldest in tenure on our Board of Directors. I cherish his friendship and staunch support.
>
> Flint is a better city in which to live as a result of his generosity.
>
> Flint is a growing and prosperous community. General Motors is happy to have contributed to this prosperity through its own growth. We recognize, too, that the support of the citizens of Flint has had a great deal to do with the growth and prosperity of General Motors.

The Flint college and cultural center project was launched —beginning with a $12-million goal for Flint's centennial year. Plans at that time called for construction of a 3,000-seat auditorium, a transportation and historical museum, an art center, a theater, a carillon, and a planetarium. Michael Gorman, editor of the Flint *Journal,* made the college and cultural development the central focus of his endeavors, and many other Flint people were inspired by the good beginnings Flint was making in improving the quality of opportunity in education and the arts for the whole community. The community-school concept had taken hold, and was being directed into levels of higher education.

In December, Mott was appointed General Chairman of the Michigan White House Conference on Education, scheduled for the next May. Late in December, it was announced that on January 11, 1955, President Eisenhower would confer the International Big Brother of the Year Award on Mott, "for his oustanding work with the Flint Youth Bureau and for broad humanitarian endeavor." Mott had been chosen for the award by the board of directors of the Big Brothers of America.

On January 10, Mr. and Mrs. Mott, Frank J. Manley, George V. Gundry, Dr. Harold W. Woughter (chairman of the Mott Foundation Coordinating Committee), Everett A. Cummings (school board president), Woodrow W. Skaff (Flint Youth Bureau president), Joseph T. Ryder (Flint Youth Bureau director), and Gerald H. Rideout were flown to Washington. Mott telephoned Mrs. Arthur Summerfield, who told him that Postmaster General Summerfield would be with the party at the White House. The next morning, the party made a tour of the official rooms of the White House, then walked outside and around to the north-west gate, where they entered at 11:30 A.M. Mott records the proceedings in his diary for the day:

> We met a large group of folks. I presume the whole party numbered as many as 40 and included Senator Potter and Congressman Dondero of Michigan, Eddie Rickenbacker, and others. At 12:30 we all filed into President Eisenhower's private office where the President was standing at his desk, and batteries of photographers, movie and still, were all ready for us.
>
> The Postmaster General took me up to the President and introduced me, remarking to the President that I was his first employer and that President Eisenhower was his last—and at both places his job was carrying the mail.
>
> After hand-shaking, a framed Big Brother Award was handed to the President by Mr. Berwind, and the President read the inscription and handed the award to me with another handshake, and then a talk lasting not over two minutes. I accepted the award on behalf of over one-thousand associates in Flint who were, I said, the ones who really did the work and deserved the award. In Flint, with a population of 165,000, we have 600 Big Brothers, each with a boy to look after, and probably at least another 600 folks working in social agencies and other program activities all very helpful to the Big Brother movement. And I finished by saying, "Mr.

President, we think you are the biggest Big Brother of all."
And for some unaccountable reason that last remark seemed
to make a great hit, not only with the President, but with the
men of the press who were present. More pictures were taken
with the President shaking hands with me, and my receiving
the award, and the party was over.

The President appeared in excellent health and spirits and
extremely affable and agreeable. He certainly has a wonderful personality. I must not forget to say that before I left the
room I introduced Joe Ryder to the President, and Joe gave
him a box of trout flies which had been tied by the boys in
his organization, and the President, being a trout fisherman,
seemed to be very pleased.

The reference which Postmaster General Arthur E. Summerfield, of Flint, made to Mott as his first employer, and "carrying the mail" was an allusion to the fact that Summerfield's
first job was as an errand boy at the Weston-Mott Company—
where his duties had included carrying the mail around to the
various offices.

Newspaper accounts of the Big Brother Award give additional details of the ceremony. As reported by William F.
Pyper, of the Flint *Journal* Washington Bureau, President
Eisenhower said, with reference to the citation on the award
scroll, "I'm going to read this because I like it." He read:

> To Charles Stewart Mott in recognition of your humani-
> tarianism in supporting youth programs in Flint, Michigan,
> which has provided a pattern for other communities to fol-
> low: Big Brothers of America, Inc., United States and Canada,
> proudly name you Big Brother of the Year 1954.
>
> Your leadership and labors in the public interest and your
> services in behalf of the youth of Flint point to the value of
> private philanthropy in stimulating communities to greater
> responsibilities for their welfare, and are in keeping with the
> highest traditions and aims of the Big Brother movement.
>
> The giving of yourself, your heart, and your concern to
> this cause is a source of lasting pride to every big and little
> brother in America.

The winter adult education program offered Flint a choice of 524 courses at 39 centers. Students who wished to do so could follow a planned curriculum to accomplish definite objectives; appointment of coordinators in major fields of adult education made possible the development of sequences of courses in related fields. Dr. Myrtle F. Black, adult education supervisor, received a distinguished service award from the Flint PTA Council for her contributions to Flint's educational progress.

Mott received an unusual and deeply appreciated honor on January 25, 1955. His diary describes it:

> Lunched with Harding and Roy at Elks. At 2:00, with previous notice, four American Federation of Labor men arrived, also a reporter and a couple of photographers. The men were Walter Heddy, President of AFL Painters Local 1052, Ralph Welborn, Secretary, Jack Niles, Business Agent, and O. J. Lilies, Vice President. The AFL man made a speech and told me that as the Union Card which they had given me a year ago had expired, they now presented me with an honorary life membership in the AFL Union. This because, not only of my participation in the tornado re-building operation, but also the Foundation program work for the people of Flint. I accepted the membership card with pleasure and told the men something of my own feelings in regard to things in general and what we are trying to accomplish in the Foundation program, all of which seemed to be pleasing to the men.

On the following day, Mott's diary mentions ". . . action of the University of Michigan Board of Regents in favor of operating a third and fourth year of college classes here in Flint, which would be in building provided by local capital." Mott had been working for such a decision for almost ten years, and he mentions that Michael A. Gorman had been devoting special efforts and activities to achieving the same end.

On February 1, Mott went to Lansing to carry out his function as chairman of the Michigan White House Conference on Education. His diary entry for the day records this incident:

204

I was presented to the assemblage by Dr. Clair L. Taylor, Michigan Superintendent of Public Instruction, and it was up to me to introduce Governor G. Mennen Williams, who sat alongside of me during the luncheon.

After making some remarks regarding educational, health, and recreational work being done in Flint, I said to the audience, "It is now my job to introduce the Governor. Last night I said to my wife that I would introduce him in the following manner — — — — And she said, 'Oh, no. Don't do that! He might not like it.' This morning I told Dr. Taylor of my conversation with my wife, and he said, 'Go ahead and do it.' " At which point the audience roared with laughter. Williams being a Democrat and Taylor being a Republican, the audience imagined all sorts of things, and this is it: "It seems strange that I should have to introduce Governor Williams, for if there is any person in the room, or in the State of Michigan who has not had his hand shaken by him, it is not the Governor's fault." That brought the house down.

On the following day (although this does not presuppose any connection between the two events), State Senator Garland B. Lane, Flint Democrat, sponsored a concurrent resolution of commendation which cleared both houses of Michigan's Legislature commending Mott's "contributions made throughout the years."

It was a season of honors for Mott; on February 12, at Founder's Day ceremonies beginning Michigan State College's centennial year, Mott was presented with a centennial award, thoughtfully inscribed. The award was especially gratifying to Mott because of his exceptional regard for Dr. John A. Hannah, president of Michigan State.

A diary entry of February 15 makes reference to another man for whom Mott has always had exceptional regard: Dr. Arthur L. Tuuri, Director of the Mott Foundation Children's Health Center.

Up at 6:30 and drove to Northern High School to attend one of Frank Manley's staff meetings with about 40 present, including Dr. and Mrs. Arthur Tuuri. He heads our Health Operations and Clinic for children, and has been called to service in the Army for 2 or 3 years, and is leaving shortly. The breakfast party this morning included a few talks telling him what we thought of him. I was delighted to present him with a Retina camera, going-away gift from the staff, while Mrs. Tuuri received an orchid, which she said was her first.

I just want to say in the diary what I said this morning—that Dr. Tuuri is undoubtedly the finest head of our Health Operation that we have ever had or ever could get . . . and we certainly will not listen to anything other than plans for him to return here when he is finished with the Army work.

On March 24, 1955, Mott went to Lansing to testify at a hearing before the House Ways and Means Committee of the state legislature, relating to a bill being considered to appropriate $37,000 to the University of Michigan to plan proposed operation of a third and fourth year of college to be carried on by the University of Michigan in Flint. Mott made a strong presentation of the case for a Flint branch, and indicated the willingness of the Foundation to make available another $1 million for a building. University of Michigan officials and the Flint men attending offered further testimony on the advantages of the project.

Special honors kept coming to Mott—including a citation from the Metropolitan Club of Stevens Institute of Technology, an award certificate from the Flint Chapter of the American Red Cross, and a certificate of merit and life membership from the American Legion. Mott began to become somewhat self-conscious about all the awards being conferred, when—as he notes in his diary—"All that I am trying to do is to enjoy myself by improving things in Flint."

The City of Flint was celebrating its hundredth birthday with a year-long centennial observance, and Mott, who had shared exactly half of Flint's first century, was eighty years old on June 2, 1955. The impetus imparted to Flint in the direction of educational and cultural development was picking up momentum impressively. Two former Weston-Mott men, Robert Longway and F. A. Bower, were co-chairmen of the college and cultural development—devoting their very

206

considerable talents, energies, and resources to the great centennial project. The Michigan legislature had passed the bill providing for University of Michigan studies and plans leading to establishment of a branch of the University in Flint to offer third and fourth years of college. Sponsors of the college and cultural development were coming forward with increasing frequency, with contributions of $25,000 or more toward completion of the ambitious plans. Mott deeded an additional 6-and-a-fraction acres of land to the board of education from his estate in the college area, "for use as an athletic field or such other purposes as you may desire." Just five years after Mott's seventy-fifth birthday party at the IMA Auditorium— at which he had pledged $1 million—the building constructed with that money (plus an additional $557,000 Mott had added to his contribution) was ready to be dedicated—and Mott had offered another $1 million toward construction of buildings for the University of Michigan in Flint.

This, then, was the background for Mott's eightieth-birthday party, in the midst of Flint's centennial year. The party was held June 2, on the campus—which, until a short time before, had been part of Mott's farm-in-the-middle-of-Flint. In the course of an impressive dedication program, Mott made formal presentation of the new Charles Stewart Mott Community Center of Science and Applied Arts—saying, in effect, "Boys, here it is." Presiding at the program was Dr. Harold W. Woughter, former member of the board of education, and immediate past president of the Mott Co-ordinating Committee. Dr. Spencer W. Myers, superintendent of schools, made formal acceptance of the new junior college building for the people of Flint. Mott's presentation talk reviewed the community-school development from elementary schools to this new college building, noting of the new Mott Science and Applied Arts Building that, "The board laid out the building so it can be used to teach trades and occupations, and at the same time it can be a valuable adjunct to the junior college and to the university."

Dr. Woughter utilized one of Mott's own phrases in mentioning that Mott, for twenty years, had been "upgrading the quality of living" in Flint by providing funds for education and recreation.

From the dedication of a completed building, Mott walked across the campus to grasp a shovel and break the ground for the new University of Michigan building which he had agreed to provide; President Hatcher of the University shared the digging in this symbolic groundbreaking.

Next, the big birthday party moved into Ballenger Field House, where some 1,200 people were present for the birthday dinner. In his diary for the day, Mott notes:

> We had a very fine dinner and the program went off beautifully. Speeches, messages, and tributes to me were very touching. Ivan Wiles presented to me a most magnificent book which must measure 30 by 24 inches, filled with large hand-painted scenes of various incidents in my life since our program was started. Also, I was presented with a very large and beautiful Service Award from the Boy Scouts of America. Another item of memory: At each table there had been left a card which each person at the table signed and these cards were collected and bound in a book which was presented to me; thus I have the signature record of everybody who was on hand this evening.
>
> Mrs. Mott was presented with a beautiful bouquet of red roses by the Stepping Stone girls.
>
> I had prepared no speech. It was just as well that I did not, for nothing that I might have prepared would have been exactly appropriate. I undertook to thank everybody who had participated in any way in all of the proceedings of the day, and especially those on the Board of Education and their staff for co-operation in our program work, without which we could have had no success whatever. Then I commented on and expressed appreciation of Frank Manley and his able and efficient staff.
>
> I also praised Roy Brownell and Harding, who have done such good work for us in the Foundation. Then I told about getting the original idea of a University of Michigan Branch in Flint from Dr. Ruthven about 9 years ago, which I was

unable to get across until Mike Gorman got behind the project, and he and Dutch Bower and Bob Longway put across the Cultural Center project and sold the idea to a large group of Sponsors who each donated $25,000 or more. It was quite apparent that the matter had been put up to them in such a way that they really wanted to make the contribution.

When I got through my talk, the Junior College A Capella Choir took over, and while they were singing, Dr. Hatcher, together with six Regents present and a number of University of Michigan faculty members, retired and put on academic gowns and caps. When singing was over, they marched into the main room where the Convocation was held, and President Hatcher conferred on me a Degree of Doctor of Laws. I was given a diploma, and proper scarf was hung about my neck . . .

At the close, all hands joined in singing Michigan's Anthem, "Yellow and Blue." Before I could get away I think more than half of the folks present crowded up front and shook hands with me, complimented me, and showered birthday greetings upon me, all of which was extremely pleasant . . .

Among the birthday greetings Mott received was one from President Eisenhower:

On your 80th birthday I join with your friends and neighbors at tonight's testimonial dinner in a greatly deserved tribute to you for a lifetime of constructive work and service. Your selection for the Big Brother Award earlier this year was a highly merited distinction. To everyone in Flint I am sure it was fitting recognition of many years devoted to the betterment of your community, your State, and your Nation.

But tonight's celebration, because of its spontaneous expression of affection and esteem by those who know you best in close association, must be a heart-warming and personal satisfaction to you.

As you look about the room this evening, I hope that you will recognize that those there represent many thousands of others who with like affection and esteem wish you long years of active, happy living.

Back in Utica, New York, the city he had left a half-century earlier—Mott was honored on his fiftieth anniversary as a member of Utica's Ziyara Shrine Temple; he received a fifty-year Shriner pin and a fifty-year medal from the Grand Lodge of Masons of New York.

Paul Gallico, in the December, 1955, *Reader's Digest*, in an article called, "Rediscovery of America," made a comparison between the Flint he had seen in 1937 and the Flint of 1955, characterizing Flint's great progress through those eighteen years in a significant phrase: "blurring of class lines." That may seem understatement for an ideal, but it does suggest the development of a community social unity and common purpose that may well sum up the whole American idea; certainly it is a remarkable tribute to the end-product, in Flint, of twenty years of Mott Foundation exploration and accomplishment toward the good community ideal.

NINETEEN

The year 1956 witnessed rapid growth of Flint's educational-cultural plans. It was announced by the Flint *Journal,* January 11, that the board of education had indicated that the new senior college building to be constructed for the use of the University of Michigan would be called the Mott Memorial Building, with a plaque to be inscribed: "Erected by Charles Stewart Mott in memory of his parents, John C. Mott and Isabella T. Mott."

In February, 1956, approval was given to the final plans for the Mott Memorial Building. Dr. David M. French was appointed dean of the University of Michigan in Flint, and it was announced that the first university classes would open in the fall of 1956, utilizing junior college buildings, and that the Mott Memorial Building would be ready by the fall of 1957.

April 11 brought a meeting of the Notre Dame Club of Flint, at which Frank J. Manley was named Flint's "Man of the Year" for "responsible Christian citizenship." Robert Sibilsky, president of the club, made the presentation, stating that Manley "has always been interested in and sympathetic with the needs of others—particularly of children and youth. But, being a man of action and a creative leader, he has never been content to just 'feel sorry.' He has constantly rolled up his sleeves and pitched in to do something to improve the situation. What's more, his dynamic example has induced hundreds of others to help."

Mott spoke forcefully of Manley's dedication to the good of the community: "What Frank Manley has done should be apparent to all citizens of Flint who have their eyes and ears open. . . . In the last analysis, the Mott program is Frank Manley . . . and its results are due to one man, Frank Manley.

I'm tickled to death that he received the award he so justly deserves. God bless Frank Manley." George V. Gundry, a member of the board of education, emphasized the contribution Manley's "zeal, spirit, and enthusiasm" had made to growth of the Mott program. Walter E. Scott, also of the board of education, noted that, to borrow industrial terminology, "we are taking an inventory of a most distinguished person." The Rev. C. C. McHale praised Manley as one "blessed with the power to influence others," and indicated how well he believed Manley had employed this blessing for the good of others. Nothing could have pleased Mott more than this public acknowledgement of the rare and fine qualities he had recognized in Manley so many years before.

A few weeks later, the Frank J. Manley Swimming Pool at Northern High School was dedicated, and a portrait of Manley was unveiled in the foyer. Mott made the formal presentation of the pool, and Dr. Spencer W. Myers accepted for the schools, mentioning that the "Mott-Manley team is unbeatable." Dr. Charles L. Anspach, president of Central Michigan College, conferred upon Manley an honorary Doctor of Laws Degree, and Dr. Wilbur E. Moore, head of clinical services at Central Michigan, read a citation honoring Manley.

At Michigan State Normal College in the June Commencement, William F. Minardo received a degree never before granted: master of community school administration. The course had been developed under a cooperative graduate training plan worked out with the Flint Board of Education and Mott Foundation and Michigan State Normal College in Ypsilanti. Appropriately, Minardo was the first to complete the work for a master's degree, since he had been Flint's first community-school director. Dr. W. Fred Totten directed the course, built around the laboratory offered by the Flint community schools, and designed to develop the wide scope of skills, techniques, and personal qualities required by this new and important vocation.

A fifty-two-day tour of Europe was sponsored by the Foun-

212

dation as an adult education experimental development. A group of twenty-seven people toured eight European countries under this plan. The steady progress of the health-achievement program was demonstrated when end-of-school-year figures showed 12,751 children—52.6 per cent of the 24,207 enrollment in public and parochial schools—in the health-guarded category, having all known medical defects corrected. Some 6,000 children were enrolled in Mott Foundation Tot-Lots for the summer—and the high point of their program, as every year, was the "Motti Gras" show. The children's theater program also showed splendid development under the guidance of Mrs. Helen Hardy Brown and Mrs. Mary Nell Humes; children are encouraged to develop dramatic characters from stories they know—improvising rather than learning lines by rote—for a kind of creative expression not otherwise experienced.

The Mott Foundation budget projected for the 1956–1957 year was in excess of $800,000—not including a $500,000 gift for construction of a new special-education building for the use of handicapped children. By mid-August, Dr. David M. French announced that the Flint College of the University of Michigan had already received two hundred applications for admission. Mott adult education classes were expanded, and in-service training for teachers was intensified.

On September 4, 1956, Mott received the distinguished service medal from the American Legion at the Legion's National Convention in Los Angeles. Mott accepted the tribute "to a fine organization of able and dedicated workers numbering several hundreds who are putting into effect in Flint what they call the Mott Program of Education, Health, and Recreation—for the purpose of not only making Flint a better place in which to live, but also to furnish an example for other communities to copy—which they are already doing."

One more award which came to Mott in February, 1957, was a reminder of the fact that engineering was a major facet of his life. The Michigan Society of Professional Engineers presented to Mott the award as Michigan Engineer of the Year, accompanied by a framed citation.

On October 8, 1956, the Flint College of the University of Michigan was officially opened; a formal convocation provided appropriate ceremonies. And the junior college opened also—with 2,247 full-time students enrolled.

The Flint College and Cultural Development raised its announced aim to $20 million and was incorporated as a nonprofit organization. Bids for the Enos A. and Sarah DeWaters Art Center were received; the total figure was over $950,000, of which DeWaters had already contributed $700,000.

Pledges of $25,000 or more were coming in at an impressive rate. In December, bids were requested for construction of a planetarium and a theater. It was announced that the planetarium would be named for Robert T. Longway, and the theater for F. A. Bower. The two men were old associates—from the days they had first worked at the Weston-Mott Company—and it was most appropriate that the two buildings named for them were to stand side by side. Members of the family of Cady B. Durham, one of the strong and able automobile production men of the earlier days, contributed a total of $325,000; it was announced that the swimming pool to be built at the college and cultural center would be named for Durham.

Early in 1957, Dr. John H. Hannah, president of Michigan State University, toured Flint at Mott's invitation to see for himself how the community schools operated and to have a look at the college and cultural development. Mott and Manley took him to Freeman School, Potter, and then to Fairview—where, since the first experimental work, a gymnasium-auditorium had been built. They visited other new schools, stopped in at Northern High School to see the Manley Pool, then came back to the junior college campus to look over the buildings there and see how fully they were being used. A newspaper story quotes Hannah as saying, "The program has accomplished wonders in bringing the residents together to work for the common good. I feel that it will have a tremendous impact throughout this state and the rest of the country." Another quotation from a different newspaper is even more sweeping: "For the first time, I am seeing an actual exemplification of a program getting the job done that so many others are only talking about. . . . I can think of nothing any person or organization could do to make better use of education than what is being accomplished in Flint."

The original $12-million goal of the college and cultural development had seemed imaginative; the later $20-million figure had seemed proportionately more unrealistic—but by mid-January, 1957, contributions had already reached $15,-167,000, and the snowball was still rolling. With a $25,000 minimum on sponsorships, 160 sponsors had already come forward. Mr. Enos A. DeWaters simplified bookkeeping on his account by adding another $300,000 to make his contribution an even $1 million.

Another sponsorship of exceptional interest came from Dr. and Mrs. Arthur Pound, honoring the memory of Mrs. Pound's father, W. A. Paterson—who had opened Flint's first carriage factory in 1869, had made roadcarts for Durant and Dort in 1886, and had manufactured the Paterson automobile from 1908 until 1921. Dr. Arthur Pound is well-known as the author of *The Turning Wheel,* the story of the first twenty-five years of General Motors, and for many other fine books. It was he who had edited the Flint *Arrow* supporting Mott's first candidacy for mayor of Flint.

On February 28, and the first two days of March, the Michigan State Department of Public Instruction and the Flint Board of Education and Mott Foundation sponsored a three-day workshop in community education—with the Flint community schools as the laboratory. Dr. Clair L. Taylor, state superintendent of public instruction, stated the theme of the event as "Community improvement through community leadership and cooperative effort."

Dr. Ernest O. Melby, national authority on community

215

education, made the first major talk of the three-day conference. His subject was "The Community-Centered School." One of his comments about Flint's accomplishment was: "You've translated into reality the ideas I've been talking about for years." He defined a community-centered school as

> ... not a community doing things for people, but an educational system which helps people do things for themselves. The key is getting people to do things. ... If we give every man, women, and child in America a chance to take active part in education, we won't have to worry about shortages of buildings and teachers. We can get anything we want. At the same time, if we have faith in our people, and respect our people, we can learn from them, and in working together they will come to respect and love each other. Think of the problems in human relations that would solve. ... I'm convinced that what really educates people is not what they hear or what they read, but what they do.

Mott welcomed the visiting educators, thanking them for their visit because, "It's useless for us to send people out to tell the story—they wouldn't believe it. The only way we can accomplish our goal is for you to come here and see what's going on."

On the second day of the workshop, Dr. Shane MacCarthy, executive director of the President's Council on Youth Fitness, spoke to the group. He defined fitness as including "not only physical improvement, but mental and moral strengthening as well." He pointed out that, as a nation, we are sports-conscious —but mostly in observer roles. He suggested that it was a community responsibility to help encourage the "simple concept of exercise" by providing opportunity and incentive.

Another speaker, Dr. Howard Y. McClusky, of the University of Michigan, pointed out that today's organization of society tends to separate people rather than to bring them together; he saw the community school as the agency to bring people back to that socially healthy neighborhood and family cooperation essential to community betterment.

216

Dr. G. Robert Koopmen, state associate superintendent of public instruction, reviewed the development of the community-school idea, concluding that the preparatory and experimental phases had been completed so that now the concept could be applied. He said: "That's why we're in Flint, where the experiment has been carried furthest. Our aim is to spread the idea to as many communities in the State as possible."

Dr. James A. Lewis, University of Michigan vice-president for student affairs, added, "It's time we start using what knowledge we have about why people and groups behave the way they do. If we want warm and friendly people, we've got to provide the kind of climate they can grow in. Schools have got to go beyond supplying knowledge. Knowledge alone won't change behavior."

The visiting educators included some 150 people from 35 Michigan communities. On the final day of the conference, Dr. Taylor asked those attending the workshop to "Make yourselves committees to find out what you can do in your communities in the light of what you've learned here." He asked if it wouldn't be appropriate to add a new meaning to the initials of C. S. Mott's given names, to make "C. S. stand for 'Community Service.'" He reminded his listeners that in pioneer days, the one-room school was the center of community activities, and added, "Here is a large city that has recaptured that pioneer concept. The idea is contagious, and I can't see any reason why it won't spread over the entire state."

Mott, Manley, and Dr. Robert K. Burns contributed to the final session of the workshop—and the visitors expressed enthusiasm about what they had seen and learned in Flint. The first workshop in community education was obviously an overwhelming success—because the visitors had not merely heard about what was being done in Flint, they had seen it happening. A survey of Flint's community schools showed an average weekly attendance of 24,000 in after-school and evening recreation activities—events scheduled outside of regular school hours—during the winter.

In April, Flint re-elected three members of the board of education—William S. Ballenger, Jr., S. S. Stewart, Jr., and Walter E. Scott—for six-year terms—which the Flint *Journal* saw as "a ringing indorsement of the policies and operations" of the board. Additional sponsorships kept coming in for the college and cultural development. A tremendous science fair was presented at Ballenger Field House. Dedication of the Guy W. Selby Community School added one more link in the chain of progress. A new library was planned to serve both the junior and senior colleges.

At the Flint Youth Bureau's thirteenth annual banquet, Director Joseph T. Ryder reported 677 Big Brothers active in the program and Dr. Ernest O. Melby re-emphasized his enthusiasm for Flint:

> To make freedom live in the world, we first must make it live in a community.... If you can build a community in which people have love, understanding, and respect for each other, you're paving the way for a sound world.... I came to Michigan and heard about the Flint program. I've been here six times in the last four months and I'm not sure even you realize fully what is going on in Flint.
>
> First I saw what a vision of the future of youth and of America Frank Manley has. Then I met Charles Stewart Mott and was deeply impressed with the insight, sympathy, and understanding of this great human being.

Dr. Melby saw the success of the Foundation program as based in the belief of its leadership that something could be done. He felt that Flint was finding the answer to the problem that had bothered him most—that with fantastic prosperity, people are not happy. He stated that the Flint Youth Bureau represented the approach to the good society in which "We must have people working with the desire to be of service to humanity."

One of the Mott Foundation activities most dedicated to such service to humanity, the Stepping Stones, paid tribute to Michael H. Hamady as guest of honor at their sixteenth annual banquet—in recognition of the meaning of the gift, back in 1943, of his $175,000 Branch Road estate as a clubhouse for the Stepping Stone clubs.

It was apparent that the second of the Foundation's two basic objectives—functioning as a pilot project for other communities—was being realized when six Flint school and Foundation staff members were invited to participate in the National Conference on Education for Leisure in Washington, D.C. Also, four of the five main speakers scheduled at the conference were authorities who had already visited Flint and commented enthusiastically on Flint's community schools.

Another school—the new Everett A. Cummings Community School—was dedicated May 20, 1957. The dedication happened to fall on the forty-seventh birthday of the man for whom the school was named, board of education member Everett A. Cummings.

With Flint voters approving continuation of a 2½-mill debt-service levy for ten years, the city could follow a planned program for construction of needed schools—particularly junior and senior high schools required by the growing population. Walter E. Scott, president of the board of education, called the favorable vote an "inspiring responsibility to board members."

The Mott Foundation's experimental developments were, as always, exploring new possibilities. A family-participation arts and crafts workshop provided an opportunity for whole families to work together on a variety of activities—pottery making, metal enameling, basket weaving, sketching, wood carving, or other arts and crafts. A new athletic program, the Flint Junior Olympics, offered 225 highly varied events, with 1,500 participants. The four-day athletic program (witnessed with great approval by Dr. Shane MacCarthy, who brought the greetings of President Eisenhower) was climaxed by a pole-vaulting exhibition by Bob Richards, and an impressive gymnastic performance by Ernestine Russell. Bishop-method sewing classes had proved highly popular in the adult education program, and plans were made for an enrollment of 1,500 in 61 such sewing classes in 30 centers.

Michigan State University announced for the fall of 1957 the initiation of a new program for developing leadership in community education by extending graduate credit beyond the master's degree toward a special degree as director of community education. Dr. W. Fred Totten, Flint's director of graduate study in the field of community education, announced that the plan was an extension of the in-service program instituted in 1954 with Eastern Michigan College.

The community-school program in Flint, by the fall of 1957, was reaching thirty-six different schools—with the services of thirty-four community-school directors.

For the college and cultural development, a $100,000 contribution was received in memory of Harry H. Bassett—the gift of his widow, Mrs. Jessie H. Swenson, and his son, Harry Hood Bassett.

In September, 1957, Flint's community-school program received new recognition. The twenty-eighth annual conference of the Michigan Association of School Administrators was built around the theme: "The Community School and the Shape of Things to Come." One of the principal speakers, Dr. Paul H. Hanna, Professor of Education at Stanford University and an international authority on community schools, visited Flint just before going to the conference and promised that the Flint story would be adequately presented. Manley also was invited to bring the pioneering Flint development before the conference.

After visiting Flint community schools, Dr. Hanna said that Flint had the most thorough and effective program he had seen.

> Some places are doing some of the things you are. Other cities have what they call community schools, but still lock up the doors at 5 o'clock each afternoon ...
> One of the chief impressions I get here is that through the Mott Foundation you've shown that the public schools are instruments for directing leadership for community improve-

220

ment. The school is the only instrument which completely represents all the people. The school offers permanent facilities and a permanent staff.

The school is the coordination agency for all resources of a community. It is more than a physical facility, but something to be used by neighbors to help themselves make the community improvements they need to do together, such as in health, recreation, and adult education.

Success of the whole system depends on a building and training leadership being available. That certainly is the key to your success in Flint.

The committee of sponsors of the college and cultural development reported that E. A. DeWaters—who had previously contributed $1 million to the project, had added an additional $362,000 to pay the complete cost of the art center which would bear the name of himself and his wife. Original plans of the center had been enlarged to provide twelve classrooms, conference, and study rooms—found necessary to meet the growing college enrollment. This added gift brought the Development within $3.5 million of its $20-million goal. Flint Junior College enrollment was 3,335—as compared with 736 in 1952.

On October 2, 1957, it was announced that the Mott Foundation budget for the 1957–1958 school year would exceed $1 million for the first time. On the same day, the Mott Memorial Building was dedicated to the use of the Flint College of the University of Michigan. Dr. Harlan H. Hatcher, president of the University, and Dr. Alexander G. Ruthven, president-emeritus, attended the ceremonies along with the regents. Walter E. Scott, president of the Flint Board of Education, presented Dr. David M. French, dean of the Flint College of the University of Michigan. Dean French discussed the facilities provided by the new building. Mott told the audience that Dr. Ruthven, back in 1946, had indicated the day was coming when the university might have to open branches off-campus and mentioned his own early efforts to get a branch of the

221

university for Flint. Meanwhile, he had joined in Flint's efforts to develop the best junior college anywhere. Both efforts had now become realities. He presented the keys of the Mott Memorial Building to Walter E. Scott, who then presented them to Dr. Hatcher. Dr. Hatcher called the new school a "manful attack on some of the problems that lie ahead for higher education." He assured his listeners that "the University of Michigan will do its best to carry on proudly in its great tradition here in Flint." Mott unveiled the bronze plaque in the lobby of the new building:

ERECTED BY
CHARLES STEWART MOTT
IN MEMORY OF HIS PARENTS
JOHN C. MOTT AND ISABELLA T. MOTT

One of Mott's interests had always been sound understanding of the fundamentals of economics. This led to a project in economic education which was started, with the backing of the Foundation, by Dr. Robert K. Burns, dean of the University of Chicago School of Business. By 1957, the project was in operation in eight colleges and universities, sponsored by the University of Chicago with the aid of a grant from the Mott Foundation. Training of teachers, development of leadership, getting the fundamentals of our economic system clearly and simply to the people—are among the objectives of the program. Dr. Burns, in outlining the application of economic instruction at the high school level to a group in Flint, pointed out that only three of every hundred high school students were taking a course in economics—and that better economic understanding of our own system is an essential tool in meeting the ideological challenge of communism. Dr. Burns said: "The future of free people depends on what happens to free enterprise and education."

In November, 1957, the Mott Foundation contributed $1 million for the construction of a University of Chicago industrial relations building to house the expanding program devel-

222

oped by Dr. Burns, centered on economic education, leadership, and communications. Mott explained the gift, as quoted in the Chicago *Sun-Times* of December 8, 1957, by saying that people "simply have not acquired the economic facts of life. Dr. Burns has a plan to get some of these facts across to the people of the United States through the Industrial Relations Center. He has a staff of 80, and they need a comprehensive single building to do their work properly. We agreed to pay for the building, not simply as a gift to the University of Chicago, which will own the building, but as a tool with which to accomplish this particular proposition."

TWENTY

One of the reasons for the effectiveness of the Foundation's programs from the very earliest days has been good communications; it does no good to offer splendid opportunities if the people who might participate do not even know the opportunities exist. Newspapers, radio, and television have always found good stories, good features, good news in Foundation activities—and have been generous with space and time. The Flint *Journal,* for example, has not only found countless news and feature stories—it has also printed schedules of community-school activities regularly. Radio Station WFDF has produced many programs in behalf of Foundation developments, including a series for several years under the general title "Opportunity Unlimited"—as well as contributing broadcast time to conduct two Mott Foundation adult education courses by radio for the whole listening area. Other radio stations and television stations have been similarly active in behalf of the Foundation.

During 1957, 826 individuals came to Flint specifically to study and observe the community-school program. They came from ten different foreign nations, seventeen different states of the Union, and eighty-eight different communities in Michigan. They included members of the President's cabinet, college presidents, deans, professors, school superintendents from large cities and small, civic leaders, teachers, industrialists, university students, Fulbright scholars, and newspaper and magazine writers and editors. The Foundation, in following the second of its two basic objectives—serving as an example—developed a program for receiving visitors and making sure they saw the real grass-roots activities that make up the reality of the community school program. All visitors were introduced to the simple, powerful, down-to-earth ideals of the program.

Visitors were taken on tours of a variety of activities, and a sincere attempt was made to help them find the answers they were looking for to the problems that concerned them most. Guests were usually entertained at breakfasts or luncheons provided by community groups in the schools they were visiting. They were invited to sit in on classes of special interest, and thus they had an ideal opportunity to talk with the community people actually participating in the activities. Visitors did not get a description of the program—they shared in it and had the actual experience of belonging to one aspect after another of it, even if only briefly. They didn't have to be told that people in vast numbers were responding—they saw this for themselves, and even felt the stirring of response in themselves to the interesting, enjoyable, informal, humanly satisfying activities—thanks to the circumstances under which their visits were arranged. Coordinators, principals, building directors, and other staff members acted as guides for groups of visitors. Foundation people were not only mindful of that second objective of the program—encouragement of outside communities to develop their own community schools—but they have always had so much pride and pleasure in the Foundation's work that they have found it a rewarding experience to help others discover the human values and real results that are evident in the program in action.

No matter when visitors come, there is always plenty to see—because the Mott Foundation program goes on around the year.

"The Flint story of education should be carried to every community in the Country. Flint Junior College is an inspiration itself, with its young, progressive faculty and dedicated administrative staff. People in Flint have a right to be proud of their College and Cultural Development—there is nothing quite like it in the world." This was the comment of Dr. Jesse P. Bogue, executive secretary, when members of the American

Association of Junior Colleges visited Flint for a conference, and to learn about the educational program.

Others were equally generous with their appreciation.

On March 19, Dr. Kevin McCann, special consultant to President Eisenhower, arrived in Flint for a three-day review of the community schools, Mott Foundation, and college and cultural development. This was the result of a visit which Mott, his son Harding, Manley, and Dr. Spencer Myers had made to the office of Marion B. Folsom, Secretary of Health, Education, and Welfare, earlier in March. It had then been planned for Dr. McCann to visit Flint and make a report to President Eisenhower and Secretary Folsom on the relationship of Flint educational development to proposed national programs for improved education. Mrs. McCann accompanied her husband to Flint.

On the evening of their arrival, the McCanns were invited to attend the annual-report meeting of the Mott Foundation Co-ordinating Committee. The next day, they first visited the Potter School, where they had breakfast served by a mothers' club, and then toured the new Tuuri-Mott Special Education Building for handicapped children. In the afternoon they toured the college and cultural development, and that evening they were guests at the Industrial Executives' Club, where Dr. McCann was asked to talk to the audience of some 2,000. He spoke in enthusiastic terms of what he was seeing in Flint, indicating that never in all of his life and experience had he been in a community where such remarkable things were carried on in recreation, in health, and community education.

The next morning, the McCanns visited Jefferson School, where they saw community-school activities in action. Mott notes in his diary that the McCanns were so interested that they could have spent the whole day there. Before 10 A.M. they drove to Pierce School, where they sat in on a meeting of school principals, community-school directors, and administrative staff members. Elmer L. Galley, Mott Foundation science consultant, discussed the current emphasis on teaching more

226

children to be scientists. Galley's theme was: "We must develop understanding of the hearts of men as well as of the hearts of atoms." Human understanding was vital to world survival, he said—so he advised caution in trying to push students into science, and suggested that we "search out our talented children. But let's encourage them to follow their natural interests, whether they lie in art, music, or science." He offered a well-organized group of practical guides in improving the quality of science teaching.

What Dr. McCann thought about what he had seen in Flint was indicated in his comments at the Pierce School seminar that morning. The Flint *Journal* quoted from Dr. McCann's remarks:

> After 10 years of searching, all of a sudden I see a pattern that looks like the answer to the biggest problem of our time. . . .
>
> In Flint I've seen for the first time what looks like a community-wide frontal attack.
>
> Evidently you have the elements here common to all American communities. But you're the only people I've seen—and I've observed education in a lot of cities—who have put all the elements together and come up with a pattern which should be common for the whole United States.
>
> I'd just like to sit down now and try to figure out how your ideas of community education can be spread.

In April, 1958, five hundred members of the Michigan Rural Teachers Association held their three-day annual convention in Flint—with "Community Education" as the theme and the Mott Foundation as host. Just two days later, the state department of public instruction, Flint Board of Education, and Mott Foundation sponsored the second annual community education workshop—in which there was heartening testimony from representatives of communities attending the first workshop the previous year, now reporting that the "Flint influence" had produced encouraging beginnings of community-school programs in their areas. These good reports came from the

227

Clio and Dye schools near Flint, and three other communities farther away: Pontiac's Will Rogers School, Vicksburg's community schools, and the schools of Holland, Mich. Testimony on the results to date was enthusiastic in each instance—and there were some 150 representatives of thirty-five communities attending this second workshop.

Mott found his days busier than ever, with never quite time enough to go around. At the annual banquet of the Michigan Education Association in Lansing, he was given a distinguished service award, which he accepted in behalf of Manley and the Foundation staff. And then, to demonstrate how strongly he felt that the credit should be passed on, he opened a carton he had brought along, and took from it a large sterling silver tray on which was inscribed, "Frank J. Manley, Spark Plug and Director of Mott Program, in appreciation of service— Charles Stewart Mott Foundation, April, 1958." Manley had no inkling of such a presentation, and, as Mott notes in his diary, "was pretty well overcome." Mott then presented Mrs. Manley with a sterling silver coffee set.

Flint became the 1958 host for the National Science Fair; Manley made recreational and other facilities of the Foundation available to the visiting contestants from everywhere, and special events were arranged to make their visit to Flint enjoyable, with teen clubs as hosts.

The first graduating class of the Flint College of the University of Michigan was honored in a convocation June 13, 1958; on the next day, the seventy-six Flint graduates joined the rest of the University's graduating class at Michigan Stadium at Ann Arbor.

Recognition of Mott Foundation Director Manley's concern for physical fitness and for constructive youth activities came in the form of his appointment by President Eisenhower as a member of the President's Citizens Advisory Committee on Fitness of American Youth. Shane MacCarthy, executive director of the President's Council on Youth Fitness, designated Manley as one of those who had assumed initiative in

228

developing youth-fitness programs. Other members of the committee included General Mark W. Clark, Clarence L. Munn, George Romney, Arthur Godfrey, Robert W. Sarnoff, and a number of other men of accomplishment. Appropriately, the announcement of Manley's appointment reached the newspapers just one day after the final figures on the completed school year's Mott Foundation Health Achievement Program, showing 15,860 of 27,000 pupils (58.7 per cent) in the health-guarded category at the close of the nineteenth year of work with Flint school children.

As detailed earlier in these pages, Mott had attended an appreciation banquet in honor of Harlow H. Curtice in Flint on September 25, 1935. On that occasion Mott had felt that there should have been a "strong and direct statement" which he did not find in the references to Curtice, and so he wrote such a statement and showed it to Michael Gorman, Editor of the Flint *Journal,* who printed it under the title, "TRIBUTE PAID CURTICE IN SPEECH THAT WASN'T MADE." Mott sent Sloan a copy of the "speech that wasn't made."

Just twenty-two years and eleven months later, Mott attended a meeting of General Motors Directors in New York, August 25, 1958, followed by an appreciation dinner at the Union Club in honor of Curtice, retiring as president of General Motors. Mott had in his pocket a copy of the 1935 "speech that wasn't made," and before the dinner, Alfred P. Sloan, Jr., said to Mott: "Stewart, you're such an old director and know so much about Curtice I would like to have you tell the directors something about him." Mott agreed to do so, pleased that at last the "speech that wasn't made" *would* be made—and in circumstances that would add infinitely to its impact. However, Sloan apparently forgot all about calling on Mott—and again the "speech that wasn't made" wasn't made. Back at his hotel after the dinner, Mott once more mailed a copy of the "speech that wasn't made" to Alfred P. Sloan, Jr.

In that 1935 speech Mott had made a "strong and direct statement" recognizing the same exceptional qualities in Curtice that were to make him an eminently successful president of General Motors. Mott's respect, admiration, and friendship for Curtice have been unwavering over the years. Curtice has always had that quality which Mott also found in Nash, common sense; at the same time, he has had an element of boldness, dash, creative imagination, and courage reminiscent of Durant, disciplined by a down-to-earth quality of realism; these plus dedication to the concept of progress (as embodied in his splendid statement: "Anything and everything can be improved"). And beyond these, Curtice has had the capacity for decision and the remarkable prescience which have always been characteristic of Mott. As the head of the business, he exercised brilliantly the functions Mott had defined: ". . . to sort the wheat from the chaff, to hold up a standard to work to, and to make decisions of prime importance."

The acquisition of the J. Dallas Dort home on Kearsley Street, immediately across from the new location of the Flint Public Library, provided a touch of historic continuity to the college and cultural development, as well as adding a music center to the project. This impressive Georgian mansion built in 1906 by Durant's partner in the old Durant-Dort Carriage Company may well serve as a distinguished link to some of the glories of the past for Flint; it has been designated as the J. Dallas Dort Music Center. Dort was the driving force of civic improvement activities for Flint in his lifetime; it is most appropriate that his beautiful home be part of today's college and cultural development.

The Mott Foundation was host to a State Pilot Leadership Workshop for elementary school science consultants in September. This three-day conference was sponsored by the Michigan Department of Public Instruction and its science education curriculum committee.

In September, also, *The Saturday Review* carried Robert Lewis Shayon's "Report from the Grass Roots," in which Flint's community schools, and the contribution Manley has made to educational opportunity in Flint, were given much credit.

230

A gift of $1 million from the Mott Foundation for construction of a library to serve both colleges brought the contributions of the Foundation to the college and cultural development to almost $4 million.

The death, on October 11, 1958, of Michael A. Gorman, Editor of the Flint *Journal* for thirty years, was a major loss to Flint in general and to the college and cultural development in particular. Among the many tributes to Gorman's memory from friends everywhere is this from Mott: "Mike's untimely passing was a sad blow to all of his many friends and a great loss to the City of Flint, in whose growth and development he was so interested. In the College and Cultural Development he was the spark plug. It had become his prime interest and he seemed more concerned in its completion than in his own life. He will be greatly missed."

Flint's third annual community education workshop, in the latter part of October, brought 250 representatives of Michigan communities to Flint to learn first-hand about the community-school program. As in the previous workshops, distinguished authorities indicated their belief that Flint had found answers to the most vital problems of our time through the revitalization of education in the community-school program. There were also enthusiastic reports from representatives of communities that had been making progress in developing their own community-school programs after learning about Flint's accomplishment.

Among 1958 visitors to Flint was Gen. Edwin Norman Clark, member of the executive committee of the President's Citizens Committee on Youth Fitness, who made a careful study of the Mott program.

In an enthusiastic letter to Mott, General Clark made many comments about the effectiveness of the Foundation. Here is one paragraph from his impressive letter:

> Since returning to New York I have thought a great deal of what I have seen and heard during my trip to Flint. I have asked myself why this near-miracle is happening in Flint and

not happening in our other American communities. Frankly, I am convinced that the approach to education, to community life, and to fitness of your youth and your adults in Flint, is the approach which must be copied and put into operation throughout America. It is immaterial whether it should be pulled out into America by other communities and by their responsible government officials, or pushed out by you and the Mott Foundation, who know so well what you have accomplished. Both things should be done as quickly as possible. I for one, am going to have some conversations with some of my associates who are interested in the problem of youth fitness, both here and in Washington. I further hope that you will allow me to return to Flint soon so that I may gain a better knowledge of your activities and successes. I want to thank you, Frank Manley, and your associates in Flint for the great pleasure and for the great inspiration which have been given to me, and by which I have gained much. It must be a source of great satisfaction to you to see the Mott Foundation Program in full flower in Flint.

In the college and cultural development, Flint's new public library was completed. The aesthetic stature of the project was enhanced by the gift of a $500,000 collection of Renaissance art objects of great distinction, by Mrs. Everett L. Bray. Additional sponsorships for the development were announced from time to time. The board of education decided to name the new Flint Junior College science building for Michael A. Gorman.

On December 3, 1958, Mott participated in the dedication of the Tuuri-Mott Building which had been constructed with the aid of a special $500,000 Foundation grant. It had been built as part of Durant School, which is since known as the Durant-Tuuri-Mott School. The building is specially adapted to the education and rehabilitation of handicapped children. In the course of the dedication, board of education president Walter E. Scott read a citation honoring Mott and presented him with a gigantic framed scroll listing awards previously made to him. The scroll states that the "Mott Foundation Program has enabled the Board of Education to undertake, on behalf of the citizens of Flint, programs and services that have brought national and international distinction to the community. The City of Flint has become, in fact, a model for the Nation." The scroll then lists the organizations and individuals who have awarded distinctions to Mott.

In his diary for the day, Mott notes: "Condensed report of so-called address as follows:"

I am afraid that my merits have been overstated.
I admit my guilt of helping Flint folks,
But—they themselves have helped themselves:
First, by the ideas and energies of Frank Manley,
Second, by a sympathetic and co-operative School Board,
Third, by Frank's wonderful Staff,
Fourth, by a grand P.T.A. and understanding public.
Time does not permit me to tell you
All that I think about Frank Manley.
Regarding Dr. Tuuri, he is simply the best ever—
Loved by the medical profession, his assistants, the folks
he serves, and by all of us.
Have I covered this point?
Then there is Cleo Popp and her devoted staff.
When Frank came to me regarding
The need for this building, I listened
Until he finished and then said:
"O.K. I am sure that Flint would
Construct this building some day,
But—we can't wait. Let's do it now—while we're alive.
And it's done, and we're all happy.

The last weeks of 1958 were shadowed for Mott by the death, on November 25, of Charles F. Kettering, a man Mott had always liked and admired to the highest degree. They had been close friends, working together for many years. Mott was in Bermuda when the news of Kettering's death came. He made arrangements to reach Dayton, Ohio, for Kettering's funeral, at which he was an honorary pallbearer.

The last entry in Mott's diary for 1958 is the listing of the twelve Kettering statements printed on the small calendar Kettering had sent him at Christmas the year before with a "Kettering idea" under each month. One of these idea-statements is:

> With willing hands and open minds, the future will be greater than the most fantastic story you can write. You will always under-rate it.

TWENTY-ONE

It would be difficult to find more appropriate words to begin the last section of this book than those offered in the Kettering Calendar for 1959, sent out by Eugene W. Kettering, with one of his father's inspired perceptions for each month of the year, including:

> Nothing ever built arose to touch the skies unless some man dreamed that it should, some man believed that it could, and some man willed that it must.

Dreaming . . . believing . . . and willing . . . have been going on in Flint since 1819—but never at a greater pace, and with richer and wider fields of accomplishment than in 1959. The remarkable gains of 1958 continued with gathering momentum. More sponsors joined the college and cultural development; construction proceeded on new buildings; three new schools were planned; the first Pilot Leadership Workshop in High School Science Education was held in mid-January; adult education class enrollments kept growing; and there were more and more visitors to Flint. A publication of the United States Information Service at the U.S. Embassy in Brussels had published an article about Flint community schools which had been made available in several languages to visitors to the World Fair at Brussels. There had been 4,000 visitors to Flint in 1958 to learn about the educational program—with representatives from sixteen states and nine foreign countries, and in 1959 they kept on coming.

The thirty-seventh yearbook of the American Association of School Administrators, *Educational Administration in a Changing Community,* speaks of the Flint community-school program's remarkable level of effectiveness, and credits Flint's development of a set of principles to administer such programs.

235

Dr. Myrtle F. Black, in reviewing the book, notes that most of its recommendations "are in accordance with programs and philosophies already established in Flint," and that the Flint system "has assumed the stature of a laboratory and leadership training center for other places striving to build more effective school-community relationships."

On March 10, 1959, delegates from forty-six cities in twenty-three states met in Flint for the first National Community School Clinic. In addressing the clinic, Dr. Lynn M. Bartlett, state superintendent of public instruction, paid tribute to the world fame of Flint's successful community-school program. Later in the year, Peter Clancy, assistant director of the Mott program, wrote a report about this first clinic for publication in the *Journal of Health—Physical Education—Recreation,* describing the months of planning for the event, and the program conducted for the 250 people from many states attending. The experiences and responses of the participants are described, as they actually visited Flint's community schools and talked with the neighborhood people whose community life was so actively centered in the schools. C. C. Trillingham, Los Angeles County superintendent of schools, summarized the clinic at the final session, stating:

> The community-school concept has been tremendously successful for Flint. . . . I hope that all of us may take back with us a clearer vision of what an all-out community commitment to education can do, a renewed courage to utilize fully all of our community resources, a deepened belief in the importance of all of our people young and old, along with a desire to serve them better, and a realization that the battle for universal education will not be won in Washington or our state capitals, as important as they are. The battle will be won in local neighborhood schools across this land, where we have dedicated and competent teachers working with interested and understanding parents and where the big job of administration and school boards is to provide the necessary wherewithal for doing the kind of job that needs to be done. To me, this is the lesson at Flint.

In Mott's diary for March 24, 1959, the following aside is of special interest:

Regarding small cars, it was about fifteen years ago that I wrote to G.M. President, C. E. Wilson, regarding the desirability and market for small cars and even sent specifications of one that I thought would fill the bill. I showed the letter to Ket and he said it was exactly what he had in mind, but, although since then I have sent copies of the above-mentioned letter to various men in General Motors, no interest seems to have been shown in a small car of the type I described. It was essentially a low-priced transportation job, which Ket called the "Market Wagon."

The world leader of the Salvation Army, Gen. Wilfred Kitching, visited Flint and toured the college and cultural center; he cabled Mott in Bermuda, stating that he was "deeply impressed by your contributions to the well being of this community." Among the amazing variety of Mott-program courses offered, one was announced on "How Best to Use Retirement," but Mott, approaching his eighty-fourth birthday, was as "unretired" as ever. General Motors contributed $650,000 to Flint's YMCA building fund, as announced by John F. Gordon, president of the corporation. Expansion of the Foundation's summer adult education courses was planned.

At the close of the two-day annual conference of the Adult Education Association of Michigan, in Flint, in May, 1959, Dr. Myrtle F. Black was elected to the board of directors of the association. The relationship between adult education and industry in Flint was outlined by Joseph A. Anderson, general manager of AC Spark Plug Division, in a talk to the conference. Manley, Dr. Black, and George V. Gundry, of the Flint Board of Education, also spoke to the conference, and the association presented its award of merit to Mott.

On his eighty-fourth birthday, Mott found himself in the midst of a typically busy day. That evening, he and Mrs. Mott attended the annual dinner meeting of the Flint Chamber of Commerce. An enormous birthday cake was wheeled in, and

237

the group sang "Happy Birthday." Mott made an off-the-cuff response.

On the next day, June 3, 1959, Mott notes in his diary:

> I recommend you read Admiral Rickover's book, "Education and Freedom." I'll say that his opinions as given in his book are right down the line, and very sensible and timely. Last night I talked with new President of Board of Commerce and also Harding, and I would like to see if we can't get Rickover here to talk before the Board of Commerce, or a larger meeting. He is one of the brightest geniuses in the country, highly educated, and I would like him to give a synopsis of his book about which I think everyone should have a knowledge. I would like to ask the Admiral's critics to tell me in detail where they think his book is mistaken in facts and fundamentals.

On June 25, Mr. and Mrs. Mott and their two younger children, Stewart and Maryanne, met Mr. and Mrs. Manley, Mr. and Mrs. Harding Mott, and Mr. and Mrs. Everett Cummings, in Chicago to attend the dedication of the new Mott Building at the University of Chicago. Manley and Dr. Robert K. Burns presented talks about the work of the Foundation, and the architect turned the keys of the building over to the chancellor of the university.

Receiving a YMCA award for service to camping on June 30, Mott mentioned being camper number 101 at the first YMCA camp ever opened. The 1959 award was made at the Flint YMCA's Camp Copneconic—345 acres at a lake given by Mott years earlier. On July 1, the YMCA reached its $2.6-million building fund goal.

In July, Mott attended a meeting at the junior college concerned with working out a plan to carry on organized industrial training and retraining, so that men looking for work would be qualified to fill jobs requiring special skills, and men already employed could be trained to advance to better jobs. The committee was organized, with an excellently diversified membership, under the chairmanship of Edward T. Ragsdale, former general manager of Buick. Of this plan, Mott notes in his diary:

It just so happens that this is the program that caused me to promote the building of our Science and Arts Building. We are already training graduate nurses, IBM operators, stenographers, cooks, dressmakers, etc., and today's program is calculated to go a lot further. It presents many difficulties, but we think something can be accomplished which could be nationwide. All present seemed to be enthusiastic, and agreed to serve on this committee to which other important men will be added.

On September 10, Mott went to the Flint Junior College to attend graduation ceremonies for seventy-four adults who had not completed high school in their younger days, but who had taken Mott-program high school credit courses to earn the diplomas being awarded. Mott congratulated the graduates, told them how pleased he was to be present at their graduation, and expressed the hope that they would continue their education with the more than nine hundred adult education courses being offered.

Mott has always been interested in the work of the Genesee County Chapter of the Michigan Society for Crippled Children and Adults, and has felt that Mrs. Peggy McWhirter, executive secretary, has done an excellent job. On October 21, Mott offered a Foundation gift of $100,000 to construct a much-needed building for the organization—to be located on the Durant-Tuuri-Mott School grounds.

In the final days of October, Flint was host to the fourth annual community education workshop, which again brought hundreds of visitors to learn the Flint community-school story. Mott talked to the workshop group at Freeman School on the evening of October 28. The next day, Dr. Jess Davis, president of Stevens Institute of Technology, and Dr. Fulton Cutting, vice-president, visited Mott—and he was glad to have them see Foundation activities in action.

Dr. Paul J. Misner, superintendent of Glencoe, Illinois,

239

schools, and past president of the American Association of School Administrators, talked to the workshop visitors on October 29. He submitted four observations about the community school:

1. The community school provides us with the only acceptable means of achieving educational purposes within the framework of democratic ideals and traditions;
2. The community school is the means whereby the resources essential for a good educational program can be mobilized with optimum effectiveness and economy;
3. The community school is the most promising means of achieving dynamic curriculum programs geared more effectively to changing social needs and conditions; and
4. The community school presents teachers and administrators with new and challenging opportunities for leadership.

At a panel discussion that evening Mott was especially delighted with the enthusiastic report of Mrs. Louis Asaro, recreation chairman of the PTA Council, and member of the City-School-Community Committee, Roseville, Michigan. Roseville representatives had attended a Flint workshop, had come back for more information, ("We needed community schools and needed them bad.") had sponsored bus-load visits to Flint, and had asked Mott staff members, including "Mr. Frank Manley, who has been a god-father to us," to come to Roseville and tell the story. They presented a program-plan to the city. There were setbacks, problems, obstacles. They thought funds to work with would be included in the city budget—"$10,000 to start. We knew we couldn't start big"— but found the funds not in the budget because of a hitch in the program-plan submitted. "So again we called upon . . . Mr. Manley." Manley, as always, was helpful in practical ways. There was a budget hearing: ". . . we jammed the City Hall. Have you ever tried saying *no* to about fifty screaming females? Well, don't! Because they couldn't, and we were granted $10,000 to start our community-school program. I can remember that night so well. All of us were so happy—it was like a new baby being born. We have always said that Flint was like a big mother, always giving birth to other communities." There were still roadblocks. But the school custodians helped. The school board helped. They found a building director. Manley had said that when they got a building director, they could send him to Flint for training if they wanted to (*"If* we wanted to! Yes, we wanted to, because we knew our building director would get the very best training possible where it all started—in Flint.") The building director returned from his training in Flint, explained the program, and "That happy feeling came over us. We made it! We in Roseville had community schools. . . ."

Mrs. Asaro addressed the others present who wanted community schools, too:

> I hope in some small way this will help others to realize that you, too, can have community schools. It's not an easy hill to climb. You will have pitfalls; you will have some who don't think you need it; you'll also have people saying we can't afford it. Also, you'll hear Flint has Mr. Mott. Yes, they have got Charlie Mott, but we should be thankful that we have the privilege to be able to see the wonderful things he has done so that we can go home and say we want community schools, too.
>
> You don't need a Charlie Mott; you need only to be determined to say *we're going to have community schools* and work towards it, and someday say with a happy feeling, "We have community schools in our town," because Flint is still a big mother, and we in Roseville know she will continue to give birth always.

On the strength of that report alone, the workshop would have been a notable success.

The November, 1959, issue of *Educational Leadership in Michigan,* published by the Michigan Association of School Administrators, devoted its opening page to a story, " 'Proof of the Pudding Is In the Eating'—Flint Program." The article points out how different Flint is today from the way it was even fifteen years ago, because, "The character of the community has been uplifted." Specific evidence is cited to show why many people believe the community school movement is responsible for the improvement . . . with more adults enrolled for evening education and recreation courses than children in regular school . . . with the juvenile-delinquency rate in Flint not showing the rise reported elsewhere . . . with such experimental ventures as retraining of unemployed people for new positions . . . with demonstrated popular support for education, including voters' passage of school-expense measures . . . with both locally focused courses and others relating to the broader scope of man in the modern world . . . with the remarkable *esprit de corps* of the Flint teaching staff.

The December, 1959, issue of *The Journal of Educational Sociology* is devoted completely to a report of the First National "Community-School" Clinic—with Peter L. Clancy (assistant director of the Mott program) and Milton A. Gabrielson as issue editors. This comprehensive 68-page report explains the background, development, and current status of the Mott Foundation's activities, and includes the talks given by Harding Mott, vice-president and business manager of the Foundation; Dr. Ernest O. Melby, and Howard Y. McClusky, as well as the panel-discussion contributions of Mrs. Fred L. Keeler, Dr. James P. Lewis, Dr. Lewis Barrett, and Dr. C. C. Trillingham. There are reports, also, on reactions of participants, postclinic evaluation, and a bibliography on the community school. In Harding Mott's greeting to the visiting educators, he said:

Now, there is nothing so powerful as a right idea, and as you can see, our budget has expanded from $6,000 to its present amount of over a million dollars a year. This right idea has also helped encourage the late W. S. Ballenger to establish his trust fund for endowing chairs of learning at the junior college. This in turn inspired other leading citizens of the Sponsor's Committee of the College and Cultural Center to further expedite the completion of the over-all $25,000,000 project that many of you have seen. This right idea also caused the tax-payers of this city to levy many millions of dollars against themselves to provide many of the buildings that you have seen in the city today. This building we are in now is just a sample of the last model that rolled off the line. We certainly are indebted to the Board of Education for its vision and raised sights in providing such outstanding leadership for the Flint school system. Further, this leadership has caused the state legislature to support a branch of the University of Michigan on the college campus....

Mott's diary in recent years has made frequent reference to the development and operation of the basic-economics program. On December 16, 1959, Mott and Dr. Burns attended a meeting at Bryant Junior High School gymnasium at which about 700 people who had taken the adult education basic-economics course received their certificates of completion. Manley opened the meeting, and Mott and Burns functioned as a panel to answer questions. Mott was very conscious of the necessity of accurate, clear, careful answers to the questions—some of which were on the complex and ponderous side. He maintained his contention that sound economics is common sense above all, with such comments as, "Everybody knows that if you continue to spend more than you take in, you'll go bankrupt and be thrown into the street." He noted that several elements threatened trouble for our economy in the long run from increase of the national debt; from imbalance in foreign trade, reducing our gold reserve; from continued high tax rates that inhibit consumer spending and investments in productive enterprises, and from rising prices and costs. He commented that the course just completed was the best way he had ever observed for people to learn basic economics—because the trained discussion leaders did not tell the students what to think, but posed problems and let the classes work out the answers.

The Mott Foundation swept into 1960 with a tabloid-catalog of more than 900 classes for winter adult education . . . evening college, high school, pre-high school . . . special interests, program services . . . music, arts, crafts, drama . . . Bishop sewing and home arts . . . trades and mechanical skills . . . business education . . . recreation. Enrollments for the 1958–1959 year had totaled an amazing 77,644.

Again in 1960, Flint was host to the National Community School Clinic—co-sponsored by the Mott Program of the Flint Board of Education and the American Association for Health, Physical Education, and Recreation. Some 200 educational leaders from many states attended the three-day clinic on March 15, 16, and 17. Dr. Ernest O. Melby and Dr. Howard Y. McClusky brought their own appreciative insights to consideration of community-school problems, as they had done in previous workshops in Flint. Each visitor was given a kit of background materials, several opportunities to share in community-school activities, and all the help the Flint staff could provide in finding answers to questions and problems in organizing and developing community schools.

Typical of the Foundation's close working relationship with other organizations and agencies in Flint was the city's 1960 Michigan Week observance. Harding Mott was regional chairman, Karl Schwartzwalder and Ralph Whittier, of AC Spark Plug Division, were Genesee County co-chairmen of the celebration, with Marvin Sitts, of the Foundation staff, as coordinator. A full week of community-participation activity was scheduled—chiefly centering in and near the College and Cultural Center.

In 1961 and 1962, activities have been even more impressive, with a choice of more than 1,100 adult education and recreation classes offered in Flint's community schools, and new pilot projects under way.

On June 2, 1962, Charles Stewart Mott attained his eighty-seventh birthday. The partnership between Mott and Manley—making up the essence of the Foundation program—is still very much a going concern. In fact, it goes about as rapidly and purposefully as any human enterprise observable.

The Foundation built, and opened in September, 1962, one

244

of the finest health centers anywhere, the Mott Children's Health Center, next to Flint's Hurley Hospital. This is at once a recognition of community need, and a tribute to Dr. Arthur L. Tuuri, the center's director.

In 1926, Mott established the Foundation ". . . for the purpose of supporting religious, educational, health, and recreational activities for public benefit."

Certainly the Foundation has lived up to that objective.

In the process of doing so, it has made Flint a better place to live, and has established patterns which other communities are increasingly finding to be worth following.

It has developed its own medium by which to function: the community school, which solves those most basic of problems —communication with people, opportunity for people, participation by people—providing the universal solvent of common interest in the natural, democratic, publicly owned community center, the school.

So broad is the total program that it cannot accurately be defined more narrowly than to call it a *Foundation for Living*.

For each man—for Frank J. Manley as for Charles Stewart Mott—it is also a *personal foundation for living*—the foundation stone, the living rock, upon which the house of his life is built.

Dr. Melby has well said of these men, "But actually beyond their contributions, there has been developed in Flint an enterprise which has an on-going internal spirit. It isn't only what these people do. It's the way they do it. It's the spirit in which they do it."

The Foundation derives from the lives of these two men who share a common concern for all people, and the most warmhearted and practical determination to set workable patterns by which people can help themselves with their own—and the world's—most critical problems.

Charles Stewart Mott has been *hurrying* for many years now —to accomplish through the Foundation as much as possible while he is alive to guide and observe.

245

In his diary for June 30, 1959, there is a fascinating entry, involving a dear friend of more than forty years, Floyd Allen, a regular recipient of the daily diary.

> I had a funny dream the other night. It was that the venerable Floyd Allen and I had attended the funeral of a contemporary octogenarian, and had gone to the cemetery some miles out of town. And when the burying was completed, the venerable Floyd turned to me and spoke.
>
> FLOYD: "C. S., how old was the deceased?"
> c. s.: "About eighty years old."
> FLOYD: "C. S., how old are you?"
> c. s.: "I supposed you knew that I am younger than you, and I am eighty-four."
> FLOYD: "Well, C. S., it hardly seems worthwhile to go back home, does it?"
>
> But we did return home. Floyd has retired from active life —leading "the life of Riley" and visiting foreign climes and, at present, Alaska. While old man Mott is working days and nights, and Sundays, not knowing enough to quit.

Charles Stewart Mott, at eighty-seven, is still under the compulsion of a lifetime: *to get things done.* And those *things* are predominantly new and improved ways for the Foundation to do an even-better job of helping others help themselves.

The Mott family crest bears the motto: *Spectemur Agendo,* meaning, *"Let us be known by our deeds."* Quoting it, Charles Stewart Mott says, "Applying it to our work through the Foundation, I would add a phrase: *'Let us be known by our deeds—and not by our money.'* "

INDEX

AC Spark Plug Division of GM, 33, 85, 151
Adams, Floyd, 102, 107–108, 126, 147
Addison, Chris, 116
Adult Education Association of Michigan, 237
Adventures of a White Collar Man (Sloan), 13, 91
AFL Union membership card, 204
Alcoholism, prevention and cure, 186
Aldrich, F. A., 6
Allen, Floyd, 246
American Association for Health, Physical Education and Recreation, 244
American Association of School Administrators, 235
American Automobile Association, 24
American Ball Bearing Co., 22
American Legion, 206, 213
American Red Cross, 99, 206
Anderson, H. W., 160
Anderson, Joseph A., 181–182, 187, 237
Anspach, Dr. Charles L., 212
Applewood, 89–90, 103–104, 118
Arizona, trips to, 89, 102, 106
Armstrong, Robert, 6
Armstrong Spring Company, 6, 87
Art and music, 89
Asaro, Mrs. Louis, 240–241
Autocar Co., 20
Automobile Club of Utica, 24
Automobile Old Timers, 181
Automotive Giants of America (Forbes and Foster), 92–97
Axles made by Weston-Mott, 4, 22

Bacon, Harold D., 133–134, 168, 197
Bahlman, Dr. Gordon, 152
Baker, E. K., 42
Ballenger, William S., 5, 41, 44, 147, 182, 187, 242
Ballenger, William S., Jr., 218
Ballenger Field House, 208
Barrett, John M., 187
Barrett, Dr. Lewis, 242

Barton, Henry L., 84
Bassett, Harry H., 29, 41–42, 75, 85, 87, 92, 191
Begole, C. M., 41, 44
Bermuda, 111, 137
Big Brother movement, 158
Big Brother of the Year Award, 201–203, 209
Bills, Dr. Mark W., 187
Bishop, Arthur G., 5, 28, 74, 132
Black, Dr. Myrtle, 133–134, 203, 236–237
Board of Education, 119–122, 196–197, 208, 218, 232–233, 237
    Co-ordinating Committee, 196, 200
Bogue, Dr. Jesse P., 225
Bowen, Wilbur P., 113
Bower, F. A., 32, 146, 152, 155, 206, 209, 214
Boy's club work, 101, 157
Boy Scouts, 98, 199, 208
Bray, Mrs. Everett L., 232
Briscoe brothers, 26
Brown, Helen Hardy, 213
Brown-Lipe Co., 22, 35, 87
Browning machine guns, 151
Brownell, Roy E., 79, 98, 103, 105–106, 126, 147, 156–157, 208
Brownson, Rear Admiral Willard H., 18
Brussels World Fair, 235
Buffalo World's Fair, 14
Buick, David D., 27
Buick Motor Company, 1, 4–5, 27, 49, 70, 74
    expansion, 29–39, 70, 74
    presidents, 58, 85, 87, 109–111
Burns, Dr. Robert K., 217, 222–223, 238
Burr, Dr. C. B., 68–69
Burroughs, Mr. and Mrs. James, 103, 107
Butler, Aimee Mott, 98

Cadillac Company, 6, 22, 33, 37
Camp Copneconic, 102, 106–108, 238
Camp for boys, 102, 106–108, 147, 169–170, 174, 179, 200

248

249

Parkland community school, 186
Patterson, Alton R., 133–134, 183
Paterson, W. A., 26–27, 84–85, 215
Paterson Company, 30
Pecora, Ferdinand, 103–104
Peerless automobile, 37
People's Party, Flint, 59–60
Pero Lake, 102
Physical education program, 114
Pierce-Arrow, 37
Pierce community school, 189, 195
Pollock, Mrs. Milton, 144
Pontiac Division, 86, 102
Potter, E. D., 146
Potter community school, 189, 195
Pound, Dr. and Mrs. Arthur, 215
President's Council on Youth Fitness, 216, 228, 231
Probation cases, 150
Public affairs, interest in, 93–94, 102
Pyper, William F., 203

Radio station WFBE, 197, 224
Ragsdale, Edward T., 238–239
Rankin, Francis, 6
Rawlings, Ruth, 105
Rawlings, Sarah and Junius, 105, 131
Rawlings Health Center, El Paso, 150
Reader's Digest, 210
Recreation Council, 116
Remington, Frederic, 89
Remington Arms Co., 29, 75
Remington Automobile and Motor Co., 23–24
Reo automobile, 37
Retraining program for workers, 238
Rickover, Admiral Hyman, 238
Rideout, Gerald H., 202
Riggs, Professor, 52
Roosevelt, Mrs. Franklin D., 127–128, 198
Roosevelt, Theodore, 56
Roosevelt community school, 186
Roseville, Michigan, 240–241
Rotary Club, 117, 145, 147
Rubel, Ellen, 106
Russell, Ernestine, 219
Ruthven, Dr. Alexander G., 159–161, 176, 178, 187, 221
Ryder, Joseph T., 158, 174, 202–203, 218

Saginaw County distinguished service award, 198
Sarvis, Arthur H., 146

Saturday Review, 230
Schwartzwalder, Karl, 244
Science teaching, 226–227, 235
Scott, Walter E., 150, 212, 218–219, 221–222, 232
Selby, Guy W., 218
Shayon, Robert Lewis, 230
Sibilsky, Robert, 211
Sitts, Marvin, 244
Skaff, Woodrow W., 202
Sloan, Alfred P., Jr., 13–14, 68, 78–79, 81, 85, 91–93, 109–111, 132, 147–148, 180, 191, 193, 229
Adventures of a White Collar Man, 13, 91
Small cars, 237
Sobey, Albert, 92
Socialist party in Flint, 47–51
Society of Automobile Engineers, 41
Somes, Russel V., 159
Spanish-American War, 14–18
Sportsmen's Clubs, 114
Star automobiles, 86
Stepping Stone Program, 144–145, 157, 169, 174, 179, 218–219
Stevens Institute of Technology, 10, 13–14, 137, 206, 239
Alumni Award Medallion to Mott, 168
Stewart, Col. Charles, 8
Stewart, Isabella Turnbull, 8
Stewart, S. S., Jr., 187, 218
Stewart, William F., 6
Stewart Body Company, 6, 30
Stoddard-Dayton cars, 37
Strikes, sit-down, 132–133
Suffrage movement, 54–55
Summerfield, Arthur E., 203
Swenson, Mrs. Jessie H., 220

Tanner, Floyd, 136
Taucher, Mrs. E. A., 90
Taylor, Dr. Clair L., 205, 215, 217
Tennant, John S., 76
Thorne, Willis, 103
Time magazine, 151, 188
Tornado, 196–197
Tot Lot program, 182, 213
Totten, Dr. W. Fred, 187, 212, 220
Trillingham, C. C., 236, 242
Tuuri, Dr. Arthur L., 196, 205–206, 245
Tuuri-Mott Building, 232, 239

Union Industrial Bank defalcations, 100–101, 103
United China Relief campaigns, 151

253

ACKNOWLEDGMENTS

For assistance in the preparation of this book, the authors wish to express particular indebtedness to the editor, staff, and files of the Flint *Journal;* Doubleday & Company, Inc., for quotations from *Adventures of a White-Collar Man,* by Alfred P. Sloan, Jr., in collaboration with Boyden Sparks; the B. C. Forbes Publishing Company, for quotations from *Automotive Giants of America,* by B. C. Forbes and O. D. Foster; Dr. Arthur Pound, author of *The Turning Wheel,* for a wealth of background material and for the most generous of professional and personal assistance; Mr. Frank J. Manley, Miss Margaret Yambrick, Mr. William F. Minardo, and other members of the staff of the Mott Program of the Flint Board of Education for consistent helpfulness; Mr. Walter E. Scott for insight, information, and advice; Mrs. Marion Gordon for creative suggestions as well as help in the reading of proofs; Mr. C. S. Mott and his own personal staff for making available a remarkable collection of letters, documents, and records.

254